EARLY TRAVELS IN INDIA

EARLY TRAVELS IN INDIA

BEING

REPRINTS OF RARE AND CURIOUS NARRATIVES OF OLD TRAVELLERS IN INDIA IN THE SIXTEENTH AND SEVENTEENTH CENTURIES

JAMES TALBOYS WHEELER

GYAN

Published by

Gyan Publishing House
5, Ansari Road
Daryaganj, New Delhi-110002
Phone: 011-47034999, 9811692060
E-mail: books@gyanbooks.com

Distribution Network
gyanbooks.com
India, USA, Canada, UK, Australia

ISBN: 978-93-7097-515-6 (HB)

First Published, 1864

2nd Impression 2025

Printed at: Gyan Press, Delhi.

EARLY TRAVELS IN INDIA
Author James Talboys Wheeler

EARLY TRAVELS

IN

INDIA.

EARLY TRAVELS IN INDIA,

BEING

REPRINTS OF RARE AND CURIOUS NARRATIVES OF OLD TRAVELLERS IN INDIA, IN THE SIXTEENTH AND SEVENTEENTH CENTURIES.

FIRST SERIES,

COMPRISING

"PURCHAS'S PILGRIMAGE" AND THE "TRAVELS OF VAN LINSCHOTEN."

CALCUTTA:
PRINTED AT THE "ENGLISHMAN" PRESS, 2 HARE STREET,
AND PUBLISHED BY R. LEPAGE & Co.

1864.

PREFACE.

In consequence of the difficulty which has been experienced in collecting at a reasonable price and within a reasonable compass, the works of old Geographers and Travellers respecting India, an arrangement was made with Mr. J. O'B. Saunders, the Editor of the "Englishman" for publishing from time to time in his *Saturday Evening Journal*, such old descriptions of India and especially such old travels in this country, as were both curious and rare, accompanied by such explanatory notes as might be useful to the general reader. The present volume consists of a reprint in a book form of the first series of Old Travels, which have already appeared in the *Saturday Evening Englishman*, consisting of "Purchas's Pilgrimage," and the "Travels of Van Linschoten;" and by way of indicating their scope and character, it may be as well to extract the following introductory paragraphs, which appeared in the *Englishman* at the time when the publication was first commenced.

"In order to begin as nearly as possible with the beginning of the East India Company, we propose to confine ourselves for the present to those very early and graphic narratives of travels which were undertaken in the reigns of Queen Elizabeth and James the First, when the East India Company was agitating for its first Charter, which it finally procured on the 30th December 1600, and when the first few fleets of adventurers were despatched to the Malabar Coast and the Spice Islands. For centuries before that period, India had been the land of fable, but even the truth when told was almost as marvellous as the reckless fictions of the Middle Ages. The wonderful stories of Sir John Mandeville and others about the men with two heads who peopled the region now known as Orissa and Masulipatam, had still not quite died out; whilst strange accounts of the Indian Kings had become as familiar to the people of England as household words. The nursery story of Blue Beard has, we believe, been traced to the annals of a Hindoo King of the Dekkan; whilst the story of the King of Cambay, who fed upon poisons, until his very breath was deadly, so much so that a wife died every night, and he was compelled to marry another doomed fair one every morning,—a story by the way which has been preserved in Hudibras—this very story, we say, is still to be identified as applicable to a King of Guzerat who flourished in the fifteenth century, and was named Mahmood Begarra. The more veritable tales of social life in India were, as already indicated, almost equally attractive: and the grave old ministers of Queen Elizabeth might be shuddering at the accounts of the poor widows who burnt themselves with their dead husbands, whilst the maids of honour were giggling over the scandalous reports of the ladies of Malabar, who married as many husbands as they pleased, and kept them all in perfect control. But the grand charm about India was its wealth, and every traveller who visited the country at this period brought back accounts of its riches,—its gold, silver and jewels—its silks, and cottons, and stately edifices,—which alone were sufficient to inoculate the gravest London citizen with a desire to do a little trade with such wealthy idolaters. A voyage round the Cape in those days was, however, a very different thing from what it is in our time. It occupied generally a year or two. It involved frequent fights with the natives of Africa, or Madagascar, or Johanna, or with the inhabitants of any other spot where it was found necessary to take in fresh provisions, or water. Then, again, if an English vessel fell in with a Portuguese vessel ,or a Dutch merchantman, there was not unfrequently a battle ; and, not to mince matters, sea captains in those days were as much pirates as they were traders, and so long as they brought home good cargoes and treasure, few questions were asked, though very many stories were told.

"But we do not intend to forestall any of the old world narratives which we shall continue publishing in our *Saturday Evening's Englishman.* All that we wish to do is to intimate the character and age of the republications which we have just commenced. It seems that in the year 1626, just after the accession of Charles the First, and within a very few years after the publication of the authorised version of the Bible, the Reverend Samuel Purchas published his once famous collection of Voyages and Travels over the world, know as 'Purchas's Pilgrims;' and about the same time published also a digested account of the different countries in the world, which was drawn up from the voyages and travels, and which was called 'Purchas's Pilgrimage.' Old Purchas was a character in his day, and deserves some notice. He was born in 1577, and was thus a boy of eleven years of age when the Spanish Armada was threatening the coasts of England. From an early age, he was passionately fond of voyages and travels, and having spent a life in collecting them, and ruined himself in printing and publishing them, he died two years after the publication, hopelessly in debt. The difference between the *Pilgrimage* and the *Pilgrims* is thus described by himself. 'The *Pilgrimage* being mine own in matter, though borrowed, and in the form of words and method; whereas the *Pilgrims* are the authors themselves, acting their own parts in their own words.'

"The collection entitled 'Purchas's Pilgrimage' consists of five very large and closely printed volumes in folio, which are at this time excessively rare. The bulk of this great collection is perhaps taken up with America, Africa, Europe and Northern and Western Asia; but still India does find a very good place; and all the old travels of Stevens, Fitch, Raymond of Raymond, Sir Thomas Roe, Davis, Terry, Coryat, Hawkins, Michelbourne, and a host of others, are either given at full length, or in the form of a judicious and readable abridgment.

"But it will be seen that we have not begun with the actual travels, but with what good old Purchas calls his 'Pilgrimage,' and which comprises a good account of India, as it was in the reign of Jehangeer, about a generation before England heard of Oliver Cromwell, or India heard of Aurungzebe. After that has been carried to a conclusion, we shall be able to decide whether our readers are sufficiently interested to render it worth our while to continue the republication.

"In order, however, that the public may have some general notion of the history of India at the time these accounts were written, it may be as well to enter into a little introductory detail. The Mogul Empire at Delhi was only just growing to the dimensions of an Empire. Bengal had only very recently been conquered by the Mogul, having been very recently an independent kingdom. The Rajpoots were still formidable. The Mahrattas were really unknown. The whole of India to the southward of the Nerbudda River and Vindhya Mountains, was altogether independent of the Mogul. The Deckan was in the hands of the independent Mussulman kings, who were as prepared to resist the Mogul on the north, as they were to fight the Hindoo sovereignties further south. Calcutta, Madras, and Bombay had literally no existence at all, as far as Europeans were concerned. There was an English factory at Surat, and another at Pulicat, and these, we believe, were the only permanent settlements which the English at this time possessed in all India. The Dutch were rather more fortunate, and the Portuguese were more so, inasmuch as their possessions included their famous city of Goa, and the surrounding territory. But still most of the matter in our published sample will have proved tolerably familiar to our readers; and, at any rate, they will be amused at this juncture to read what old Purchas has to say of Bootan.

"With these preliminary remarks we beg to introduce old Samuel Purchas to the notice of our *Saturday Evening* readers, and should our published sample please the public taste, we can only say that for some time to come, at any rate, we shall have a supply constantly on hand."

Such were the observations published when the republication of the "Pilgrimage" was commenced, and it was gratifying to learn that the readers of the *Saturday Evening's Englishman* took a large interest in these quaint and suggestive old narratives. Accordingly, it was arranged to republish in order the Travels of Van Linschoten, Sir Thomas Roe, and Fryer: and here again it may be as well to reproduce the following paragraphs in which the arrangement was made known to the public.

"In accordance with a promise made last week in our *Saturday Evening's Englishman*, we shall, to-morrow evening, commence the republication of three of the rarest and most interesting books of old travels in India, in continuation of Mr. Samuel Purchas's 'Pilgrimage' which has already appeared in that journal. The three narratives we have selected are those of Linschoten's travels in the year 1583; Sir Thomas Roe's Embassy to the Court of the Mogul in 1615-16; and the travels of Dr. John Fryer between the years 1672 and 1676. Before, however, commencing the reprints, we think it advisable to point out the distinguishing characteristics of each separate book of travels, and to explain, as nearly as possible, the condition of India at the different periods indicated.

"John Huighen Van Linschoten visited India just sixteen years before the old East India Company received their first Charter from Queen Elizabeth of blessed memory. He was a Portuguese, and consequently made Goa his head quarters; and his travels are chiefly interesting from the light they throw upon the character of Portuguese administration in Goa, and upon the domestic life of the Portuguese in this country in the days when their power and wealth were still very great, though fast fading away before the suicidal bigotry of the successors of Charles the Fifth. The Portuguese lived like grandees, whilst freely intermarrying with the ladies of the country; and, judging from our author, the lives of both sexes were luxurious and vicious in the extreme. A new Portuguese Viceroy was sent out every three years, but during that period a very considerable treasure could be hoarded. Every household had a number of slaves; and ignorance, superstition, and arrogant pride prevailed everywhere. Conversions went on largely, for the priests seem to have accommodated themselves pretty well to the tastes of their flocks, provided, only, that no man or woman who had been once christened, fell back into heresy and heathenism. Duels were frequent, and affronts were often revenged by assassination in the open streets; whilst the ladies are said to have indulged themselves with as many lovers as they pleased. But then they were all religious after their own bigoted fashion, and any one who imbibed false doctrine was handed over to the Goa Inquisition, there to be dealt with as seemed most meet for the good of his or her soul. Linschoten's descriptions of the Natives are also exceedingly life-like, and will be found interesting as referring to a part of India which is still far from being generally known."

Such then are the Travels now submitted to the public in a book form. Meantime however the republication of Roe and Fryer's narratives is still going on in the *Saturday Evening's Englishman*, and will in due course be printed as a second series uniform in every way with the present volume. As the readers of the First Series may like to know something about what is to follow after, we extract the following notices of the authors which were originally pnblished in the *Englishman*. :—

"The narrative of the Mission of Sir Thomas Roe in 1615 and 1616, from James the First of England to the Great Mogul, Shah Jehan, introduces us to a somewhat different state of things from that exhibited in the pages of Van Linschoten. The East India

Company had now been sending out annual ships for some sixteen years, and though, as yet, Calcutta, Madras, and Bombay had no existence, yet the Company had established a Factory at Surat and carried on a considerable trade. There, however, they suffered much from the rapacity of the Mogul Governor at Surat, and, accordingly, King James was induced to send a somewhat pompous embassy with presents to the Great Mogul in order to propitiate that mighty potentate and induce him to keep his Governors of Provinces in better order. The narrative of Sir Thomas Roe is, therefore, most interesting from the description it gives of the manners and customs of the Mogul court, and the strange conviviality and ideas of amusement which prevailed in those times. Wine and women, hunting and rebellion, seem to have been the chief pursuits of the nobles; whilst every courtier passed his days in the dreariest uncertainty, from the fact that his life and fortune depended upon the will of a drunken Sovereign, who was himself in strict subordination to a virago Queen. We do not wish to forestall any of Sir Thomas Roe's anecdotes or descriptions, but still he has told one good story which will bear repetition. Amongst the presents for the Emperor was a large picture of Venus and a Satyr, in which the Goddess was represented as pulling the brute savage by the nose. This picture was a poser for his Majesty, whose conscience inclined him to the belief that the painter was ridiculing himself for being led by the nose by the beautiful Noormahal. Fortunately, his Majesty's attention was somewhat diverted by other matters, and especially by the promise of the Ambassador to bring him some bull dogs next time he came; otherwise the Royal wrath might have manifested itself in a disagreeable manner towards King James' Ambassador.

"The third book of travels which we hope to present to our readers, is the latest in point of time, but, perhaps, the most interesting of the three. Dr. John Fryer visited India some years after the English and Dutch had fairly established themselves in this country, and when the English were in possession of the cities of Madras and Bombay. In those days, the whole of the Madras Presidency was only about four miles long and half a mile broad, but it was a subject of great pride and exultation at home that the Company of merchants should possess a city with a Mayor and Corporation in the gorgeous Ind. At that time, again, the Native government was going through a transition state. The famous Arungzebe was sitting on the throne of the Moguls, and he was busily engaged in carrying out his grand scheme for conquering the Dekhan and extending his power over the whole of India. Meantime, the measures which he took in this direction were already arousing the old nationality of the Hindoos, and a mysterious power rapidly appeared, which is known to history as the rise of the Mahrattas. During the stay of Dr. Fryer in the country, the Mahrattas had been transformed from a mean band of robbers to a sovereign power; and the Doctor was lucky enough to penetrate to the mountain Fort at Rairee, and secure an interview with the great Sivajee himself, the first of the Mahratta Rajahs. Dr. Fryer is also amusing from the fact that he was one of those curious, gossipping, self-satisfied men, who pick up a vast amount of petty information which would escape more thoughtful and scientific minds, and which is always interesting and entertaining. In a word, he is a very Boswell amongst travellers, giving his opinions upon the religion and philosophy of the Hindoos, with all the self-sufficiency of a doctor in a big wig; and at the same time being just as exhaustive upon the subject of prickly heat and musquitæ bites, as upon the customs of the Rajpoots, or the religion and rites of the Parsees. By a second piece of good fortune, he was introduced, in his professional capacity, into the apartments of the ladies of Sivajee, where he felt their pulses under a curtain, and bled some of their arms without seeing their faces. An amusing scene occurred, however, which must have been exceedingly gratifying to the Doctor's curiosity. Whilst he was bleeding one of the ladies, the others were so anxious to see the strange man, that they overturned the *purdah* and fairly exhibited themselves; but even under such circumstances the Doctor employed his eyes so well during the moment or two which elapsed before the *purdah* could be hung up again, that he saw they had been eating mangoes and sweetmeats and amusing themselves with needlework. The worthy Doctor also travelled through the Dekhan and the Carnatic, and his observations upon what he saw are as instructive as entertaining."

In concluding these remarks the Editor of the Travels must return his best thanks to Mr. J. O'B. Saunders, through whose liberality the arrangement has been carried out, by means of which the present volume is submitted to the public at a moderate price in a separate shape, and in a convenient form.

J. TALBOYS WHEELER.

CALCUTTA,
13*th December*, 1864.

CONTENTS.

MR. SAMUEL PURCHAS'S DESCRIPTION OF INDIA.

TRAVELS IN INDIA BY VAN LINSCHOTEN.

MR. SAMUEL PURCHAS'S

DESCRIPTION OF INDIA

250 YEARS AGO.

CHAPTER I.

OF BENGALA.

THE Kingdome of Bengala is very large, and hath of Coast one hundred and twentie leagues, and as much within Land. *Francis Fernandes* measureth it from the Confines of the Kingdome of Ramu or Porto Grande to Palmerine, ninetie miles beyond Porto Pequene, in all six hundred miles long. The River Chaberis (which some call Guenga, and thinke to bee the ancient Ganges) watereth it; it is plentifull in Rice, Wheat, Sugar, Ginger, Longpepper, Cotton and Silke; and enjoyeth a very wholesome ayre. The inhabitants neere the shoare, are (for the most part) Mahumetans, and so also was the King, before the Great *Mogore* (one likewise of his owne Sect) conquered Him. Gouro (*a*) the seat Royall, and Bengala are faire Cities. Of this, the Gulfe, sometimes called *Gangeticus*, now beareth name *Golfo di Bengala.* Chatigan (*b*) is also reckoned amongst their Cities. They

(*a*) Gour was the ancient capital of Bengal. It's ruins may still be traced by the river Ganges some distance above Moorshedabad.

(*b*) Chatigan is evidently the modern Chittagong.

are a most subtile and wicked people, and are esteemed the worst slaues of all India: for that they are all Theeues; and the Women, Whores; although this fault is common through all India, no place excepted. They have a custome, neuer to dresse or seeth meat twice in one pot, but have euerie time a new one. Whensoever they are found in Adulterie, they have their Noses cut off, and are thence forwards narrowly looked to, that they keepe not each others company. The Portugalls have here *Porto Grande* and *Porto Pequino*, but without Forts and Gouernment; euery man liuing after his owne lust: and for the most part, they are such as dare not stay in their places of better Government, for some wickednesse by them committed.

In Bengala are found great numbers of *Abdas* or *Rhinocerotes*, whose horne (growing up from his snowt,) Teeth, Flesh, Blood, clawes, and whatsoever he hath without and within his bodie, is good against poyson, and is much accounted of throughout all India. The skinne upon the upper part of this Beast, is all wrinkled, as if hee were armed with shields. It is a great enemy of the Elephant. Some think that this is the right Vnicorne, because as as yet there is no other by late travellers found, but onely by heare-say. Onely *Lodovicus Vertomannus* saith, he saw a couple of those other Vnicornes at Mecca; one whereof had a horne of three Cubits, being of the bignesse of a Colt of two yeeres and a halfe old; the other was much lesse; both sent to the Sultan of Mecca for a rare present out of Æthiopia. *Gesner* in his Booke of Foure-footed Beasts, citeth this testimony, and some others, whereby he perswadeth, that there are diuers sorts of these Vnicornes, but it cannot seeme otherwise than strange, that in this last hundred of yeeres, where in the World hath un-veyled her face more than euer before; none of credit (that I have heard) hath affirmed himselfe to haue seene this Vnicorne, but in picture. And in picture they haue lately abused *M. T. Coryate,* (*a*) who writing that he saw Vnicornes at the Mogors or Mogols Court (which, as some that were there, told me, were Rhinocerotes) they haue published the same with picture of the Painters Vnicorne, with a long horne out of his forehead, whereas this groweth out of the middle of the Nose and is but short, the length of a man's hand being a large Hornes measure. That which is reported of their vertue against poyson, proceedeth from the hearbs which Bengala yieldeth; for in other places they are not neer the price of these. There are here also certain wild goats, whose hornes are in account against venome; as I myself (saith *Linschoten*) haue proved.

The Kings of Bengala, in times past, were chosen of the Abassine or Æthiopian slaues, as the Soldans of Cairo were sometime of the Circassian Mamalukes. Northward from Bengala lyeth the Kingdome of Arracan, before mentioned. The great *Can* subdued these parts and the Kingdome of Mien, about the yere 1272 while *Marcus Paulus* (*b*) liued there. Arracan, Chandican, and Siripur are by *Fernandez* placed in Bengala, as so many Kingdomes; Patane or Patenaw (*c*) by *Fredericke* and *Fitch* reckoned to another Bengalan Kingdome; which our Countryman Master *Fitch* calleth the Kingdome of Gouren: so that vnder this name, Bengala, are comprehended many Seigniories; all, or the most part now subject to the *Mogor*.

(*a*) Master Coryat, as he is generally called, is well known for his travels to the Mogul Court, in the early part of the seventeeth century. He is said to have been half cracked, but his adventures are amusing enough.

(*b*) Marcus Paulus is better known by his name of Marco Polo.

(*c*) Patna.

CHAPTER II.

OF GANGES AND THE SUPERSTITIONS THERE OBSERUED.

Ovr maps seeme not to describe the Riuer Ganges (so will wee here terme it with *Ortelius*, *Castaldus*, *Barrius* and all our later Trauellers, both Merchants and Jesuites), according to the due course thereof. For Chaberis they bring from the North, enclining to the East, Guenga from the West, but Master *Fitch*, which continued fiue months in passing downe first in Jamena (*a*) from Agra, which falleth into Ganges, and then in Ganges it selfe to Bengala (although he confesseth it may be done in shorter time) saith it commeth from the North-West, and runneth East into the sea. Some call Chaberis, Ganges ; and some hold Guenga to be Ganges ; and some make but one Riuer of them both ; and hence may happily arise in part, that seeking of Ganges so farre off. Both Ganga and Ganges are in sacred account (saith *Barros*) and therefore the Mahometan Kings will not suffer the superstitious washing of the Ethnikes therein without a Custome or Imposition. (*b*)

There is in Ganges a place called *Gongasagie*, that is, the entrie of the Sea, in which are many fishes called Sea-dogs. They which are weary of this World, and desire to haue a quicke passage to Paradise, cast in them-

---

(*a*) Jumna.

(*b*) These speculations which now appear so absurd, were to be expected at a time when the Ganges was scarcely so well known as the sources of the Nile are in the present day selues here to bee devoured by these Fishes ; perswading themselues that the next and readiest way thither is by their jawes.

Ganges, ouerflowing his bankes, in times past, drowned many Villages, which so remaine, and hath changed his wonted channell ; the cause that Tanda (a Citie of trafficke, where the people goe naked to the waste) standeth now a league from the Riuer. It watereth a fruitfull Countrey, and populous, and (as the Ocean's high Collector) receiueth into him many Riuers by the way, some no lesse than its selfe, so that in the time of raine, you cannot see from the one side of Ganges to the other. The superstitious opinion conceiued in those parts of this Riuer, appeareth by the reports of all. *Emanuel Pinner* at Cambaia obserued many to resort thither on Pilgrimage, sometime out of that citie foure thousand ; and was told by the Gouernour of Bengala, vnder the *Mogor*, then at Lahor, that there came thither sometime three hundred thousand or foure hundred thousand Pilgrims. And addeth, that not long before his comming to Cambaia there assembled there, to this deuout iourney, fiftie thousand people. Happy they esteeme that man which washeth himselfe therein and secure of saluation, if at the point of death hee may drinke of this water. He conferred with one *Gedacham*, a great man, which had been on this holy voyage, and had there weighed his Mother three times ; first by her weight in Siluer ; secondly in Gold ; thirdly in Pearles, all which he gaue to the poore. A brother of his, called *Rau*, being to goe to the great *Mogor*, offered one hundred and fiftie thousand *Pardaws*, that his Pagods or idols should send him good successe. Theymake an Image also to this Riuer, whereunto they doe divine honor. The King of Calecut, and the other kings of Malabar keepe a solemne feast euery twelue yeeres, in honor of this Riuer ; because that long since, a certaine *Brachmane* (falsly accused) fled vnto Ganges, and there led an austere life twelue yeeres, worshipping that Streame and his Idoll, to whom, when hee purposed to returne home, after those twelue yeeres expired, that image of Ganges appeared, and said, that on the last day of *February* he would appeare in a Riuer of his owne Countrey, and cause the waters thereof to arise, and run backward in witnesse of his innocencie, and bade him assemble all the Lords of Malabar to the sight, which accordingly came to passe, and the memorie thereof is by this Feast solemnized.

Bannaras (*a*) is a great Towne on Ganges, to which the Gentiles out of farre Countries come on pilgrimage. The men are shauen all but the crowne. Alongst the water side are many faire houses, in which stand images of euill fauour, made of stone, and wood, like Leopards, Lyons, Monkeys, Men, Women, Peacocks, and Deuils, with foure armes and hands, sitting closelegged, and holding somewhat in their hands. There are diuers old men, which on places of earth, made for that purpose, sit praying, and they giue the people (which by breake of day, and before, come out of the Towne, to wash themselues in Ganges) three or foure strawes which they take, and hold them between their fingers where they wash themselues : and some sit to marke them in the foreheads, and they haue in a cloth a little Rice, Barley, or Money, which they giue to these old men. After that, they goe to diuers of their images, and giue them of their sacrifices, those old men in the meanewhile praying, which maketh all holy. They haue one idoll called *Ada*, with foure hands and clawes. On certaine great carued stones also they powre Water, Rice, Wheat, &c. They haue a great place like a Well, with steps to goe downe, wherein the water standeth foule and stinketh, by reason of those many flowers, which they continually

(*a*) Benares.

throw there into. Many people are alwayes therein, with imagination of pardon for their sinnes, because *God* (as they blaspheme) washed himself therein. They gather vp the Sand in the bottome, as a holy Relike. They pray not but in the water, and wash themselves ouer-head, lading vp water with both their hands, and turne themselues about, and then drinke a little of the water three times, after which they go to their gods in their houses. Some of them will wash a place which is their length, and then pray vpon the earth, with their armes and legs at length out, and will rise vp and lye downe, and kisse the ground twentie or thirtie times, but will not stirre their right foot Some use fifteene or sixteene pots, little and great, ringing a Bell, while they make their mixture ten or twelue times; and make a circle of water about their pots, and pray; others sitting by, one of which reacheth them their Pots. They say over these pots diuers things many times, which done, they goe to their gods and strew their sacrifices, which they thinke are very holy, and marke many of them which sit by, in their foreheads, esteemed as a great gift. There come fiftie and sometime an hundred together, to this Well, and to these Idols. About their idols, in some houses, sitteth one in warme weather, to blow the winde with a Fan vpon them. And when they see any company comming, they ring a little Bell, and many giue them their almes. None of these idols haue a good face. Some are blacke, and haue clawes of brasse; and some ride on Peacocks or other Fowles. One there is alwayes attended with his Fan, to make winde, which (they say) giueth them all things, both food and rayment. Here some are burned to ashes, some scorched in the fire, and throwne into the water, when they are dead; the Foxes presently eat them. The Wiues doe burne with their husband when they dye; if they will not, their heads are shauen, and never any account is made of them after. If a man or woman be sicke, and like to die, they will lay him before their idols all night; and that shall mend or end him. And if hee doe not mend, that night his friends will come and sit a little with him, and crie, and after will carrie him to the water side and set him vpon a little raft made of reeds, and so let him goe down the riuer. The chiefe idols are very euill-fauoured, their mouthes monstrous, their eares gilded and full of Jewels, their teeth and eyes of gold, siluer, glasse, coloured blacke, with Lampes continually burning before them. Into their houses or Temples you may not enter, with your shooes on. When the scorched Indians are throwne into Ganges, the men swim with their faces downwards, the women with their faces vpwards; which I had thought they had by some meanes caused, but they denied it. The people goe all naked, with a little cloth about their middle. Their women are exceedingly on their necks, armes, and eares, decked with rings of Siluer, Copper, Tinne and Iuorie hoopes; they are marked with a great spot of red in their foreheads, and a stroke of red vp to the crowne, and so it runneth three wayes. Their marriages are in this sort: The man and the woman come to the water-side where standeth a *Bramane* or Priest, with a Cow and a Calfe, or a Cow with Calfe; these all goe into the water together, the *Bramane* holding a white cloth of foure yards long, and a basket crosse bound with diuers things in it. This cloth he layeth vpon the backe of the Cow. And then he taketh the Cow by the tayle and saith certaine words. Shee hath a Copper or a Brasse pot-full of water. The man holdeth his hand by the Braman's hand, and the wiue's hand by her husbands, and all haue the Cow by the tayle. Then they powre water out of the pot vpon the Cows taile which runneth thorow all their hands, and they lade vp water with their hands and then the Brachmane tyeth their clothes together. After this, they goe round about the Cow and Calfe, and giue somewhat to the poore there attending, leauing the Cow and Calfe for the Bramans vse, and offer to diuers of their idols mony ; then lying downe vpon the ground, they kisse it diuers times, and go their way. Between this and Patanaw are diuers Theeues, like the Arabians, without certaine abode.

CHAPTER III.

OF PATANE, COUCHE, ORIXA, BOTANTER, CANDECAN.

PATANE or Patanaw, (*a*) is a greate Towne and long, with large streets, simple houses of earth, couered with thatch, the people tall and slender, many old; sometimes a Kingdome, now subject to the Mogor. They haue gold, which (as in America) they dig out of the Pits, and wash the Earth in great Bolls. The Women here are so decked with Siluer and Copper, that it is strange to see, and by reason of such Rings vpon their Toes, they can weare no shooes. Here I saw a dissembling Prophet, which sate vpon an Horse in the Market place, and made as though hee slept, and many of the people came and touched his feet with their hands and then kissed their hands. They tooke him for a Great Man, but I saw he was a lazie Lubber, and there I left him sleeping. The people here are great Praters and Dissemblers. As I came from Agra downe the River Jemena,(*b*) I saw also many naked Beggars, of which the people make great account; they call them *Schesche*. Here I saw one, which was a monster among the rest, wearing nothing on him, with a long beared, the hayre of his head couering his priuities. The nayles of some of his fingers were two Inches long; for he would cut nothing from him. Neither would he speake, but was accompanied with eight or ten which spake for him. When any man spake to him, hee would lay his

(*a*) Patna.
(*b*) Jumna.

hand vpon his brest, and bow himselfe, but speake he would not to the King. The King of Patanaw was Lord of the geatest part of Bengala, vntill the Mogoll slue their last King. After which twelue of them ioyned in a kinde of Aristocratie and vanquished the Mogolls (it seemes this was in the time of *Emmaupaxda*) and still nothwithstanding the Mogolls Greatnesse are great Lords, specially he of Siripur, and of Ciandecan, aboue all *Maasudalim.(a)* Nine of them are Mahumetans. Thus *Fernandes.* These Pataneans seeme by the Iesuites report to come of the Tartars.

In those parts they had many strange Ceremonies. Their Bramans or Priests come to the Water, and haue a string about their necks made with great Ceremonies, and lade up Water with both their hands, and turne the string first with their armes within, and then one arme after the other out. Here also about Iemena, the Gentiles will eate no flesh, nor kill anything. They pray in the water naked, and dresse their meate and eate it naked; and for their penance they lye flat vpon the earth, and rise vp and turne themselues about thirtie or fortie times, and vse to heaue vp their hands to the Sunne, and to kisse the earth with their armes and legs stretched out along, their right leg being alwayes before the left. Euery time they lye downe, they score it with their fingers to know when their stint is ended. The Bramans marke themselues in their foreheads, eares, and throates with a kinde of yellow geare, which they grinde; euery morning they doe it. And they haue some old men which goe in the streets with a boxe of yellow powder, and marke them which they meet on their heads and necks. And their Wiues doe

---

(a) It should be borne in mind that Bengal occupied a very different portion in reference to the ruling power in the Mussulman period, to what it has occupied under British rule. As regards Delhi it was an outlying province, and never was thoroughly conquered until 1592, in the reign of Akbar, only a very few years before the present account had been drawn up.

come ten, twentie, and thirtie together to the water-side, singing, and there doe wash themselues, and vse their ceremonies, and marke themselues on their fore-heads and faces, and carry some with them and so depart singing. Their Daughters bee marryed at, or before, the age of ten yeeres. The men may haue seuen wiues. They are a craftie People, worse than the Iews. The way from Bannaras to Patanaw is a faire and fertile Countrey, beautified with many faire Townes.

I went from Bengala into the Countrey of Couche,(a) which lieth fiue and twentie dayes journey Northwards from Tanda. The King was a Gentile named *Suckel-Counse;* his Countrey is greate and lyeth not farre from Cauchin China. All the Countrey is set with Canes made sharpe at both ends, and driuen into the Earth; and they can let in the water, and drowne the Countrey knee-deepe. In time of Warre they poyson all the waters. The people have eares, which be maruellous great, of a span long, which they draw out in length by deuices when they bee young. They are all Gentiles and will kill nothing. They haue Hospitalls for Sheep, Dogs, Goats, Cats, Birds, and all other liuing Creatures. When they bee old and lame they keepe them till they dye. If a man catch or buy any quick thing in other places, and bring it thither, they will giue him mony for it, or other victuals, and keepe it in their Hospitalls or let it go. They will giue meat to the Ants. Their small mony is Almonds, which often times they eat. We passed thorow the Countrey of Gouren, where we found but few villages, and almost all Wildernesse (for we chose this Desart way for feare of theeues,) and saw many Buffes, Swine, and Deere; grasse longer than a man, and very many Tygres.

Orixa is the next Countrey, which hath beene a Kingdome, but conquered by the King of Patanaw, and both

(a) Cooch Behar.

since by *Echebar.*(*a*) Orixa stands sixe dayes South-west from Satagan.(*b*) There is much Rice, cloth of Cotton, and cloth made of grasse, called Yerua like silke. (They speake of the like in Virginia.) Through this Kingdome (*Fredericke* writes) a man might haue gone with Gold in his hand without danger while the old King reigned, who so befriended Merchants that he tooke no custome of them. And there were laden in the Porte of Orisa yeerely fiue and twentie or thirtie Ships, with Rice, Lacca, long Pepper, Ginger, Mirabolins, and the Yerua aforesaid made of an herbe growing in the Woods wild, then gathered when the boll is growne round, as bigge as an Orange. In the Hauen of Angeli are yeerely many Ships laden with many kindes of commodities. Satagam is a faire Citie, (for a Citie of Moores) and very plentifull, sometime subject to Patanaw. In Bengala such is the estimation of Ganges, that they will fetch of it a greate way off, though they haue good water neere; and if they haue not sufficient to drinke, they will sprinkle a little on them, and then they are well. From Satagam I trauelled by the Countrey of the King of Tippara, with whom the *Mogor* hath continuall warre. The *Mogores*, which be of the Kingdome of Recon and Rame, be stronger than this King of Tippara. Foure dayes journey from Couche is Botanter,(*c*) and the Citie Bottia. The King is called *Dermaine*; the People are tall and strong; the Country greate, three moneths journey, and hath in it high Mountaines, one of which a man may see sixe days journey off. Vpon these Mountaines are people with eares of a span long; otherwise they account them Apes. Hither resort many Merchants out of China and Tartaria. From Chatigan in Bengala I went to Bacola, the King whereof is a Gentile; thence to Senepare

(*a*) The Mogul Emperor Akbar.

(*b*) Chittagong.

(*c*) This account of Bhootan ought to be especially interesting at the present time.

and after to Simergan, where they will eate no flesh, nor kill no beast, and thence to Negrais in Pegu and Colmin. Thus farre hath our Countreyman led vs in the view of so many superstitions of these Bengalans, and their Northerly Neighbours.

In that part of Botanter, which is next to Lahor, and the *Mogor* the People are white, and Gentiles. Their garments are close girt to them, that a wrinkle or pleit is not to be seene, which they neuer put off, no, not when they sleepe, as long as they are able to hang on; their head attyre is like a Sugar—loafe, sharpe at the top. They neuer wash their hands, lest say they, so pure a Creature, as the Water, should be defiled.(*a*) They haue but one Wife; and when they haue two or three children, they liue as brother and sister. Widdowers and widdowes may not marry a second time. They haue no Idols nor Townes. nor King in those parts of Botanter.(*b*) They haue their Sooth-sayers, which they ask counsell of. When any is dead, they resort vnto these Wisards, to know what is to be done with their dead. They search their Bookes; and as they say the word, they burne them, or bury them or eate them, although they vsually feed not on man's flesh. They also vse dead men's skulls instead of dishes, as in *Thebet*, wee haue obserued the like custome. They are liberall Almes-giuers. They liue on Weauing and making Clothes, which they sell at Calamur and Negariot in Summer, for in their Winter they cannot passe for Snowes. They are like in colour and haire to men of these parts. The Bengalans haue a Tradition or Fable amongst them, That this Riuer commeth out of Paradise,(*c*) which was

(*a*) This description of the Bhootanies is, we believe, generally confirmed by the accounts brought back by Mr. Eden's mission; but whether their distaste for washing themselves is to be ascribed to a religious veneration for the water, or to a philosophic disregard of dirt, must be a matter of opinion.

(*b*) Much the same in the present day.

(*c*) Here we have traces of the old legend in the Ramayana, which relates how the goddess Gunga fell from heaven upon the head of Mahadeva.

proued by one of their Kings, who sent men vp the streame, till they came to a pleasant Ayre, still Water, and fragrant Earth, and could row no further. Hence happily grew this conceit, that this Water should wash away sinne, and that without it they cannot be saued. This Riuer hath in it Crocodiles, which by water are no lesse dangerous then the Tygres by land, and both will assault men in their Ships. There is also a little small Beasts which by his barking maketh the Tyger to run away.

The King of Candecan (which lyeth at the mouth of Ganges) caused a Iesuite to rehearse the *Decalogue*: : who when he reproued the Indians for their polytheisme, worshipping so many *Pagodes* : Hee said, That they obserued them but as, among them, their Saints were worshipped : to whom how sauoury the Iesuites distinction of *douleia* and *latreia* was for his satisfaction I leaue to the Reader's judgement. This King, and the others of Bacala and Arracan, haue admitted the Iesuites into their Countries, and most of these Indian Nations.

CHAPTER IV.

OF THE GREAT MOGOR, OR MOGOLL.

SECTION I.—*Of the Mogors Countries ; and of Melabdim Echebar.*

THE Great Mogor (according to Boterus) hath vnder his subiection seuen and fortie Kingdomes, which lie betweene Indus and Ganges on the East and West, and betwixt Imaus and the Ocean, contayning all that which the Ancients called *India intra Gangem* or *India Citenor.* Hee is called of the people the Great Mogor, for the same cause that the *Ottoman*-Turkes are called Great. The style of him that was King, when the Iesuites imparted to vs these Relations, was *Mahumeth Zelabdim Echebar,* King Mogor or Mogoll ; for so they call him in the Countrey, and not Mogor, as the Iesuites. This Mogoll seemes to argue their Tartarian Originall from the Moai Tartars of which see our Tartarian relations. The true Mogors, or Mogols, liue on the hither side of Indus, in the Kingdome of Quabul, or Cabul, which is under the brother of *Echebar* ; against whom *Anno* 1582, hee led a strong Armie, in which the Iesuites say, were fiue thousand Elephants armed. These weare plates of Iron on their foreheads, carrie foure Archers, or else foure Gunners, with great Peeces ; and goe not before the Armie, lest they should hinder their fight, or (being hurt) disturbe the rankes ; and therefore are set in the Rere, a Sword bound to their trunke, and Daggers fastened to their great teeth. King *Echebar* was borne in the Prouince of Chaquata, which hath Indostan on the South, Persia on the West, the Tartars East. Their Language is

Turkish; but the Courtiers to this day speake Persian. *Baburxa* his grand-father chased the Parthians vnto Bengala, before possessors of the Region of the Mogors; after whose death, the Parthians, or (as they are now called Pataneans, of Patanaw before mentioned) recouered themselues, and warred on his sonne. (*a*) Their descent is from *Tamerlane* whose third sonne was *Miromcha*, grandfather to *Abusayd* who slue *Abdula*; successor to *Abdelatife* which had slaine *Oleghbek*, the sonne and successor of *Mirzah Charrok* the fourth sonne and first successor of *Tamerlan*. Sultan *Hamed*, sonne of *Abusayd*, obtayned Maurenahar, and after him *Babor* his sonne, which in the yeere 1500 was dispossessed by the Vsbechs, yet still possessed Gaznehen, and some parts of India, succeeded by his sonne *Homayen*,(*b*) the father of this *Achabar*. Thus *Mirkand*. The Iesuites say, they are Parthians, descended of *Cingis* (therefore rather to be called Tartars;) *Achabars* grandfather they call *Baburxa*, which by his sword entred Industan, and chased those Tartars into Bengala. But they againe preuailed after his death; insomuch that *Achabar's* father *Emmaupaxda* (as the Iesuite's report) (*c*)

(*a*) These historical data are very curious. The real facts are as follows:—The three first Mogul Emperors at Delhi were Baber, Humayoon, and Akbar, and their reigns synchronized very nearly with those of Henry VIII, Edward VI, Mary, and Elizabeth in England. Baber, called in the text Baburxa, carried on a war with the King of Bengal, and defeated the Afghans in the Army of the Bengal sovereign; and the identification of the Parthians with the Afghans, strange as it appears to modern eyes, is by no means far from the truth. The movements of the ancient Parthians bear, however, a stronger resemblance to those of the Mahrattas than to those of the Afghans; but old Purchas is quite right as regards locality, for whether the Parthians were Mahrattas or Afghans, it is certain that their homes were in the region now known as Cabul and Candahar, though their light horse occasionally swept westward as far as the confines of Syria.

(*b*) Humayoon.

(*c*) This is a mistake. Humayoon was the father of Akbar. It will be remembered that when Humayoon had been driven out of his dominions, and was residing in the desert of Scind, he thought proper to fall desperately in love with a young lady whom he saw in his step-mother's Zenana, and in spite of the remonstrances of those around him, married her at once. The consequence was that Akbar was born in the middle of the desert, whilst his father was proceeding towards Persia, and had no presents to give on the occasion except a single pod of musk which he broke and distributed amongst his adherents in honour of the joyful occasion.

being driuen to great straights by the Parthians, Tartars, or Pataneans, was driuen to aske aide of the *Sophi*, or Persian King; which he obtained, with condition of submitting himselfe to the Persian Religion. The Mogors speake the Turkish language. The Empire of this Mogor is exceeding great, contayning the countries of Bengala, Cambaya, Mendao, and others, comprehended by some vnder the name of Industan. This Mendao is said to be ten leagues in circuit, and that it cost the Mogor twelue yeers siege. Agra and Fatipore are two Cities in his Dominion, great, and full of people, much exceeding London; and the whole space, betweene, is as a continuall populous Market. Many Kings he hath conquered, and many haue submitted themselues and their States voluntarily to his subiection. Twentie Gentile Kings are numbered in his Court, which attend him, equalling the King of Calecut in power. Many others pay him tribute. In his Countries are many Spices, Pepper, Ginger, Cassia, and others; many precious Stones, Pearles, Metals of all Sorts, Silkes, Cotton, Horse, and other Commodities, which yeeld him many millions yeerely beyond his expences. About the yeere 1582 the Iesuites first entred there; after whose report, his Dominions were then as followeth since much more enlarged. Eleuen great Riuers run through his Dominions; Taphi, Haruada, Chambel, Iamena, Ganges; the other sixe, are Indus or *Schind* (as they call it) and Catamul, Cebcha, Ray, Chenao, Rebeth, tributaries to Indus. The whole Mouarchie enuironeth nine hundred leagues. King *Echebar* hath many Lords; each of which is to maintayne eight, ten, twelue or fourteene thousand Horse in readinesse for the warre, besides Elephants; of which in the whole Kingdome are said to bee fiftie thousand. Himselfe can further bring of his owne into the Field fiftie thousand Horse, and Foot-men innumerable. To those Lordes hee alloweth certaine Prouinces, for such Militarie seruice: for hee is

Lord of all nor hath any else possession of any thing, but at the will of the King. Once a yeere they appeare before the King, where they present a view of those their enioyned Forces. Many millions of Reuenue doe besides accrew unto his Coffers; yet his Port and Magnificence is not so great, as of many other Princes, eyther for Apparell, Diet or the Maiestie of his Court seruice. Hee cannot write or reade, but heareth often the Disputations of others, and Histories read before him, being of deepe iudgement, piercing wit, and wise fore-cast.

In execution of Iustice hee is very diligent; insomuch, that in the Citie where hee resideth, he heareth all Causes himselfe; neither is any malefactor punished without his knowledge; himselfe giuing publike Audience twice euery day: For which purpose, he hath two wide Halls, or rather open Courts, and in them Royall Thrones, where hee is attended with eight Councellors, besides Notaries. Yet doth hee stand, and not sit; and at other times sit on Carpets, after the Turkish manner, notwithstanding his Chayre of Estate standing by. He hath twelue Learned men alway about him, which ordinarily reason and dispute in his presence, or relate Histories. Hee is a curious discourser of all Sects. Hee is both Affable, and Maiesticall, Mercifull and Severe; delights himselfe in diuers Games, as fights of Buffals, Cockes, Harts, Rammes, Elephants; Wrestlers, Fencers, Dances, Comedies, and in the Dances of Elephants and Camels, thereto instructed. In the midst of these Spectacles he dispatcheth serious affaires. He delights in Hunting, vsing the Panther to take wild Beasts. Hunting Dogs hee had none. They vse tame Harts to take the wild, with Nets fastened to their hornes; wherewith they intangle the other. When hee goes to warre, hee will cause a whole Wood to bee round beset with men, hand in hand; sending others in, which raise the Beasts, and driue them into the others armes; which, if they let them goe, are punished, to make sport that way. He was skilfull in diuers Mechanicall Trades; as, making of Gunnes, casting of Ordnance, hauing his Worke house in the Palace for that purpose. But we haue obserued, that this is common to all Mahumetan Priests and Princes, the Great Turke, yea, the Great Chalifa himselfe (as *Tudelensis* writes of his Times) practising some Mechanicall Mysterie. Theeues and Pyrates He punished with losse of the hand; Murtherers, Adulterers, Robbers by the high way, with empaling, hanging, or other deaths; not executed, till the Sentence had been thrice pronounced: Loued and feared of his Owne; Terrible to his Enemies; Affable to the Vulgar; seeming to grace them and their Presents, with more respective Ceremonies than the *Grandes*; of sparing Dyet, scarce eating Flesh aboue foure times in the yeere, but feeding by Rice, White meats, and Electuaries; sleeping but three houres in the night; curiously industrious. (*a*)

This King detesteth the Mahumetan Sect, which, as you heard, his Father embraced for his aduantange; and therefore hath ouerthrowne their Moschees in his Kingdome, razing the Steeples, and conuerting the rest into Stables, and more trusteth and employeth the Gentiles in his affaires than the Moores; whereupon many of them rebelled against him, and stirred vp the Prince of Quabul,

---

(*a*) This is a very fair description, though in antiquated language, of the Emperor Akbar; and the remarks which follow respecting his religious views are strictly in accordance with what is known of this monarch from other sources. Akbar seems to have believed in what is called natural religion, but to have had no faith in revelation of any kind or sort. He was fond of listening to religious controversy, and a good story is told of his having on one occasion paid great attention to an angry and lengthened dispute between some Portuguese Missionaries and some Mussulman Moollahs, and to have suggested that the rival parties should settle the question by leaping into a great fire, the one with the Bible and the other with the Koran, when the victory should be adjudged to the party who was preserved from the flames. Accordingly a great fire was kindled, but the cantroversialists. though perfectly ready to consign their opponents to eternal fire in another world, seemed to have an accountable objection to leaping into a furnace on this side of the tomb. Accordingly each party offered to jump in provided the other party commenced, and as neither party volunteered so each party was enabled to say how much it would have done had it not been for the cowardly backwardness of the other party.

(*a*) his Brother, to take Armes; against whom *Echebar* opposed himselfe (as is said,) and caused him to retire into his owne Countrey. It is vncertaine what Religion hee is of, some affirming him to bee a *Moore*, some a *Gentile*, some a *Christian*, some of a fourth Sect, and of none of the former. Indeed it appeareth that he wauereth, vncertaine which way of many to take, able to see the absurdities of the Arabian and Gentile professions, and not able to beleeue in the mysteries of the *Christian Faith*, especially the *Trinitie* and *Incarnation*. Hee hath admitted the Iesuites there to preach, and would haue had them by miracle to haue proued those things to him, which they (elswhere so much boasting of miracles) wisely refused, when hee demaunded that the *Mulla's* or Priests of the Mogores, should by passing throw the fire, make tryall of their Faith. He hath many Bookes and Images, which the Christians there doe vse, and seemeth to haue great liking to them, vsing the same with great reuerence. But his Religion is the same (it seemeth) with that of *Tamerlane*, his predecessor, to acknowledge *One God*, whom varietie of Sects and Worshippings should best content. Hee caused thirtie Infants to bee kept (like that which is said of *Psammetichus*, King of Egypt) setting certaine to watch and obserue that neither their Nurses, nor any else, should speake vnto them, purposing to addict himselfe to that Religion, which they should embrace, whose Language these Infants should speake; which accordingly came to passe. For as they spake no certain Language, so is not he settled in any certaine Religion. Hee hath diuers Idols sometimes brought before him among which, is one of the Sunne; which early euery morning, and three other times a day, at noone, euening, and in the night, he worshippeth. He worshipped also the Image of CHRIST and OUR LADY, which hee set on the

(*a*) Cabul.

crown of his head, and wore Relikes about him.(*a*) He is addicted to a new Sect, as is said, wherein he hath his followers which hold him for a Prophet. The profit which they haue by his gold, addicteth them to this new Prophet. Hee professeth to worke Miracles ; by the water of his feet curing diseases. Many Women make Vowes vnto him, either to obtaine children, or to recouer the health of their children ; which if they attaine, they bring him their vowed Deuotions, willingly of him receiued, yea, euery morning as he worshipped the Sunne, so he delighted to be worshipped himselfe of the people : to whom hee made shew of himselfe at a window ; and they kneeling performed like Ceremonie to him, as to their Idols : and he was thought to entertaine men skilfull in diuers Sects and Religions ; that of euery one hee might take somewhat to, the constitution of a new one. He hath three sonnes ; *Sciec* the eldest, he which is honoured with the title *Gio*, and called *Sciecigio*, that is, the Soule or Person of *Sciec* ; he much fauoureth the Iesuites : the second, *Pahari : Dan*, or *Daniel*, is the youngest. Some call them by other names. His Presents are exceeding great, besides his Tributes and Customes. Hee mentions One, which in their presence offered his Vassalage, and withall a Present, valued at two hundred thousand crownes and more ; a Horse with furniture of Gold and Iewels ; two Swords, and the Girdles of like worke ; Camels, Carpets, &c., taking himselfe dignified in the acceptation of his Present. Himselfe after often bowings, and touching the ground with his head comming nerer, was searched, whether hee had any weapons, and then was admitted to touch his foot, *Echebar* laying his hand on his necke, and allowing him to stand with his other Nobles. The King's sonne, Sultan *Morad*, at the same time offered a Present of fiftie Elephants, worth a hundred and fiftie thousand Duckats ;

(*a*) All pious lies told by the Jesuits for the delectation of their admirers in Europe.

one Chariot of Gold, another of Siluer, others of Mother of Pearle, with other things of great value. The Vice-Roy or Gouernour of Bengala, followed with another Present, esteemed worth eight hundred thousand Duckats, *viz*, three hundred Elephants. Almost dayly hee receiueth such Presents, especially at a certaine Feast called Nerosa ; in which one Great Man was thought to present him neere the worth of one Million of Gold.

CHAPTER IV.

SECTION II.

Of the Conquests and death of Echebar, and of his Sonne and Successor Selim now reigning.

OVR Relations of *Echebar* or *Achebar*, his Rites Humane and Diuine, as also of his Possessions and Greatnesse, wee have alreadie seemed long; yet cannot be so satisfied, without further satisfaction to the Reader, if he be (such as he of whom wee write) curious and desirous to know remote Affaires and farre distant Occurrences. Great *Echebar* added vnto that Greatnesse which his Father left him, the Kingdome of Caxemir,(*a*) of Sinda, of Guzzarat, of Xischandadan, (*b*) and a great part of Decan, with all the Tract of Bengala. Such was his felicitie, that it grew into a Prouerbe, *As happie as Echebar*; seldome attempting any thing, without prosperous successe; I speake of worldly happinesse. Euen in Nature's treasures hee was rich, both Wit and Memorie; this so happie, that of many thousands of Elephants which hee had, hee knew the names; yea, of his Horses (to each of which hee gaue names) of his wilde Beasts and Harts, that hee kept in a place appointed; and euen of his Pigeons, which hee kept for sport. Yet, was not this happinesse so perpetuall, but that he had some, especially domesticke, Crosses. His second sonne, Sultan Morad, being sent into Guzzarat,

(*a*) Cashmere.
(*b*) Few things are more puzzling than the identification of names of places in these old travellers. This unpronounceable name must be left to our readers without even an attempt at explanation.

against Melic King of Decan(a) (sometime Lord of Chaul) was slaine, with many other Commanders; which newes was then brought to *Echebar*, when hee was celebrating their New yeeres Festiuall (the day that the Sunne enters into *Aries*) whereupon hee sent thither another of his sonnes. Another time, when hee was solemnizing the Sunnes Festiuall, on Easter day, 1597 (about which time the King of China sustained the like Casualtie) Fire fell from Heauen vpon his Tent, richly adorned with Gold and Iewels, and consumed it to ashes, with all the Tents adioyning, together with his Throne of solide Gold, valued at 100,000 Duckats, consumed or melted: from whence it proceeded to the Palace; which being of Timber, was for the most part brought into ashes. Some millions of Treasure there reserued, could not bee there preserued from this flame; which made a Streame of Gold and Siluer, mixed with other Metalls, runne alongst the streets. For this cause, hee forsooke Lahor (where hee had built the Iesuites a Church, and where hee kept his Court, as hee did before at Fatepore, and sometimes at Agra) and went to Caximir, or Cascimir, a Kingdome which a little before he had subdued. This yeelds not to any Indian Region, in goodlinesse and wholesomenesse, being encompassed with very high Mountaines, couered most part of the yeere with Snow; the rest a delicate Playne diuersified with Pastures, Fields, Woods, Gardens, Parkes, Springs, Riuers, euen to admiration. It is coole, and more temperate then the Kingdome of Rebat, which adioyneth to it on the East. Three leagues from Caximir is a Lake, deepe and beset round with Trees, in the midst thereof an Iland and thereon hee built a Palace. The countrey hath store of Rice, Wheat and Vines, which they plant at the foot of the Mulburie, the same Tree seeming to beare two Fruits. Had they not beene at Contentions amongst themselues,

(a) Better known as Malik Amber who reigned at Ahmednuggur.

hee could neuer haue conquered so strong a Kingdome. In times past they were all Gentiles; but three hundred yeeres before this, the most of them became Mahumetane. This Countrey he left when Summer was past, and returned to Lahor, losing many Elephants and Horses in the way, both by Famine then oppressing the Countrey, and the dificultie of the Passages; the Elephants sometimes, in the ascent of Hils helping themselues with their Trunkes, leaning and staying themselues, being burthened, thereon, as on a staffe. The Prince, which is now King, was assaulted by a fierce Lioness, as he rode on a Female Elephant, which yet hee wounded first with a Dart, then with a Shot, and lastly smote her with the hand-Gun itselfe; wherewith being overthrowne, a Souldier came in and slew her, but with loss of his owne life. The next yeere, 1598, *Echebar* went to Agra, chiefe Citie of a Kingdome, which hee had also conquered, a hundred leagues from Lahor towards the South, passing that way to Decan. Hee had eight hundred Elephants, and seuen thousand Camels, to carrie his Tents and Prouisions; yea, his Secretarie had at the same time seuen hundred Camels, and seuentie Elephants for his own furniture; and therefore it is lesse maruaile of the Kings. The King conducted in this Expedition aboue a thousand Elephants, instructed to fight, and a hundred thousand Soldiers. Hee passed the Mountaines of Gate, by almost impassable Passages spending sometimes a whole day, in passing the space of a Musket shot. One of his Captaines went before him with fiftie thousand, who tooke one of the Decan's strongest Holds, and made easie way to the Conquest of the rest of Melics Dominions, which hee left in the Gouernment of his sonne. Brampore fell into his hands being destitute of defence. This was *Anno* 1600. *Miram* the King thereof had forsaken it, and betaken himselfe to Syra, a strong Hold both by Nature and Art. It was seated on the top of a Hill, which reacheth fiue leagues, enuironed with a triple Wall, so built, that one might be defended from the next. Within, was a Well of running Water, and all necessarie Prouisions for threescore thousand persons, for many yeeres. It had three thousand great Peeces of Ordnance. In this Castle (according to the Country custome) the next of the Bloud Royall were kept with their Families; nor might depart, except (the Throne emptie) the next Heire was hence deliuered, much after that which is written of Amara, in the Abassens Countrey, and it seemes borrowed from thence; so many slaues of those parts being here entertained, and some in the highest Employments. At this time, besides King *Miram*, there were seven of these Princes. The Gouernour was an Abassine, with seven other Vnder-Commanders, all renegado Mahumetanes. The Mogoll layde siege thereto, with almost two hundred thousand men: but more preuailed (as before in Melics Countrey) with Bribes, and Promises, then Force. Thus inuiting *Miram* to a Conference, swearing, *By the King's head* (accounted an inuiolable Oath, as is that, *By their Father's head*) that hee should be permitted safe returne: Some of his Councellours perswaded him to goe; hee went, with a kinde of Stole on his necke, hanging to his knees, in token of subiection: And comming before the *Mogoll*, bowed himselfe, but was cast to the ground by some of his Captaines, and forceably detained. The Abassine Gouernour sent his sonne to demand performance of *Achebar* his promise, who being questioned of his Father the Abassen, and the hopes to obtaine the Castle, freely answered for his Father's fidelitie, and that if *Miram* were not restored, they should not want a Successour; with which libertie he prouoked the *Mogol* to cause him to be slaine; which his Father hearing, strangled himselfe. And the walls were soon after battered (at least entred, and a breach made through the open gates) by golden shot; none of these seuen for feare of treason, daring to take the Royall Soueraigntie. These with the King, were dispersed into diuers parts of his Kingdome and maintenance allowed him. Thus remained *Echebar* Lcrd of these parts and longed to adde the rest of India, whatsoeuer is betwixt Indus and Ganges euen to the Cape Comori, to his Dominion.

He writ a Letter about this time to the Vice-Roy of Goa beginning thus (I mention it to shew you his Titles which hee arrogated) *The Great and Mightie Lord of the Law of* MAHOMET, *The Re-nowned and Great King, Vanquisher of the Kings, his Enemies, Obserued aud honoured of Great Men, Exalted aboue other Kings in ample Honour and Dignitie, The onely Man for Gouernment, amongst all the Princes of the World. His Ambassage to* ARIAS DE SALDGANA, *&c. The ninth day of Franard* (the first moneth of the yeere beginning at the Æquinoctiall Vernall) *in the fortie sixe yeere viz.*, of His Reigne. At this time dyed the Gouernour or Vice-Roy of Lahor, which left to the King (who is Heire Generall and Successour of euery man's wealth) three millions of Gold coyned, besides other Gold, Siluer, Iewels, Horses, Elephants, furniture and goods almost inualuable. This also for a taste of the meanes accrewing to this King's Treasure. *Echebar* returning to Agra gaue libertie to the Iesuites to conuert as many as would to Christianitie.

The King of Candacar or Candahar, not able to defend himselfe against *Abduxa*, King of the Vsbechs surrendered himselfe and his Kingdome to *Echebar*. The particulars of his other Conquests I cannot relate; His last victory I know not whether to impute to his happinesse or not. It was against his Sonne, in which the griefe to haue such an enemy could not but be more than the glory of the exploit. This happened, *Anno* 1602. *Echebar*, being forced to giue ouer his Decan Conquest, by his Sonne's vntimely challenge of the Scepter, who weary of his Father's long life, stiled himselfe King, and his Father the Great King. Armies were gathered on both sides, on both sides were sent Letters and Messengers. The Mother of *Echebar*, being ninetie yeeres old, laboured a peace, but not preuailing, fell sicke, which caused him to returne from this expedition against his Sonne. But her body not able to ouercome the disease yeelded to death. Her Sonne shaued his head, beard, and eyebrowes, and mourned after the country fashion in blue, his Nobles doing the like three dayes. Her huge Treasure which shee had bequeathed to her children and Nephewes, the King seized on. The Prince was perswaded to come to his Father without an Army, which he did, and after some rebuke, was reconciled, and remained content with the Kingdome of Cambaia or Guzzerat. He seemed much addicted to the Iesuites, and obtained his Father's License for a Temple at Agra, to the building whereof hee gaue a thousand pieces of Gold.

On the twentie seuen of October *Anno* 1605, *Echebar* dyed in the Climactericall yeere (63) of his age, and fiftie of his reigne. In his sicknesse, *Selim* the Prince (*a*) (whom some suspected of dealing as the Turkish *Selim* had done with his father *Baiazet*) came not into the Presence; and much consultation was amongst the Great ones to conferre the Succession vpon *Cuffero* his sonne. But the issue was that vpon his Oath to maintaine the Law of *Mahomet*, and of full pardon to his Sonne and all his Partakers, hee was brought into his Father's presence. *Echebar* was past speech, but made signes that hee should take the Royall Diademe, and gird himselfe with the sword hanging at his bed's head. The Prince performed the solemne Iordam or Rite of Adoration, with the head bowed to the Earth, and, his Father signing with his hand that hee should depart

(*a*) Prince Selim is known in history as Jehangeer, the lover of the celebrated Noormahal, distinguished in Thomas Moore's poem of the "Light of the Harem." The readers of Lalla Rookh will remember that there was a slight coolness between the happy pair, which according to the poet, was somewhat unaccountable, but according to history, seems to have arisen from the ardour of the royal lover who murdered Noormahal's first husband, and then forcibly married her immediately afterwards. No doubt such an energetic proceeding proved the strength of the attachment, but still a little coolness on the part of the lady was perhaps excusable, and, at any rate, was in strict accordance with modern notions of propriety.

did so; as did his Father presently after out of the world. His body was carried on the shoulders of his Sonne and Nephew out of the towre where he lay, the wall being broken (after the fashion) for passage, and a new gate there erected; and being brought into his Garden, a league from thence, was interred with small attendance, neither the King, nor his Nobles (except *Coffero* and a few others) wearing mourning habite. So little was He in his West, a little before the great Terrour of the East. Eight dayes after *Echebar*'s death, the Prince entred the Palace, and seated himselfe in the Throne, the people crying *Padiausa*, or *Padasha lamat*, GOD saue the King. His first endeauours were to giue contentment to the Mahumetans; causing their Moschees to bee purged, and their Rites to bee established; yea, hee tooke a new Name, NVRDIN MOHAMAD IAHANVIR, that is, the *Splendour* of MAHOMET's *Law, Subduer of the World*. And by this Name IAHANVIR or (as our Countrey-men, lately come from thence, pronounce it) IAHANGERE, hee is vsually called, and not by his ancient Name SELIM.

In Aprill after, his sonne rebelled, and (taking the Title of SVLTAN IA, that is, Sultan the King) brought into his partie two Great Men, and so went to Lahor, which (not being admitted entrance) hee besieged eight dayes; or (as others say) presented himselfe with his forces (about twelue thousand) before it, without any great hostilitie offered him. His Father in person pursued him, which being rumor'd, so dismayed the sonne that he fled, hauing euen then put some of the King's men to rout. For by a notable strategeme hee lost the day, the aduerse Generall sending many with flying tales into the Princes Armie, buzzing the neerenesse and Greatnesse of the Kings power, and seconding the same (like GIDEON's Policie) with multitude of Trumpets and Drummes, scarred them and notwithstanding the Princes gaine saying, hee was by his owne almost compelled to flight. Hee tooke his way towards Cabul, and being to passe a Riuer, the Captaine of the place caused all Boats to be taken away, and commanded the rowers, that if the Prince came, they should fasten the Boat (as by mischance) on a Shelfe or Iland of sand in the middle of the Riuer, which being done, they should seeme to call for helpe, and so giue notice. This was done, and the Gouernour came, and after due reuerence (promising all fidelitie and securitie, wherein hee was vnfaithfully faithfull) brought Him into the Castle, and sent the King word thereof, who sent presently and brought Him in fetters together with his company. The King bitterly checked him, committed him to prison. Some adde, that hee sealed vp his eyes. Others say, that his eyes were put out. But their eyes were not put in (only eares put on) that say so; for hee hath lately been freed, and hath the vse also of his eyes, as I have been tolde from the eyes of diuers. His two great Captaines had a strange punishment, the one sowed vp close in an Oxe-skinne, the other in an Asse-skinne, both new flayed, that drying they might withall straightly pinch in their Prisoners in a close and narrow Little case. The next day they were carried through the Citie on Asses, their faces to the tailewards, the one conspicuous with his Oxe-hornes, the other with his Asses-eares; The shame and ignominy so pierced one of them, that hee fell down dead; his head was cut off, and the pieces of his dismembred bodie were set vp in diuers places. The other by way of fauour, was permitted to haue water powred on his hide, which brought a worse euill, by the heate of so neere a Sunne, causing a filthy stinke, and multiplication of Vermine, till at last his pardon was procured. Two hundreth of the Prince's Souldiers, were set on both sides the way, as hee should passe to be executed. He caused his second Sonne to be proclaimed Prince, as his Father had before transferred the Title from him to This his Son.

There was a famous Prophet of the Ethnikes, named

Goru, esteemed there of his Sectaries as the Romish Pope is of the Popish Romanists ; with him, as a man famous for Sanctimony did the Prince consult, who in adulation adorned his head with a Diadem, which in an Ethnike to a Mahumetan was strange ; but hee coloured it with the Gentilisme of the Princes Mother. Vpon this *Goru* was committed, but vpon promise by an Ethnike of 100,000 pieces of Gold, to bee payd to the King, hee was pardoned. Hee that vndertooke this, hoped on the King's pardon, or that *Goru* would procure this summe, which failing, hee seised, on all hee had, not sparing his wife and children : adding tortures also to extort money from him, and taking away his meate, thinking him rather a miser than a begger. Thus in varietie of misery the flattering Prophet lost his life : and his Suretie also thinking to escape by flight, was taken and slaine, his goods all confiscate.

This King at first made great shew of zeale to *Mahomet*, which since is cooled, and his Religion seemes to bee the same with *Echebar's*. Contrary to the Mahumetan practice, hee delighteth much in Images, as of CHRIST, the Virgin, and other Saints, with which his chambers and publike roomes are stored ; and to all his Letters and Charters, besides the Kings Seale, addes the Images of CHRIST, and the Holy Virgin, engrauen in a paire of tongs (as it were) of Emeralds, with which hee seales his Letters on both sides the pendent waxe. The last newes that wee haue from the Iesuites (of whom we haue borrowed allmost all the former Relations) is of Captaine *Hawkins* comming to the Court, and kind entertainment of the King, who made him (say they) a Gentleman of foure hundred Horse, and assigned him thirtie thousand Rupies stipend : adding other reports of his pride, obstinate heresie, and supplantation of the Portugals ; with other things of Him, and those of the Ascension were wracked, partly true, partly false. I haue thought good to set before you in the next seruice, some of Captaine

Hawkins obseruations whiles hee staied there, and after of other our Countrey-men, which now haue a settled trade in these vast Dominions. Obserue by the way that the Iesuites to the last, doe accuse Captaine *Hawkins* of his obdurate heresie, contrarie to the calumnies of some that say hee became deuoutly Popish at their perswasion.

CHAPTER V.

THE RELATIONS OF CAPTAINE HAWKINS, EMBASSADOR THERE.

MASTER *William Hawkins* being Captaine in the Ship called the *Hector*, after a long and tedious voyage (from March 1607 to the foure and twentieth of August 1608) arriued at Surat, subiect to the *Mogor* or *Mogol* (so he calleth him) and after much kindnesse offered, and indignities sufferred, by reason and treason of the Portugals (who had by bribes and slanders wrought the Vice-Roy or Deputie, called *Mocreh Chan* against him) passed thence to Agra, to the Court, as Embassadour, with a Letter from the King of England. *Peniero* a Iesuite, before in this Booke mentioned (obserue the *Conuersions* and conuersations of that Societie in those parts) like a worthy Factor for his Nation, had proferred to *Mocreh Chan* fortie thousand Rials of Eight, to send them to *Daman*, that so he might become their prisoner, and the English negotiation might be hindered ; and now, when the name of an Embassadour had protected him from such courses, plotted with him to ouerthrow his iourney, both by detraction of necessarie forces to assist him in a way so full of Out-lawes and Rebels, and suborning his Trudge-man and Coach-man, to poyson or murder him by the way ; which was not farre from effecting. The Portugals had also dealt with the Lord of Cruly, to bee readie with two hundred Horsemen to assault him in the way ; so that hee was forced to hire a strong conuoy for the securitie of his person. Being come to Agra, hee was brought with great State to the King, (a) who kindly entertained him, and sware by God, and by his Fathers soule, to performe the Kings Maiesties request, in the Letter contained, notwithstanding the deprauation thereof by the Iesuite, to whom the King had giuen it to reade. He promissed also to allow him three thousand and two hundred pound a yeere, or foure hundred Horse (for so they reckon all their fees, much like the Turkish Timariots) and caused him to take a wife of the Countrey, the daughter of an Armenian Christian, called *Mubarikesha*, sometimes a Commander in the Warres of *Ekbar Padashar*, Father to this present *Mogor* or *Mogul* whose name is *Selim*. This King is so fickle and inconstant, that what hee had solemnly promised for an English Factory, was by the Portugals means reuersed, and againe promised, and againe suspended, and a third time both graunted and disanulled: so that the second of Nouember 1611 Captaine *Hawkins* departed from Agra, and the last of December came to Cambaya, where hee heard of English shipping, in which hee passed first to the Red Sea, after to Sumatra and Bantam, and dyed on the Irish shoare in his returne homewards. Whiles hee kept at Agra his liuing assigned him by the King was much impaired by the Officers, who appointed to him such places where Outlawes and Rebels liued, so that hee neuer received aboue three hundred pound. His attendance whiles hee was in fauour, was honourable and neere the King; so that the Mahumetans enuying a Christian such dignitie, became his priuie enemies, and assistants to the Portugals; which was increased by a Present the King sent him publikely, being a wilde Boare, killed in his hunting-Progresse and by him and his eaten. The insolencies of the Guzarates, it they may bee suffered, and as much basenesse of their

(a) The king Jehangheer.

deiected cowardly courages, being kept in awe (which is also the disposition of all the Indian Ethnikes, both white and blacke) the Portugals pride and treachery; the fittest places for our Indian traffique, whether wee follow the colours of *Mars* or *Mercury*; and other his diligent obseruations I omit. But so I cannot, the rarities of the *Mogols* Court, customes, puissances, wealth, and gouernment (notwithstanding our former Discourse) hauing met with so rare a guide. For the greatnesse of his State; hee reporteth that his Empire is diuided into fiue great Kingdomes, the first named Pengab, the chiefe Citie whereof is Lahor; the second, Bengala, and Sonargham the mother Citie; the third, Malua, the chiefe Seat Vagain (*a*); the fourth Deckan, in which Bramport is principall: and so is Amadauer in the fifth Kingdome, which is Cambaya. Hee hath sixe principall Castles for the keeping of his treasure, at Agra (which is in the heart of all his Kingdomes) Guallier, Neruir, Ratamboore, Hassier, Boughtaz. There are three Arch Rebels, which with his forces he cannot call in, *Amber Chapu* in Deckan; in *Guzerat*, the sonne of *Muzafer*, sometime their King, called *Bahador*; and *Raga Rahana* in Malua. Hee hath fiue sonnes, *Sultan Cuffero, Sultan Peruis, Sultan Chorem, Sultan Sharier, Sultan Bath*; two young daughters, and three hundred wiues, of which foure are principall. None hath the title of *Sultan*, but his sonnes. *Mirza* is also ascribed to his brother and children; *Chan*, as a Duke. Their degrees and titles are according to their proportion of Horses allowed them; foure are of the *same* of twelue thousand, the King, his mother, eldest sonne, and one of the blood Royall, called *Cham Azam*. Of the *fame* of nine thousand Horse are three; these are as Duke; Marquesses of fiue thousand, of which are eighteene; Earles of three thousand; Vicounts (so may wee paralell them with our titles of

(*a*) The famous old city of Oogein the capital of Malwa.

honour) two thousand; Barons of one thousand Horse: Knights, foure hundred; others fewer, to twentie; all which are called *Mansibdars*, men of liuing or Lordship, of which are three thousand. Of *Haddies*, which receiue monethly pay, from sixe Horse to one, are fiue thousand. Officers of Court and Campe, sixe and thirtie thousand, as Gunners, Porters, Water-men, Cookes, Gardiners, keepers of Horses, Elephants, &c., whose wages are payed them monethly, from ten to three Rupias. A Rupia is two shillings of our coyne. His Captaines or Mansibdars are to maintaine upon their allowance, and haue in readinesse at a seuen nights warning, three hundred thousand Horse.

The King's reuenue of his Crown-land, is fiftie Crou of Rupias; euery Crou is one hundred Leckes, and euery Lecke a hundred thousand Rupias; all which in our money is fiftie millions of pounds (*a*); a summe incredible, and exceeding that which is said of China. His daily expences are fiftie thousand Rupias, for his owne person, as apparell, victuals, and other houshold expences, with the feeding of sundry sorts of beasts, and of some few Elephants; his expences on his women by the day amount to thirtie thousand Rupias.

In his Treasurie of Agra are in Gold, of Seraffins Ecberi (which are ten Rupias a piece) threescore Leckes. Of another sort, which are one thousand Rupias each, twentie thousand pieces; and ten thousand of another sort halfe the value. Of Toles (euery Tole is a Rupia of Siluer, and ten of those Toles is the value of one of Gold) thirtie thousand. Of another sort of ten Toles, fiue and twentie thousand. Of another sort of fiue Toles, fiftie thousand.

(*a*) The revenues of India, which were said to amount to fifty milions under the Moguls, are now about forty-five millions. The amount must indeed have seemed enormous to our author, as the regular revenue of England at that time could scarcely have exceeded a single million. Bernier, however, estimates the revenue of Shah Jehan, the successor of Jehangheer, at twenty three millions sterling.

In Siluer, of Rupias Ecberi thirteene Crou. Of a kinde of coyne worth a hundred Toles a piece, fiftie thousand. Of another halfe as much one Lecke. Of thirtie Toles a piece, fortie thousand pieces. Of twentie Toles a piece, thirtie thousand pieces. Of ten Toles a piece, twentie thousand pieces. Of fiue Toles a piece, fiue and twentie thousand. Of Sauoys (each of which is a Tole and a quarter) two Leckes. Of Iagaries (whereof fiue make sixe Toles) one Lecke.

In Iewels of Diamants one Batman and a halfe ; a Batman is fiue and fiftie pound weight English ; these are rough, and of all sorts and sizes, but none lesse than two Carrets and an halfe. Of Ballase Rubies, two thousand. Of Pearles, twelue Batmans. Of Rubies of all sorts, two Batmans. Of Emeralds of all sorts fiue Batmans. Of Eshime, which stone comes from Cataya, one Batman. Of stones of Emen, a kinde of red stone, fiue thousand. Of all other sorts, as Corall, Topazes &c. the number is innumerable.

Of Iewels wrought in Gold, two thousand and two hundred Swords, the Hilts and Scabberds set with rich stones ; two thousand Ponyards. Of Saddle Drums of Gold, set with stones, vsed in Hawking, fiue hundred. Of rich brooches for their heads, in which their feathers are set, two thousand. Of Saddles of Gold and Siluer, set with stones, one thousand. Of Tuikes, fiue and twentie. This is a great Launce couered with Gold, and the fluke set with stones : and are carried when the King goeth to warres instead of colours. Of Kittasoles of State to shadow him, twentie. None else in his Empire may haue any of any sort carried for his shadow. Of Chaires of State, fiue, and of other sorts which are of siluer and gold, one hundred. Of rich glasses, two hundred. Of Vases for Wine set with Iewels, one hundred. Of drinking Cups, fiue hundred, of which are fiftie very rich, as of one stone &c. Of Chaines of Pearle, and other Chaines, of

Rings with Iewels &c. are infinite which the Keeper onely knowes. Of all sorts of Plate wrought, as Dishes, Cups, Basons &c. Two thousand Batmans. Of Gold wrought, a thousand Batmans.

Of Beasts; twelue thousand Horses; as many Elephants, fiue thousand with teeth, the rest female and young. Camels, twentie thousand; of Oxen for seruice, ten thousand. Of Moyles, a thousand. Of Deere for game, three thousand. Ounces for game, foure hundred. Hunting-Dogs, foure hundred. Lyons tame, an hundred. Buffles, fiue hundred. Hawkes, foure thousand. Pigeons for sport, ten thousand. Singing-Birds, foure thousand. Hee hath also Armour to arme fiue and twentie thousand men at an houres warning. All this concerning his Treasure, expences, and monethly pay, is in his Court or Castle of Agra; and euery one of the Castles, aboue named, hath a seuerall treasure: and so hath Lahor also, which was not mentioned. And if any censure this Story for want of truth, and Mee for want of iudgement, in relating such fulnesse so fully: for it, I must leaue it to the Authors credit; for my selfe, I was induced by the raritie of the subiect (not easie in this distance to be knowne, nor by Trauellers, except such as this Author, whose Embassage, and exceeding grace with the King, for the greatest part of his residence, might further his Intelligence herein) besides the rarenesse of the Copie, whereof I know but one, and that written by himselfe. Time may make further triall. Nor may any measure those parts of the Indies for wealth in these kindes, with our Europæan, or any other: and that which so many Kings and States had in many ages stored together, by the euent of warre became *Ecbars*, the father of this *Selim*: of which you haue heard of the incredible wealth of the King of Cambaia alone. Besides, if you obserue his customes, it makes it so much neerer credite. For when any Nobleman dies, all deuolueth to him: and well is it with the wife and children, if he bestoweth the Land, and what he pleaseth, on them, and the fathers Title on the eldest sonne. (a) One dyed in my time (saith our Author) named *Raga Gaginat*, on whose goods the King seized, which besides Iewels and other treasure, amounted to three score Maunes in gold, euery Maune is fiue and fiftie pound weight. None likewise may come before the King with any Petition emptie-handed: and on certaine Festiuall dayes they bring him rich Presents, as before is said. India, besides Mines, must needes be rich in money, for all Nations bring it, and carrie commodities for it: so that once in twentie yeeres it commeth to the King. All Lands in his monarchy are his, giuen and taken at his pleasure. Escheats are many by reason of his seuritie. And of those Lands which he giueth in Fee the third part still remaines to the King; and of the Crowne Lands two thirds, the rest to the Occupiers. For Presents and Mortuaries wee have before given diuers instances. And my iealousie hath made mee verie inquisitiue of such as have liued there in the Ministerie, Factorie, Souldiorie, all which affirme that Captaine *Hawkins* hath written with the least.

Of all sorts of his wealth (except Coyne) is brought daily a certaine quantitie before him, for which purpose his Beasts, and all things of value, are diuided into three hundred and threescore parts; so that the same things come but once in the yeere to his view. Hee hath three hundred Elephants royall for himselfe to ride on, which are brought with pompe, richly couered; twentie or thirtie men going before with Streamers, his female with her yongling or yonglings following, besides foure or fiue other young ones attending as Pages. These are dispersed amongst the great ones to ouer see them, the King allow-

(a) This was the fact. The estate of every nobleman, inclusive of all personal property, became on death, the absolute property of the crown, and a provision for the widows was left entirely to the generosity of the Mogul Emperor.

ing them for it, but scarcely sufficient, and they dare not make shew of them in euill plight. One of them eats ten Ropias euery day in Butter, Graine, Sugar, Sugar-canes, &c., they are very tame. I saw one take vp the Kings owne sonne by his appointment, being a child of seuen yeeres. There are thought to be in this Empire fortie thousand Elephants, of his, and his Nobles; of which, twentie thousand are trained for warre.

When the King rides in progresse, his Tents are in compasse about as large as London, two hundred thousand people vsually following his Campe. (*a*) This King is esteemed the greatest Emperour in the East. Hee hath many Dromedaries, whose swiftnesse auailed his Father much in his sudden Expedition of warre. Those valiant Captaines which *Ecbar* had, *Selim* hath by tyranny much diminished. Fiue times a weeke hee commands his Elephants to fight before him, which often in their comming in, or going out, kill many: & if any be but wounded, and might escape, yet hee commands him to bee cast into the Riuer, saying, Hee will curse him as long as he liues, and therefore best to dispatch him: Hee delights to see men executed, and torne with Elephants. Of these tyrannies he reckons many particulars which he saw; and some for no fault, but for his lust set to fight with the Lyon, and one valiant man to buffet with a very fierce Lyon, without any weapon offensiue or defensiue. If any of his subiects haue any precious stone of value, and make not him the offer of it, it is death to him; hee must haue the refusall of all, and yet giues not the worth by a third part. That Iewell hee weareth this day, is not worne againe till that day twelue-month; all his Iewels being proportioned to such a course. All his seueritie and tyranny cannot cleere (perhaps this causeth them) his Countrey of Out-lawes. There is one betweene Agra and

(*a*) The London of those days was perhaps scarcely one-tenth of the size of the modern metropolis.

Amadauar, which commands as much Land as a good Kingdome; he is strong, twentie thousand Horse, and fiftie thousand Foot, and keepes on the Mountaines. Men can scarcely trauell for Out-lawes. The often shifting of men from their lands, makes them exact more cruelly in the time they hold them, grinding the face of their poore Tenants in ruefull manner. If they continue but sixe yeeres, they raise a great state; sometimes they hold not half a yeere. If any be employed in warres and businesses in another place, he must forgoe his land here, and be assigned it there. The King's allowance otherwise is exceeding, as for euery Horse twentie Ropias a moneth for the warres, and for so many more which hee hath of *Fame*, hee is allowed two Ropias a moneth for the maintenance of his Table.

Concerning the King's Religion and behauiour, it is thus. In the morning about breake of day, hee is at his Beades, his face to the Westwards, in a priuate faire roome vpon a faire Iet-stone, hauing onely a Persian Lambe-skinne vnder him. Hee hath eight Chaines of Beades, euery of which containeth foure hundred; they are of Pearle, Diamants, Rubies, Emeralds. Lignum aloes, Eshen and Corall. At the vpper end of this Iet-stone are placed the Images of Christ and our Lady, grauen in stone. Hee turneth ouer his Beades, and saith so many words, to wit, three thousand and two hundred, and then presenteth himselfe to the people to receiue their Salames or good morrow, for which purpose multitudes resort thither euery morning. This done, hee sleepeth two houres more, then dineth and passeth his time with his women; at noone, hee sheweth himselfe again to the people, sitting till three or foure aclocke to view his pastimes, by Men and Beasts, every day sundry kindes. At three all the Nobles in Agra, whom sicknesse detaineth not, resort to the Court; and the King comes forth in open audience, sitting in his Seat-Royall, euery man standing in his degree before him:

the chiefe within a Red raile (which was allowed to ovr Author, hauing but fiue before him) the rest without. This Red raile is three steps higher then the place where the rest stand. Men are placed by officers: there are others to keepe men in order. In the middest, right before the King, standeth an Officer, with his master Hang-man, accompanied with fortie others of the same profession with hatches on their shoulders, and others with whips. Here the King heareth causes some houres euery day; and then departs to his house of prayer; which ended, foure or fiue sorts of well-dressed meates are brought him, whereof hee eateth what hee likes, to stay his stomacke, drinking once of his strong drinke. After this he comes forth into a priuate roome, where none may come, but such as himselfe nominates. Two yeeres together ovr Author was one of the Attendants. In this place he drinkes other fiue cups, which is the portion that the Physicians allow him, after which he eateth Opium, & then layes him downe to sleep, euery man departing home. When he hath slept two houres, they awake him, and bring his supper to him, thrusting it in his mouth, not being able to feed himselfe. This is about one of the clocke at night; and so he sleepeth the rest of the night. In this cup-space he doth many idle things; but nothing without writing be he drunken or sober. For he hath writers by course which write all, not omitting his going to the stoole or how ought he lieth with his women, and with whom; to the end, that when he dieth, those writings may be brought forth; and thence what is thought fit may be inserted in their Chronicles.

When any poore men come to demaund Iustice of the King, they goe to a certaine rope fastened to two pillars, neere where the King sits; this rope is full of Bels, plated with gold, and with shaking the rope, the King, hearing the sound, sends to know the cause, and doth Iustice accordingly.

While ovr Author was with him, hee made his brothers children Christians, not for zeale (as the Iesuites thought) but in policie (to disappoint a Prophecie of certaine learned Gentiles which fore-told their succession in the Kingdome) to make them odious to the Moores. God take the *wise in his craftinesse*, and conuert this peruerse policie to their true Conuerison.

One of his sonnes, *Sultan Sharier*, of seuen yeeres, could not by diuers cruelties purposely inflicted on him by his father, be forced to cry, pretending his Nurses instructions to the contrary.

Hee keeps many Feasts in the yeere, but some principall; one called Nourous, or New-yeeres day. Then hath he a rich Tent pitched, curiously and costly wrought, two acres of ground in compasse, so richly spread with silke and gold Carpets, and preciously hanged, as is more admirable then credible. There are roomes also for his Queenes to see vnseene, round about, so that in all it may bee fiue acres. Euery Noble-man makes his roome each striuing to excell other in cost. The King will come, to which of them he effects, and is sumptuously feasted and presented; But because hee will not receiue any thing as a Present he allowes as much as the Treasurer values it, which is halfe the worth. Thus all prouide and present. At this Feast commonly euery mans state is augmented; it beginneth at the beginning of the Moone in March. Some foure months after is the Feast of his Birth-day, which euery one strieueth to honor with his richest Apparel and Iewels; after many Palace-pastimes, hee goeth with the greatest pompe to his Mothers, to whom euery Noble-man presents a Iewell. After banket ended, hee weigheth in a ballance of gold against himselfe in one scale, other things of diuers sorts to the worth of ten thousand pound, which is giuen to the poore; but his richer Subiects present him that day tenne times as much. On his Fathers Funerall-day is solemnized a Feast at his Sepulchre, where himselfe meaneth to bee buried with all his posteritie; at which time much meate and money is giuen to the poore. It hath beene fourteene yeeres in building, and is thought will not bee finished in seuen yeeres more; notwithstanding three thousand at least be daily at worke thereon. But one of our workemen will dispatch more than three of them. It is by his description three quarters of a mile about, made square, hath seuen heights each narrower then other, till the top, where his Hearse is. At the vtmost gate before you come to the Sepulchre is a stately Palace in building; the compasse of the wals ioyning to the gate, &c. may be at least three miles: it is foure miles from Agra.

The Kings custome is euery yeere to make a hunting progresse of two moneths; but when hee comes forth of his Palace, if he mounts on a horse, it is a signe of his going to the war; if on an Elephant or Palamkin, it is but a hunting iourney.

CHAPTER VI.

OF THE SETLING OF THE ENGLISH TRADE, IN THESE PARTS, AND OF THE TWO SEA FIGHTS BETWIXT OURS, AND THE PORTUGALS.

We haue heard how by the Portugals working the English trade was disanulled in the Mogols Dominion, Captaine *Hawkins* despairing of any good that way, and leauing the Countrey. The Iesuites had closely wrought *Mocrab Chan* against him, with other great men ; and one of them (*Pinnerus*) was employed in publike Embassage betwixt the Vice-Roy of Goa and the Mogoll, to the same effect : The Portugals alledged the league was broken, because the English were entertained ; Neither could the Mogol easily lose their frendship, because they were then Masters at Sea : and could haue hindered him and his from all Marine trades. *Andreas Hartadus de Mendosa*, the Vice-Roy had forbidden the Merchants their Cambayan trade, and alreadie hostilitie had begun on both sides : both ceasing with the departure of the English. Sir *Henry Middleton* came to Surrat, after his Red-Sea-disasters, in expectation of trade, but found nothing but dissembling, so that after much losse of time, he was driuen with his Ships to seeke new aduentures, to repaire the losses which by Turkish treachery & the Mogals inconstancie and falsehood he had sustained. Hereupon he returned to the Strait of Aden, and intercepted the Ships that came from the Mogals Country to this Turkish Trade, easily stopping the mouth of the Turke, and cutting off the Mogols Nautike hands in hindring the mutuall Traffike of their Subiects : so weake in those Seas are these Two, iustly called GREAT, the Greatest indeed, and most puissant Princes (all things considered) in the Vniuerse. Yet did not the English make prize of them, only they set prices to them of their English commodities, and exchanging them at their prices for such Indian goods as they had brought thither (both estimated as they were worth in India) making them further allowance of two in the hundreth. One Ship of this company, called the Rehemee, had one thousand fiue hundred persons in her. Many haue cauilled this forced trade, not considering that they had first found both fraude and force at the Turkes handes, and at the Mogols much expence and losse of time and goods contrary to Couenant, which I see not how the Law of Nature and Nations might not warrant them to make good; the King himselfe being wronged, and they armed with the Kings Commission, and their owne power. And perhaps others would haue taken all without any goods giuen in exchange. Certaine it is, that the euent (which those Mahumetans make the rule of equitie) was good, the Cambayan Merchants so terrified, that when *Gen. Best* ignorant of these passages) not long after came to Surrat with the Dragon, he was promised good dealing; *Mill Ieffe*, one of the chiefe Merchants of Surrat affirming, *that they must else burne all their ships, and giue over their trade by Sea.* So true was that obseruation of Captaine *Hawkins* (an Actor, perhaps Author, in this businesse) of these people, insolent, if suffered, and base, if curbed. (*a*)

On the third of October, 1612, *Sheke Suffe*, Gouernour of Amadauaz, chiefe Citie of the Guzzurats came to Sur-

---

(*a*) The truth of these observations will be evident to all residents in India, as much now as then. Notwithstanding the supposed power of the Mogul, even he was alarmed at the immense power of the British merchant navy which could thus defy the Turk and the Mogul at the same time. Half a century before Clive landed in Madras, Sir John Child, the Chairman of the East India Company, arranged the details of an expedition which even in the time of Aurrungzebe would have been felt at Delhi. Unfortunately for him the expedition was mismanaged, and consequently failed altogether.

rat, and thence to Swally, and on the one and twentieth, concluded upon certaine Articles, with the English Generall, which I haue read in his owne Relations, too tedious to bee here inserted. Not so the famous fights betwixt him and the Portugals, who had alreadie in their insulting insolent hopes swallowed the English, but Dragons are harsh morsels, and of ill digestion. Master *Canning*, an English Merchant, had beene prisoner with the Portugals, but in a confident brauery, the Vice-Roy commanded to set him on shoare at Surrat, that *hee might goe helpe his countrey-men fight, and then wee will take their ship, and the rest of them altogether.* But not altogether, nay, not at all, could hee performe this, with all his great Fleet of foure huge Gallions, with fiue or sixe and twentie Frigates; the Dragon being assisted onely with the Osiander a little Ship (scarcely a Ship, I had almost called her a little Pinnasse) but of great performance in this Fight. *Nunno d'Ancuna* was Admirall of the Portugals, who by the Sabandore or Treasurer vnder the Mogoll in those parts, an experienced Man, who had a little before come aboord the English to spie out their strength, was counselled not to aduenture present fight, with such present courages, but to keepe betwixt them and the shoare, to hinder them from watering, and so (like another *Cunctator*) to weary the English, and force them from thence. But *Ancunas* high pride disdained stratagems, and *scorned (forsooth) to spend a weekes prouision on his Men hindring ours, whom hee could force in an houre.* Thus, on the nine and twenteith of Nouember, came hee in sight with his Fleet, with Red colours displayed, where hee recieued an vnwelcome welcomming by the Dragon, which after the Generals encouraging speech, went to meet them, and when he came betweene the Admirall and Vice-Admirall, opened his fierie mouths, and in a thundering Dialect gaue them the first salutation. The other two were not yet come vp, nor could the Osiander get cleere of her Anchor. But the next morning the fight was renewed, and three of the Gallions driuen on ground, not a man of them daring to looke aboue Hatches, and had beene their left but for the Frigates; the Osiander danced the Hay (saith one) about them, or played like a Salmon (my friend Mr. *Nathaniel Salmon*, was Master and Commander in her) swimming, frisking lightly (but not with light effect) leaping about these huge Whale carkasses, which in the afternoone got a-flote, and continued the fight till night. In the night they manned a Frigate, with six or seuen score of their best men, thinking to haue fired the English, but found both Fire and Water conspire against themselues to their destruction: the Osiander keeping diligent watch, and with a shot sinking them; there were eightie-foure of them taken vp drowned. The shallownesse of the Bay gaue occasion to the Dragon, which drew much water, to remoue to the other side, neere vnto Mendofrobag, or Medhafrbadh, sometime a faire Citie, and walled, ruined by the Mogols warres. Here was a Castle of the Razbooches (some call them Reisbuti) which haue beene the Natiue Lords of that Countrey, now as it were out-lawes, spoyling and robbing, besieged by Sarder Chan, a Great Man of the Mogols, who had many thousands in his Campe, which all became witnesses of the English valour, Spectators of the Portugals confusion. Sarder Chans Tent was stately and spacious, couered aboue with Cloth of Gold, on the floore with Turkie Carpets. Hee sent a Horse, and two Vests wrought with Silke and Gold to the Generall, and foure Vests for foure other of his company. Himselfe would not stirre out of his Tent, till he had taken the Castle, but gaue Them licence to take view thereof. But the Portugals approaching with their force, the Mogols by many Arguments dehorted the English from the fight, which yet they presently made good before many thousand gazing, admiring, astonished Eyes, the Portugals being forced to cut their Cables, and to escape by flight, being swifter of sayle then the English. Thus the Portugals wanted a *Hercules* for this Dragon (more watchfull then the Hesperidan, more terrible then the Lernæan) or, a Medæa to Charme this, as sometimes the Colchian (these three Dragons the Poets faine Monsters, begotten of *Typhon* and *Echidna*, but none of them breathing Fire, nor roaring Thunders, like this fell Indian Dragon here spoken of.)

In these fights, after Master *Salmons* reckoning, the Dragon spent sixe hundred thirtie nine, and the Osiander three hundred eightie seuen great shot, besides three thousand small. The great Mogoll, which before thought none comparable to the Portugall at Sea, much wondered at the English resolution, related to him by *Sardar Chan*. The Portugals lost by their owne Confession, one hundred and sixtie, by others report, fiue hundred men (the *Sabandar* reckoned three hundred aud fiftie) in these fights; the English three men, and the arme of another shot off. The Articles agreed on before by the Gouernour, were confirmed by the Kings *Firma*, which they receiued Ianuary the eleuuth; Captaine *Best*, returned to Swally, December one and twentieth, and sent Letters of this successe for England by land, but the Messenger with his Indian, were both poysoned by two Friers in the way homewards; another Letter sent by a Mariner, came to the Companies hands in very good season; and they sent forth foure ships hither, besides three to other places, vnder the Command of Generall *Downton, viz.* The New yeeres Gift, the Hector, the Merchants Hope, and the Saloman.

These leauing England in March, on October the fifteenth following, 1614, anchored at South Swally, not farre from Surat; where they found the Countrey in Armes against the Portugals, which had a little before taken a Ship of the Mogols, in which was said to bee three millions of Treasure, and two women bought for the Great

Mogol. They also tooke a Guzzarate Ship worth one hundred thousand pounds, with seuen hundred persons therin, at the barre of Surat (notwithstanding their owne Passe granted them) and sent them to Goa. The Decanims laid siege to Chaul, and *Mocrob Chan* was to doe his vtmost for his Master the Mogol. The Moores on all hands, sought their Destruction; and they were driuen to send away many hundreths of the Banyans out of their Townes, to free themselves of vnprofitable Mouths; three Barkes of which came to Surat, others to Cambaya. *Mocrob Chan* laboured very earnestly with the Generall, to ingage himselfe in that warre against the Portugalls, which because he could not doe (except in a defensiue quarrell) by his Commisson, the *Nabab* (so they call this *Mocrob Chan*, then Vice-Roy or Gouernour of the Countrey about Surat; the Iesuites interprete *Nabab*, supreame iudge) was strange to the English and offered the Merchants some hard measure; yea, the Iesuites which were with *Mocrob Chan*, tooke occasion from this refusall to counterfeit a Letter from the Vice-Roy, threatning that except they yeelded to peace, He and his friends the English would ioyne against Surat: which suspition Master *Aldworth*, one of our Merchants, furthered, ignorant of the former; but threatning that their abuses would cause the English to ioyne with the Portugalls. Thus ticklish were the termes on which they stood. December the sixteenth, the Generall receiued a Letter, that the Portugals had burnt Goga, with many Villages there-abouts, and ten great Ships, one of which was the Reheemee, with one hundred and twentie small vessels: hee read the Letter of a Iesuite, in which the King of Spaine commanded the Vice-Roy to burne Surat, if they receiued the English. On December the seuen and twentieth, two and twentie Portugall Frigates sought to lay the Hope aboord, but by force of shot were put off. The Vice-Roy sent offer of Friendship to *Mocrob Chan*, on condition that hee would turne the English out of Surat, and suffer him to build a Fort at Swally, otherwise threatning bloudie warres. And so on Ianuary the fourteenth, came two Fleets of Frigates, and on the eighteenth, sixe great Gallions, with three lesser Ships. Two Gallies were yet behinde. The Frigates were three score, some adde fifteene more. This great force made *Mocrob Chan* to feare, whereupon hee sent a Present to the Vice-Roy, with some Treatie of peace, whereof the Vice-roy made light account, thinking first to ouercome vs (a thing not hard in his conceit) and then to treate of peace on his owne termes. Much policie was vsed on both parts, the *Nabob* complementing and sending Presents to the Vice-Roy, and our Generall also; the Vice-Roy promising much to himselfe, but reckoning without his host: and therefore when after the fight hee would haue concluded upon the conditions that *Mocrob* had offered, hee was then refused with a scoffe, that hee would not make peace with so weake an enemy, that could not preuaile against foure Merchants Ships.

On the twentieth Ianuary, their three smaller Ships had thought to haue Stemmed the Hope then riding at an Anchor neere the Barre of Swally, some distance from the rest: these, laid her aboord on the Star-boord side; and one Gally, and fiue and fortie sayle of Frigates on their Lar-boord: the Gallions followed as farre as the Sands would permit. The Admirall made to their helpe, and for the better speed cut their Cable; but the Enemies had alreadie entered (with great show of resolution) without feare or wit (saith one of the Hopes men) thirtie or fortie were entered on the Fore-castle. But the Gift in this fatall Moneth answered her Name, and gaue them for a *New-yeeres Gift* such Orations (roarations yee may call them) that they were easily perswaded to leaue the Hope, and all hopelesse to coole their hote bloods with leaping into the Seas cold waters, where many for want of a Boat, made vse of *Charons*: those that were of most hope and courage, held still their possession of the entered Hope, but with enterred hopes, and dispossession of their liues.

I know not what *Salmoneus, Dum flammas Iouis and sonitus imitatur Olympi Ære imitans nimbos and non imitabile fulmen*;

or what *Prometheus* hath taught these later Ages to steale *Iupiters* Fires, and instructed so many Cyclopean Artificers to imitate those heauenly, in hellish Thunders, and sulphurous lightnings; these Mettall Deuils, as Angels of Death, with Brazen sides, and Iron Mouths, proclaiming Destruction and Desolation to the World. These Bullets are the true fire-breathing Buls (such the Poets fained at Colchos) and this Ordnance the fire-foaming horses of *Diomedes* feeding on the flesh of men: which yet I know not whether very crueltie haue made sparing, whiles the Terror hath made men sparing in the vse of it; this Age for this cause yeelding fewer pitched battels, and in them fewer slaine numbers, then the former which neuer heard of this *cruell-mercifull Engine.*

But let vs leaue this Parenthesis. The Portugals, whether themselues by casualtie or industry, set fire on their ships, or that the fire which Master *Mullineux*, the Master of the Hope cast into one of them, after that by helpe of Fresh-men sent in the Pinace, they were got cleere of them; certain it is, that all three driuing away vpon the ebbe (the English had entered before and killed all they found) fell on fire, and running on the Sands, there offered vp themselues at once to all the Elements, the Sayles still standing embracing the Ayre, the Keels kissing her Mother Earth, till their more churlish brethren, the Fire and Water, put them out of possession, and shared all betwixt them. One of the Gallies lost her Nose with a shot, and was content after that, with their Other to look on. The Gallions rode beyond the Sands. The Frigates could not but participate in their fellowes disaduentures:

many of them, saith *Leman*, were sunke and torne in pieces. *Masham*, another of the Hopes Company, numbreth fiue and twentie thus perishing. The Hope lost three men, and had fourteene wounded, the Hector lost two. One shot of stone, which the Hope receiued was measured seuen and twentie Inches about but the hurt was by fire in her tops by one of her owne men there slain, whiles he sought to fire the Enemy. The Portugals losse is vncertaine: three hundred and fiftie men were said to be carried to Daman to be buried, besides all that the Sea and Fire had shared betwixt them, which were thought to make vp fiue hundred, some report of eight hundred, and yet themselues gaue out, not aboue fortie or fiftie, whereas the tide cast vp at one place eighteene drowned carkasses.

After this they tried experiments : First by poyson, and this was the Iesuites Iesuitisme (I cannot call it Christianitie) who sent to the Muccadan of Swally, to entice him to poyson the Water of the Well, whence the English fetched for their vse : but the Ethnike had more honestie, and put in quicke Tortoises, that it might appeare by their death if any venemous hand had beene there. But when *Virtue and virus* wanted *vires*, *Dolus* is added, and the Vice-Roy hauing two ships sent him for supply, two Iunkes, eight or ten Boates, these, or the most of them were employed with great secrecie and subtilitie to fire our ships by night : two full of fiery entrailes on the ninth of February, the next night two others chained together and towed with Frigates, and after that in the same night foure other chained together, one of which being fired with an English shot, burnt herself and fellowes, they put fire to all the rest which deuoured them all, without harme to the English. They tooke some of these Fire-workers, and one of which being examined, confessed after M. *Prings* Relation thus :

The Admirall, called *Todos los Santos*, a ship of eight

hundred tuns, had sixe hundred men eight and twentie Peeces most brasse. The Saint Benito, Vice-Admirall, of seuen hundred tuns, three hundred and three score men, twentie peeces, Saint Lorenzo, a ship of sixe hundred Tuns three hundred men, twentie peeces. The Saint Christopher likewise. The Saint Ieronim of fiue hundred Tuns, three hundred men, and twentie three Peeces, Saint Antonio, foure hundred, two hundred men, and fifteene Peeces. Saint Pedro, two hundred, a hundred and twentie men, and eight Peeces. Saint Paulo as many. A Fly-boat of a hundred and fiftie Tuns, foure score men, and foure Peeces. The two Gallies had fiue and twentie Oares on a side, and in both a hundred Souldiers. Threescore Frigates, with eighteene, and twentie Oares on a side, in each fifteen Souldiers. So great their forces and (blessed be God) so little their force. There Vice-Royes name, was *Don Ieronimo de Sauecko* sometimes Captaine of Mosambike, after that of Zeilan eighteene yeeres, and now Vice-Roy, by the Kings strait command, and others importunitie drawne into this action. Eurey day was hee braued with the English Ordnance, but neuer aduentured any other triall by fight : the English riding neere his great Fleet, and dispatching all their other affaires of Merchandise, and mending the Hope, which they sent home with this Newes when they departed from thence ; they seemed to stay for them in the way, yet let them passe without any blowes.

This won them much glory among the countrey people, *Mocrob Chan* giuing stately entertainment to the Generall, in his Tents on shoare, which one saith were a quarter of a mile about, in the midst, his owne of Crimson Sattin richly embroidered with Gold and Pearle, and coucred with Cloth of Gold ; he had many Elephants : he gaue the Generall his Sword, made (said hee) in his owne house, the Hilts of massie Gold ; (this is their custome to deseruing Captaines) and He gaue him his Girdle, Sword, and Dagger, and Hangers of as faire show, but lesse worth.

Because I haue mentioned the Iesuites Arts In these parts, let this also be added, that Master *Canning* chiefe Merchant, and Agent for the Company, writ to Surat for some others to assist him, being in great feare of poysoning by the Iesuites at the Court, and before any could bee sent, hee was dead, May the nine and twentieth, 1613. One English-man dying a little before, was buried in their Church-yard, whom they tooke vp and buried in the high-way, but were compelled by the King to lay him in his former place, threatning to turne them out of his countrey, and their buried bodies out of that Church-yard. But this later warres brought them into further miseries : being denied their stipend and therefore forsaken of their new Conuerts, who bringing them their Beades, did vpbraid them the want of their pay, one of the best Arguments (though no great miracle) where with they had perswaded them to their Religion. A French Iesuit at Amadabar begged reliefe of the English, wanting necessary sustenance. Before, the King allowed the Superior seuen Rupias a day, and the rest three. But now this and their faire Church also is denied them, and they say their holies in their chamber. *Iohn Mildnall*, an English Papist, had learned (it is reported) the Arts of poysoning ; by which he made away three other English-men in Persia, to make himselfe Master of the whole flock ; but I know not by what meanes himselfe tasted of the same cup, and was exceedingly swelled, but continued his life many moneths with Antidotes, which yet here left him at Agra, where hee left the value of twentie thousand Dolars, after through the Kings Iustice recouered by the English.

Many other Sea-fights haue since happened in diuers parts of the Indies, betwixt Our men and the Portugals, as that by Captaine *Ben. Ioseph* (in which he was slaine, and Captaine *Pepwel* succeeded in the place and quarrell) with *Manuel de Meneses*, whose Carrack was consumed with fire by themselues (as was thought) rather then so great Treasures should be made English spoyles : also in the Persian Gulfe, by Captaine *Chilling* (slaine therein) Captaine *Blithe* and others, which chaced the assayling Portugals, *Ruy Frere de Andrada* their Commander, called the Pride of Portugall getting a fall ; and since that Ormus itself taken by the Persians ; diuers other Portugals prizes, and that especially of the *Richard*, a small Pinnasse of about twentie Tuns, which tooke a Portugall Ship supposed of two hundred and fiftie; that hauing about fourteene men and boyes ; this two hundred and fiftie : These and other fights with them, and more vnfortunate with the Dutch, in those parts I haue deliuered at large in my *Pilgrims*, or Bookes of Voyages, which now together with this commeth to the publike view of the World.

CHAPTER VII.

OF THE TRAUELLS OF DIUERS ENGLISH-MEN IN THE MOGOLS DOMINIONS.

Of the Trauells of Master *Fitch* in these parts, wee haue alreadie spoken: and of Captaine *Hawkins*. In the yeere 1609, the *Assention* by wilfulnesse of the Master (as is reported) founderd in the Sea, twentie leagues from shoare, which yet they attained, being fiue and fiftie persons, in the Riuer of Gandeuee, from whence they trauelled twelue Course, or eighteene Miles to Sabay, and twelue Course more to Surrat: from thence to Daytaotote, which Citie, hee saith, could not bee conquered by the Mogols, and yielded vpon composition, hauing still a Banyan King. Sixe and twentie Course further is Netherbery, a great Basar or Market of Brazen wares, Armour and Beasts. Eight and twentie Course beyond is the Towne Saddisee on the Riuer Tyndee, which runs to Surrat, and diuideth the Bannians and Guzurats. Thence they trauelled twelue Course to a Monasterie, and the next day came to Bramport, where the Great Generall called *Can Cannawe* liueth, who on the twelfth of October returned from the Warres, with fifteene hundred Elephants, thirtie thousand Horses, ten thousand Camels three thousand Dromedaries. This Citie is farre bigger than London, of great Trade, and faire. From hence they went fifteene Courses to Caddor, fourteene to Sawbon, and thence with the Carauan many daies, leauing which they ioyned with a Can of the Countrey bound for Agra, trauelling sixe daies through a Desart, wherein are store of wild Elephants, Lions, Tygres, Cat of Mountaines, Porpentines, and other wild Beasts innumerable; but these they saw, and were forced to make fires in the nights about their Tents to guard them. These Desarts are a hundred Course long, each Course being a mile and halfe. They had in their way after they were past this Desart. the Citie Handee, where the King hath a Castle and House cut out of the maine Rock, and wrought with carued worke round about, in it fiftie Peeces of Ordnance, a Fort impregnable, and made a Prison for great Men. Heere were also two Hospitals for Captaines maymed in the Warres. The next day they came to Tamlico, which runneth into Indus, and two daies after to Agra.

He tells of Elephants fighting before the Mogol, parted with Rackets of wilde fire, made round like hoopes, which they runne in their faces: some fight with wild Horses, sixe Horses to an Elephant, which he kills with clasping his trunke about their necks and pulling them to him, breakes their necks with his teeth. Hee hath also Deere, Rams, Veruathoes, or Bezors, Lyons, Leopards, Wolues, that fight before him. Condemned persons may craue the combate with the Lyon: one he saw that at the first encounter felled the Lyon with his Fist, but was soone torne in pieces, before the King. He saw also Allegators or Crocodiles kept in Ponds for like purpose, one of which kills two stoned Horses at one time.

There are foure great Markets euery day, where things are very cheape, a Hen for two pence, a Sheepe for two shillings, a good Hog sold by the Bannians for two shillings, and other things proportionable. They craued the Kings Passe for England, who granting it under his Hand and Seale, the Secretary went with them to the Third Queene of which he is said to have ten, and a thousand Concubines, and two hundred Eunuchs which was Keeper of the Great Seale. Hence they passed fiue in number to Fetterbarre twelue Course, and twelue more to Bianie, which is the chiefe Place for *Indico* in all the Indies, where are twelue Indico Mills. *Indico* growes on small bushes, like Goose-berry bushes, and beares a seed like a Cabadge-seed, and being cut downe lies on heapes for halfe a yeere to rot, and then brought into a Vault to bee trodden with Oxen from the stalks, and so is grownd fine at the Mills, and lastly, boyled in Fornaces, refined and sorted, the best there worth eight pence a pound.

Thence they passed to Hendown, fiue and twentie Course, an ancient faire Citie, to Mogol, a small Market Towne, fourteene, to Halstot twelue, to Chatsoe twelue, to Ladanna twelue, to Mosabad eight, to Bandason twelue. Thence to Paddar, a Riuer that runnes into the Persian Gulfe, and parts the Indostans and Hendownes. Twentie Course beyond, Roree, Buckar, and Suckar, in the Riuer of Damiadee which runnes into the same Sea. At Buckar *(a)* lyes *Allee Can*, Vice-Roy of the Bulloches, a stubborne People: this Towne stands like an Iland in the Riuer. Sucker is a clothing Towne, the first of the Bulloches, and Roree the last of the Moltans, which are Mahumetans. Here they staid foure and twentie daies for a Califa or Carauan (a great company of Merchants trauelling together) because the Country was full of Theeues. Seuenteene Course from Sucker is Gorra, a Towne of the Bullochees, which (he saith) worship the Sunne, and are Man-eaters, of Gyant-like proportion, Norry, ten Course: the last Towne of the Bullochees, the next Puttans. Here for their entertainment, Aprill the first, 1610. they were beset with Theeues, twelue Fiddlers first meeting them, but their Musicke cost deere by bribes and composition, the Mogols passe hindering futher outrage. Seuenteene Course they trauelled to Daddor; foure and thirtie ouer

(*a*) The character of the Beloochees, who are here referred to by our author, has differed very little since the period when he wrote; and the changes wrought in Scinde generally, are entirely owing to the introduction of British rule. The statement further on that the Beloochees were cannibals is open to question.

the Mountaines to Vachesto ; from thence seuen and fiftie ouer the Mountaines to Candahar, a great Citie of the Puttans, where *Sander Can* resided as Vice-Roy, where are continually seuen or eight thousand Camels occupied in Trade to and fro. The Gouernour hath fortie thousand Horses in redinesse for Warre.

Richard Sill and *Iohn Crowther*, were lately sent from Azmere, Asimere or Agimere, where the Mogoll now resides to Spahan in Persia, to obtaine Trade for the English, by Sir *Robert Sherlies* meanes, which was effected. They passed by the way of Lahore, and therefore I would desire You to beare Them company, for better knowledge of the Countrey. Their way was first towards Agra, and Fetipore, which is a faire Citie, and hath in it a goodly House of the Kings, built by *Echebar*, with many spacious Gardens now it goes to ruine, much of the stone carried to Agra, much ground sowne within the Wals. April the ninth, 1614, they came to Dillee, a very great and ancient Citie, where many Kings lye buried (and as some say the Rites of Coronation are still solemnized) many Nobles and Captaines haue their Houses of Pleasure, and their Sepulchres: the vulgar sort beggarly, most Banians. On the seuenteenth, they came to Sinan an ancient Citie. On the one and twentieth to the old Citie Sultanpoare. Sixe Courses from it they passed a Riuer as broad as the Thames called Viau, which runnes West into Sinda or Indus. Here was *Pitchte Can* his Tents pitched like a little Citie: he was Embassadour into Persia. On the four and twentieth they came to Lahore. Their Report of this agrees with Master *Coryats*, whose Relation thereof is lately published. They say it is the best of India, plentifull of all things, or in Master *Coryats* words, such a delicate and euen Tract of ground as I neuer saw before (and hee hath seene a great deale, besides his European sights at Venice, and since at Constantinople, hauing added more Asian Titles to his before *Admired* Name, then the ancient

Roman *Scipio's or Cæsars* dreamt of, yea more then *Iustinian* in the Proœme of his *Imperiall Institutions* hath marshalled and mustered together; the furthest foot English-Traueller that our dayes haue had, and the longest English stile which our eares haue heard, with many rests for your wearied breath by the way—a stile indeed so high you can hardly get ouer HIEROSOLYMITAN—SYRIAN—MESOPOTAMIAN—ARMENIAN—MEDIAN—PARTHIAN—PERSIAN—INDIAN—LEGGE--STRETCHER OF ODCOMB) euen this our Odcombian Foot-Pilgrime, which makes your Pen-Pilgrime in I know not what liking or likeness, at the very mention of his Name to sympathize, and his braines to fall in Trauell as learnedly mad, scarsly able to containe wonted words and wits in this extaticall gaze and maze of that *Propatetike* Foot: ready to admire, adore and kisse, and yet (O braines, No braines) to enuy that his lowest part: For who is able to know his better parts ?*(a)* He doubts whether the like be to be found within the whole Circumference of the habitable World. A row of Trees extends itselfe on both sides the way from the Towns end of Lahore, twentie dayes iourney, to the Townes end of Agra: most of them bearing (saith *Still,*) a kinde of Mulbery. The way is dangerous by night for Theeues, by day secure. Euery fiue or sixe Course there are faire *Seraes* of the Kings or Nobles, for beautifying the way, memory of their Names, and entertainment of Trauellers, where you may haue a Chamber and a Place to set your Horses, with store of Horse-meat; but in many of them little provision for Men, by reason of the Banian Superstition. When a man hath taken vp his lodging in one of these no other man may dispossesse him. About day-breake all make-readie to depart together, and then the Gates are

---

(*a*) The foregoing paragraph is far from being a bad specimen of the so-called Euphuisms of the period. It passed for wit two centuries and a half ago, though few modern readers will be able to perceive the wit in this enlightened period.

opened, till then shut for feare of Theeues. After the Sun hath beene vp two houres, the heat makes trauell irksome.

Lahore is one of the fairest and ancientest Cities in India, standing on Indus: It containeth at the least (M. Coryat tells you) sixteene miles in compasse. Twelue daies before hee came there, he passed Indus, there as broad as the Thames at London. In the mid-way betwixt Lahore and Agra, ten miles out of the way on the left hand, a Mountainous people, are said to haue but one Wife to all the brethren of one family, as wee haue else where spoken of the Arabians. Merchants resort to this Citie out of all parts of India, imbarking their goods here in great Boats for Tutta, the chiefe Citie in Sinda, a Trade of much importance in times of Peace to the Portugals, which by this way Traded to Ormus and Persia, and this way also furnishing India with Pepper. Twelue or fourteene thousand Camels lading yeerely passeth from hence to Persia by Candahar, before the Warrs with the Portugalls but three thousand ;(a) this mountainous way, being in Winter cold, in Summer hot. The Carauans spend sixe or seuen months betwixt Lahore and Spahan. Spices are deere in Persia by reason of the long land-carriage from Masulapatan this way.(b) *Still* and *Crowther* departed from Lahore May the thirteenth and on the two and twentieth came to Multan, a great and ancient Citie, within three Course of Indus but poore ;. for which cause, they detaine the Carauans there diuers dayes, eight, ten, or twelue to benefit the Citie. They entred the Mountaines, the second of Iune, where they had brackish water : the third and fourth daies they trauelled all night, climing

---

(a) Our author seems to intimate here that the native trade had largely increased with the decline of the Portuguese power. Tatta at that period appears to have been an emporium.

(b) The commercial route for spices ran from the Moluccas to Masulipatam on the Coromandal coast, and thence overland through the heart of India and Central Asia to Ispahan.

high Mountaines, and following water-courses, and so continued till they came to Chatcha on the tenth. In all these eight dayes trauell, is no sustenance for Man or Beast except in some places a little grasse, and therfore at Lacca in the beginning of this way they hyred an Oxe to carry Barly for their Horses. On the nineteenth, they came to Duckee, another Fort of the Mogols, and the seuen and twentieth passed the *Durwas* or straits of the Hils, dangerous narrow wayes on both sides men aced by high Rocks, from whence a few with stones may stop great multitudes, and diuers Carauans are thus cut off. For the Agwans or Puttans, the Mountaine Inhabitants are a theeuish people. The second of Iuly, they came to Pesimga another Fort, and passing thence ouer a mightie Mountaine, on the seuenth came to Candahar. The Agwans are white, stout, strong, rob Carauans, sell all stragglers : but now with feare, and the gaine they get by selling their Cattell to the Carauans, they are more tractable *(a)*.

Couert saith, they weare their beards long, are not Mahumetans : their Priests weare Sackcloth, with great chaines about their middles, falling downe and praying in Sack cloth and Ashes. At Candahar they hire Camels for India, or Persia : hence into Persia the Countrey is barren, and therefore they go in smaller compainies, sometimes in two or three dayes trauell not seeing a greene thing : at their lodging-places, water, but often brackish and stinking. Hence they departed, Iuly the three and twentieth, and on the fiue and twentieth came to Cushecunna, the vtmost Garrison in the Mogols Frontiers, thirtie Course from Candahar. On the seven and twentieth they came to Grees, a Castle of the Sophies, *(b)* a Course from the Riuer Sabba, which separateth the Persian and Mogoll Confines. The people of Grees are Theeues, and the Captaine little better than a Rebell.

(*a*) This description of the Afghans is very life-like.
(*b*) Kings of Persia.

From hence they reckon their way by farsangs (*parasangœ*) fiue of which make two Courses. They trauelled August the sixth, to Farra, a Towne walled with Sundryed Brick, and stored with Water, without which here is no store, and therefore they carry it in some places, if there be good ground, three or foure miles vnder ground. Heere they vse men kindly as they goe into Persia, for feare of complaint, but in their returne to India very hardly, searching them to the skin for Gold, which to carry out, or any Siluer coyne but the Kings, is death. On the twelue day, they were faine to dig for water. On the two and twentieth they come to Deuzayde, where they pretend all to be Religious people. On September the fifteenth (I still follow *Still*) they came to Spahan, where they found Sir *Robert Sherly*, then dispatched in Embassage for Spaine from the King of Persia, by the way of Ormus for Goa, and thence to Lisbon. Hee procured the Kings Great Seale to all his Gouernours of Sea Ports, kindly to entertaine the English at Iasques, &c. dated September the thirtieth, 1615, the same day that *Sir Robert* and his Lady departed with great pompe to Siras.

Iohn Crowther returned October the twentieth, towards Lahore, and he on December the second, towards Bagdat, and thence by Aleppo for England.

William Nicols, one of the *Ascensions* company, trauelled the Mogols Countrey Eastward to Mesulopatan, (*a*) where the Hollanders had then a Factorie. *Iohn Mildnall* in his Letters, dated from Casbin in Persia, 1606. October the third, testifieth that he had beene at Lahore and at Agra, where hee presented the King with nine and twentie great Horses, at fiftie or threescore pounds a Horse, with diuers Iewels and Rings, and obtained Articles of Tra-

(*a*) Masulipatam. This was one of the oldest Dutch factories in India. The Dutch carried the famous Coromandel cotton cloths, dyed or painted by native painters, over to the Spice Islands, where they were readily exchanged for nutmegs and other spices.

ding. Of his comming since into those parts, is before mentioned from Master *Withingtons* Relations. And his Trauells are the next Trauells of our Pen ; first, from Surrat to Amadabar by Periano, Cosumbay, Barocho (a Citie walled, on a high Hill, a Riuer running by as broad as the Thames, where are the best Calicoes in the Kingdome) Saringa, Carron Boldra (a City fairer but lesse then Barocho, where *Mussaf Chan* hath three thousand horse) Niriand a great Towne where they make Indico. These are in the way from Surat to Amadabar, *(a)* chiefe Citie of Guzerat, neere as great as London, strongly walled, situate in a plaine by the Riuers side, much frequented by Merchants, Christians, Moores, and Ethnikes. The Gouernour is *Abdala Chan* of fiue thousand Horse pay. From thence hee went to Cambaya. At Serkeffe three Courses from Amadabar, hee saw the Sepulchres of the Kings of Guzerat, very faire and well kept, much visited from all parts of the Kingdome. Their Temple is very faire. A Course from hence is a goodly House by the Riuers side, and a Garden a mile in compasse. It was built by *Chon Chonnaw*, the chiefe of the Mogol Nobilitie, in memoriall of a great Victorie there obtained on the last King of Guzerat there captiued, and his Kingdome subdued, the battell was fought in this place. They lodged one night in this House, where none dwelleth. Only poore men are appointed to looke to the Garden. Hauing newes of three English ships arriued at Lowribander the Port Towne of Guru Negar Tutta (commonly called Tutta) chiefe Citie of Sinda, hee was sent thither, and December the thirteenth, came to Cassumpauo, and thence with a Caphilo trauelled on the fourteenth to Callitalowny, a faire Castle, and the fifteenth to Calwalla, a prettie Village, which *Echebar* gaue to a company of Women and their Posteritie for euer, to bring vp their children in

---

(*a*) Ahmedabad.

dancing, &c. They practised this in the Carauan, euery man giuing them money, and then impudently asked if any man wanted a bed-fellow. The next day they came to Carrya, a well-manned Fortess, and staying a day for more company because of Theeues, came the next to Deceanaura, losing one Camell stolne from them, and a man slaine. Thence to Bollodo, a Fort kept by *Newlòck Abram Cabrath*, which that day came with a hundred and threescore and nine heads of the Cælies, a robbing Nation. The next day to Sariandgo another Fort, and on the one and twentieth to Radempoore, a great Town with a Fort, where they staid to make prouision of Water, and other necessaries for their iourney through the Desarts.

On the three and twentieth they went seuen Course, lay in the Fields, and met a Carauan which came from Tutta, robbed of all their goods: on the foure and twentieth, twelue: on the fiue and twentieth, fourteene, lodged by a Well of water so salt that their Cattell could not drinke it: the six and twentieth ten Course, to such another Well; and their gaue their Camels drinke, not hauing drunke before in three days: the seuen and twentieth fourteene Course. The eight and twentieth ten, and came to a Village called Negar Parkar. In this Desart they saw great store of wilde Asses, red Deere, Foxes, and other wilde Beasts. At Parkar they met another robbed Carauan. This Towne payes Tribuete to the Mogol. From hence till you come within halfe a dayes iourney of Tutta, they acknowledge no King, but rob and spare whom they please. When the Mogol sends any Armie against them, they fire their Houses (which are made of Straw and Mortar, in forme of Bee-Hiues soone rebuilded) and flye into the Mountaines. They take for custome what they please, and then guard Passengers and Merchants loth any should rob them but themselues.

From hence they went sixe Courses, and lay by a Tanke or Pond of Fresh-water, and on the last of December, eight Courses, and lodged by a brackish Well, Ianuary the first, they trauelled ten Courses to Burdiano. The Water is brackish, and many were sicke of it; yet they were forced to make prouision thereof for foure dayes, the space of fortie Courses; and on the fifth they came seuen other Courses to three Wells, of which two were salt, the third not perfectly fresh: the next day ten Courses to Nauraquemire, a prettie Towne, where their *Raddingpore Cafila* forsooke them. He and two other Indian Merchants, with their nine Seruants, ten Camels, and fiue Camel-men remained to goe for Tutta, whither they had now three dayes iourney.

From this Paradise (so it seemed after so tedious a Desart) they departed, Ianuary the eight, hauing hired one of the *Ragi*, or Gouernour his kindred for twentie Laries (which make about twentie shillings) to conduct and conuoy them, and went ten Courses to Gundayaw, where they had beene robbed, but for their Guard. The next day were twice assaulted, and forced each time to pay fiue Laries; came to Sarruna, a great Towne of the Razbootches with a Castle: whence it is fourteene Courses to Tutta. *Ragi Bouma* the Gouernour, is eldest Sonne to *Sultan Bulbull,* (*a*) who had beene lately captiued by the Mogoll, and spoiled of his eyes, and two moneths before our comming had made an escape to these Mountaines, animating his kindred to reuenge that losse of his sight. This *Ragi* was kinde to our Author as a stranger, and made him sup with him: the occasion that they hired him for fortie Laries, with fiftie Horse-men to conduct them to the Gates of Tutta. Hereunto they were the rather perswaded by aduice of a Banian, which had then come from Tutta, who also told Master *Withington*, that Sir *Robert Sherly* had beene much abused by the Portugals, and the Gouernour at Lowribander, his House fired, and

(*a*) This allusion is of some consequence in connection with the history of the Bellal Rajahs.

his Men hurt in the night: and arriuing at Tutta thirteene dayes after, was there vnkindly vsed by *Mersa Ruflo* the Gouernour. This *Ragi* led them fiue Courses, where they lay by a Riuer side, and at two of the clocke in the morning they departed, but were led a contrary way, and about breake of day brought into a Thicket, where he made them vnlade, tooke away their Weapons and bound them; suddenly with their Camell ropes drawne close with a Truncheon, hanged the two Merchants and their fiue Men, stripped and buried them. Mee (as a farre Countreymen, not knowing the language) hee spared with my Pions or Seruants, but tooke my Horse (giuing me a iade) and fourescore Rupias from mee, sent mee twentie Course with my men vp to the Mountaines to a brother of his, where I continued two and twentie dayes a close prisoner, and then order was sent to conuey mee to Parker: but in the way was robbed of my clothes and all that I had: so that I and my men were forced to liue vpon the charitie of people by begging: onely my Horse, as not worth taking, was left me, for which I could get but foure mamoodees (foure shillings) but chancing on a Banian whom I had knowne at Amadabar, I was relieued and sold not my Horse.(*a*) Wee came to Radingpoore. May the nineteenth, and April the second, to Amadabar: thence to Cambays, and (passing the Riuer seuen Courses broad, yeerely drowning many) to Saurau, a Towne and Castle of the Razbootches(*b*) and fiue and twentie Courses further to Borocho, and passing that Riuer, to Cassimba, and thence to Surat. In all this Countrey of Sinda, no Citie of greater Trade then Tutta; the chiefe Port thereto is Lowribander, three dayes iourney from thence, where is a faire Roade without the Riuers mouth, cleere of Wormes, which about Surat, and other places of the Indies infest the

(*a*) This incident illustrates the perils of land travellers under the fostering care of native Princes.

(*b*) The Rajpoots.

ships, so that after three or foure moneths riding, if it were not for sheathing, they were not able to returne. The Ports and Roades of Sindes are free of them. In two moneths they passe from Tutta to Lahore and returne downe the streame in one. And from Agra goods may bee conueyed on Camels in twentie dayes, which is on Sinda Riuer, and thence in fiteene or sixteene dayes aboord the Ships at Lowribander, as soone as to Surat, if Theeue[8] did not make it lesse secure.

May the fourth, 1614. Master *Withington* went from Surat to Brampore, where Sultan *Paruise* lyes. It is situate in a Plaine by a great Riuer, hauing a large Castle : and thence to Agra : all which way is seuen hundred Courses. From Surat to Brampore is a pleasant and champaigne Countrey, full of Riuers, Brookes, and Springs. From Brampore to Agra very mountainous, hardly passable for Camels by Mando the neerest way : there are many high Hils and strong Castles in the way, Townes and Cities in euery dayes iourney well inhabited, the Country peaceable and cleere of Theeues. Betweene Agimere or Azmere and Agra, are a hundred and twentie Courses : at euery Course end a great Pillar erected, and at euery tenth Course a Seraglia or Place of lodging for Man and Horse, with Hostesses to dress your Victuall (if you please) three pence will pay for your Horse and Meate-dressing : there are also at euery tenth Course faire Houses erected by *Echebar* for his Women, and none else may lie in them. The reason heereof is reported, that *Echebar* wanting Children went on Pilgrimage on foot to Asmere for that purpose, at euery Course end saying his prayers, and lodging at the tenth. Agra, is a huge Towne, situate by the great Riuer Geminie or Iamena. The Castle is the fairest thing in it, compassed with the fairest and highest Wall that I haue seene, two miles about, well replenished with Ordnance : the rest, except Noble-mens houses (which are faire and seated by the Riuer ruinous.) Fatipore is decayed, but hath a very stately Temple built by Geometry; as *Echebars* Sepulchre, the fairest thing that euer I saw. I went to Ganges, two dayes iourney from Agra, the Water whereof is carryed a hundred miles by the Banians for deuotion, which say it will neuer stinke, how long soeuer it bee kept. From Agra Master *Fitch* went to Satagam in Bengala by Water. So that if you obserue all these Trauels of *Fitch, Couert, Still, Withington*, and the rest of our Countrey-men, and adde thereto the iourney of *Goes* from thence to China, with other Relations of the Iesuites before expressed, you shall haue a better Corographie of this Countrey then any of our Maps haue yet deliuered, and their want hath made me thus full and tedious. I might adde the Trauels of *William Clerke* one of the *Ascensions* Company, which serued the Mogol in his Warres diuers yeeres (and returned in the last Ship whiles these things are publishing) against the Rasboots and Decans, hauing two Horse pay, which is neere sixe pounds a moneth, and had some moneths pay allowed him before hand, that so hee might furnish himselfe: for they must buy and maintaine their Horses.

Master *Walter Payton* was Master in the Expedition, and carried Sir *Robert Sherly*, whom they had thought to haue landed at Gauder or Guador *(a)* in Masqueranno, in fiue and twentie Degrees, and six and twentie Minutes, but the people were then in Rebellion against the Persian, and by damnable treachery had possessed themselues of the Ship and all the goods, had not one *Hoge Comal*, a Surgeon amongst them reuealed this mysterie of their iniquitie: they had thus betrayed three ships before. By this villany of the Bulloches, they were forced to goe further to the mouth of Sinde, which is East and by ¼ North, in foure and twentie Degrees, and foure and thirtie Minutes. They landed the Embassador, September the nine, and twentieth, 1613, at Diul, in the Mogols Dominion,

(a) A line of telegraph now runs through the old town of Gwador on the coast of Mekran.

fifteene miles from the ship. The Portugals reported them to be Theeues, according to their custome. And when they sought for Trade in Sinda, the Gouernour had yeelded but for the Portugals, which threatned to depart if the English were admitted, whose custome hee was loth to lose, being worth, hee said, a *Lack* of Rupias, ten thousand pound English and more (which shewes the exceeding Trade of Sinda) by the yeere.

But this Countrey, and the disposition of their King, are most amply described to vs, together with the remarkable Rarities of those parts, by the *Hon.* industry of Sir *Thomas Roe*, Embassadour for his Maiestie with the Mogoll, whose Map of those parts wee heere present you; as likewise by his learned Chaplaine, Master *Edward Terry*: both whose Obseruations wee haue presented in our first Tome of Voyages. To them I referre the industrious Reader, for more ample relations of these parts, then in this Worke were conuenient to insert. Amongst other things, the Reader shall see the true course of Indus (which all Moderne Geographers haue exceedingly falsified) and of *Ganges*. *William Finch* hath also written of those parts. I thought good heere to adde that which Master *Steele* and his wife told me of the Women of those parts. Master *Steele* hauing a proiect of Water works, to bring the water of Ganges by Pipes, &c. carried fiue men with him to the Mogol, who gaue them entertainment with large wages by the day, and gaue to each an Arabian Horse. One of these was a Painter, whom the Mogol would haue to take his picture; and because hee could not speake the language, Master *Steele* (who could speake the language of the Court, which is Persian) was admitted (a thing not permitted to Men) into the Mogols lodgings, where he did sit for the said Limner. At his entrance, the chiefe Eunuch put a cloth ouer his head, that he should not see the Women (which hee might heare as hee passed, and once also saw them, the Eunuch purposely putting on a thinner cloth ouer his head) there being of them some hundreds. His wife had more accesse at *Chan Channas* Court, whose daughter (sometimes wife to the elder brother of this Mogol, and liuing still a widdow) had a desire to see the English-woman, and *Chan-Channa* intreated her husband to permit it. Shee was fetched in a close Chariot drawne by white Oxen, attended by Eunuchs; and was first brought into an open Court, in midst of which was a Tanke or Well of Water, where sate many women, slaues to *Chan-Channas* daughter, of diuers Nations and complexions: some blacke, exceeding louely and comely of person notwithstanding, whose hare before did stand vp with right tufts, as if it had growne vpward, nor would ruffling disorder them; some browne, of Indian complexion; others very white, but pale, and not ruddy; many of them seemed goodly and louely, all sitting in their sight, but rich garments on the floore couered with carpets. The Lady came forth in meaner attire, whereat they all arose and did her reuerence, with their faces to the ground. Mistresse *Steele* made her three courtsies, after the English fashion (being also in English attire) and deliuered her a Present (without which there is no visitation of great persons) and the Lady caused her to sit by her, and after discourse, entertained her with a Banket; and began familiarite with her, continued and increased with often visitations, and rewarded with many gifts, as of womens vestmeats of those parts; some of which I saw, the vpper garment like a smoke, of thin Calico, vnder which they weare a paire of breeches close aboue, the neather parts very long and slendor, loosely ruffling about their legs, of thin stuffe also; the mans garment differing from the womans, by the fastning on the side vnder the arme, whereas the womans is fastened before, both tyed with ribbands. *Chan Channa* caused his Taylor to take view of Master *Steele*, and without other measure hee made him a cloake of cloth of gold, after the English fashion very comely, which I also saw.

CHAPTER VIII.

ON THE RASBOOTS, AND OTHER PEOPLE SUBJECT TO THE MOGOL; AND OF THEIR COUNTRIES, RELIGION, AND RITES.

Thus haue we delineated this huge Giantly Body of the Mogol Empire. The Soule or Religion thereof is more inuisible. What lurking places and labyrinths the breasts of the Kings haue had in their vnknowne, curious, vncertaine Faith, yee haue heard, and may thereby guesse at the rest. As the people are manifold, so are their Rites; some of which, about Ganges, and in other parts, haue alreadie beene touched: and some hereafter, as the People and their Rites are diffused and dispersed in diuers Tracts of India, we shall elsewhere mention. Besides Christian Forreiners, the principall Religioun is Ethnike, though that of the Prince be Mahumetan.

The *Reisbuti*, *Rasboots*, or *Rasbooches*, the ancient Inhabitants of the Countrey of Sinda, are Gentiles. How strong one of them is, you haue heard Captaine Hawkins report. His name, as I haue since learned of Mr. Rogers, Mr. Clarke, and Mr. Withington, is *Ranna*; some of them affirming, that hee is lately come in, and hath sent his sonne a pledge to the Mogols Court, who for this cause, and his sake, hath beene so long resident at Azmere. But Mr. Clarke, employed in these wars, saith, That it is not a subiection, but voluntarie friendship and neighbourhood, with acknowledgement of himselfe the Inferior. A Rebell or Outlaw he cannot be called, because hee was neuer subiect; accounting the Mogoll Superior in power, but not his Lord. There are of these many Casts, or Tribes, each of which haue supreame and independent Lords: Nature building them, with little helpe of Art, impregnable Fortresses, or inaccessable Hils. One of which called Dewras, is said to haue very many populations; able on the Hill tops to gather sufficient prouisions for themselues, and the neighbour-Markets; impossible without corruption to be conquered. When any of these Casts, or Tribes, disagree, the Mogoll interposeth himselfe, professing to take part with the right. Their Countrey lies in the direct way from Surat to Agra, the wayes by Amadauar, or by Brampore, both much about, yet frequented by Merchants, for feare of them. The Countrey people are rude, naked from the waste vpwards, with Turbants differing from the Mogol fashion. Their Armes are Sword, Buckler, and Launce. Their Buckler is great, in fashion of a Bee-hiue, in which they will giue their Camels drinks and Horses prouender. Their Horses are good; swift, and strong which they ride vnshod, and back at a yeere old. A resolute people; which the Mogol faith knowes as well to die, as any in the world. They eate no Beefe nor Buffolo, but haue them in superstitious respect. The Rasbutche husband dying, the wife is burned. The manner is this: The wife accompanies the dead bodie of her husband in her best array, pompously attended with her friends and kindred, and with Musick. The fire being made, she compasseth the same twice or thrice: first bewayling her husbands death; and then reioycing, that she shall now liue with him againe; and then embracing her friends, sits downe on the top of the pyle, taking her husbands head, in her lap, and bids them kindle the fire. This done, her friends throw Oyle and other sweet Perfumes on her, shee enduring the fire with admirable patience, loose, and not bound. I haue seene many (it is Mr. Withingtons report) the first at Surat, the woman being but ten yeeres old, and not yet a woman hauing not knowne her husband, who was slaine in the wars, and his clothes brought home. Yet would she needs burne with his clothes : and the Gouernour not permitting, because shee was a Virgin, her friends intreated and bribed him there to, shee seeming impatient of that delay, and saying her husband was a great way before her, with much blind ioy entering into endlesse sorrowes. The kindred of the deceased husband doe not force this vnkind kindnesse, but the wiues owne kindred ; holding it a disgrace to their family, if shee refuse ; which shee hath power to doe : but few will ; and then shee must shaue her haire, and breake her jewels and is not suffered to eate, drink, sleepe, or company with any bodie, till her death. If, after purpose to burne, impatient of the flame, she leaps out, her father and mother will bind and burne her perforce. But such weaknesse seldome happens. In some places they obserue it, with Rites a little differing : carrying the woman in great pompe on a Pageant, and binding her to a stake, all her kindred kneeling round about her, and praying to the Sun, and their other Idols. Shee hath betwixt her legs, and vnder each arme, a bag of Gun-powder ; the fire made all of sweet Woods. Wee shall mention other Rites in other places.

The *Hendownes* possesse the Countrey North from Asmere toward the Multans : degenerate Gentiles, and refusing no manner of Flesh or Fish. They pray naked, dresse and eat their meat naked ; and where they dresse and eate their meat, make a Circle, within which none must enter during that time. Their women are brought vp from their child-hood with shackles, some of Siluer, some of Brasse, and some of Iron, on their legges, and Rings in their eares ; all which encrease with themselues, being made bigger, as thep grow ; so that in time a man may thrust his hand through the holes of their eares. Also they were Bracelets of Elephants teeth about their armes, from the wrist to the elbow. Wee haue alreadie spoken of the Bulloches, their Northerly neighbours, Sunne-worshipping, Giantly bignesse, and Inhuman humanitie, in eating mans flesh (and likewise of the Puttans or Agwans.) The Bulloches in Sinda, and vpon the Persian Gulfe (it seems of this generation) are Mahumetans, Robbers by Land, and Pyrats by Sea, whereto they adde the murther of those they rob. Their treachery to Sir R. Sherly and the Expedition, is before mentioned : which had it had expedition according to their plot, they had murthered all but the Surgeon, the Musician, the Boyes, and the Women. When I was in Sinda (saith M. Withington) they tooke a Boat, with seuen Italians, and one Portugall Fryar, this ripped vp by them, to seeke Gold in his entrails, the rest slaine in the fight. Yet there are very honest men of them in Guzerat, and about Agra.

Touching other Superstitions of this Kingdome, thus writieth *Ioannes Oranus* in the Narration of this Kingdome: Not farre from the Citie Lahor is an Idoll, resembling a woman, which they call *Nazar Coto*, framed with two Heads, & six or seuen Armes, and twelue or fourteene Hands; one of which brandisheth a Speare, another a Club. Hereunto resort many Pilgrims to worship; and hereof they tell many miracles; as, that many cut off their tongues, which are againe restored whole vnto them, but remaine mute. Some thinke our breath to bee our Soule. Some affirme, That all things are the same thing. Some, that God onely hath a being, other things are shadowes and appearances. Some thinke all things, and some, the round Circle of the World; and some, themselues, to bee God. Almost all doe hold the commigration of Soules into the bodies of Beasts. They say, the World shall last foure Ages, or Worlds; whereof three are past. The first lasted seuenteene *Laches* (euery *Laches* contained an hundred thosand yeeres) and eight and twentie thousand yeeres. Men in that World liued ten thousand yeeres, were of great stature of bodie, and great sinceritie of minde.

Thrice in this space did God visibly appeare on the Earth: First, in forme of a Fish, that hee might bring out the Booke of the Law of Brama, which one *Causacar* had hurled into the Sea: The second time, in forme of a Snaile, that he might make the Earth dry and solid: Lastly, like a Hog, to destroy one that said he was God; or as others of them as truely say, to recouer the Earth from the Sea, which had swallowed it. The second World lasted ten *Laches*, and ninetie two thousand and six yeeres; in which, men were as tall as before, and liued a thousand yeeres. God did appeare foure times: First, in a monstrous forme, the vpper part a Lion, the lower a Woman, to represse the pride of one, which gaue out himselfe for God: Secondly, like a poore Bramane, to punish a proud King, that would by a new deuised Art fly into Heauen: The third time, to be reuenged of another King, which had slaine a poore Religious man, he came in the likenesse of a Man, named *Parcaram*: and lastly, like one *Ram*, the sonne of *Giocorat*, which had slaine *Parcaram*. The third World continued eight *Laches* and foure thousand yeeres, wherein men liued fiue hundred yeeres; and God appeared twice in Humane likenesse. The fourth Age shall enduer foure *Laches*, whereof are alreadie passed foure thousand sixe hundred fourescore and twelue yeeres. They say God will also appeare in this Age. Others imagine, That he hath alreadie appeared, and that *Echebar* is hee. Some hold, That those ten Appearances were but creatures, which had received Diuine power. They themselues easily perceiue the vanity of these *Chimœras*, and monstrous opinions, but will not leaue them, lest they should (at the same cast) lose their Wealth and Superstition together.

In the Countrey of the Mogor they have many fine Carts, carued and gilded, with two Wheeles, drawn with two little Buls, about the bignesse of our great Dogs in England, and they will runne with any Horse, and carry two or three men in one of those Carts. They are couered with Silke, or fine Cloth, and be in vse as our Coaches in England.

But we will shut up this too great discourse of the great Mogols Greatnesse, in the words of the Worlds Greatest Foot-post. He tels vs, from the very Mogols Court, That this present Prince, is a man of three and fiftie yeeres of age, of complexion middle, betwixt white and blacke, in a more expressiue Epitheton, Oliue; of a seemely composition of bodie, of stature little vnequall to Mine, but much more corpulent (hee neuer trauelled so much on foot, nor ten moneths together with fiftie shillings expence.) His Dominion is little lesse then foure thousand English miles: which, if it come short of the Turke in Geometricall dimension of ground, it is with a great pleonasme supplied by the fertilitie of his Soyle, and in the vnion of all his Territories. Againe, hee exceedeth him in Reuenue (a great deale more then M. *Coryats* reckoning); hee presenteth himselfe thrice euerie day: at the rising of the Sunne, which hee adoreth by the eleuation of his hands; at noone, and at fiue of the clocke in the euening: but he standeth in a roome aloft, alone by himself, and looketh from a window that hath an embroidered sumptuous Couerture, supported with two siluer Pillasters, to yeeld shadow vnto him. In feeding of his Beasts, hee spendeth at the least ten thousand pound sterling a day; and keepeth a thousand women for his owne body, whereof the chiefe is *Normal.* I haue bin in a Citie in this Country, called *Detee*, where *Alexander* ioyned battell with *Porus*, and in token of his victory erected a brasse Pillar, which remaineth there to this day. There arrived foure English ships at Surat, and in the same Sir Thomas Rowe, the English Embassador to the Mogol: the news whereof came to Asmere, October 8, 1615, and did much refocillate M. Coryas spirits (as did M. Brownes verses from Amadavars) and so I hope will yours.

CHAPTER IX.

OF CAMBAYA, DECAN, AND THE NEIBOURING NATIONS.

ALTHOUGH we might seem to haue spoken sufficiently of the Cambayans alreadie, in our former Mogol-Relations; yet, as better knowne, wee haue allowed them a Chapter here by themselues. Cambaya is also called Guzarat; containing in length, from the River Bate to Circam, a Persian Region, fiue hundred miles of Sea-coast, being on other parts enuironed with the Kingdomes of Dulcinda and Sanga, on the North; Mandao, on the East; on the West, Nautacos, or the Gedrosians. The Sea, and the Confines of Decan are the Southerly bounds. It hath in it, by estimation, threescore thousand Populations, or inhabited Places, watred with many Streames, the chiefe whereof is Indus, which diuideth it in the middle, running from Caucasus, or Naugrocot, and after nine hundred miles iourney, with two nauigable mouths disemboquing itselfe into the Ocean. This Countrey is very fertile, not yeelding to any other in India, in the fruits, which the Earth and Trees bring forth, besides their store of Elephants, Gems, Silke, Cotton, and such like. The people are of an Oliue-colour, and goe naked, except about their priuie parts. They eate no Flesh, but Rice, Milke, Barley, and other life-lesse Creatures. The Inhabitants are, for the most part, Gentiles; and so were their Kings, vntil the Mahumetan Superstitions preuailed. There are vp within the Land, People called *Reisbuti,* (*a*) which are the natural Nobles of this Kingdome, chaced by the Moores

(*a*) Rajpoots.

to the Mountaines, whence they make often excursions and spoyles in the Country; and the Cambayans pay them tribute, that they might liue in peace: of these is spoken alreadie. Their chiefe Sea-Townes are Daman, Bandora, Surate, Rauellum, Bazuinum; and within Land, Cambaya, Madabar, Campanel, Tanaa, &c. Surat (now an English Factory) hath a Castle of Stone, with good Ordnance: The Houses are faire, of Stone and Brick, square, with flat roofes: they haue goodly Gardens, with Pomegranats, Pome-Citrons, Melons, Limons, Figs all the yeere long, curious Springs of fresh Water. The people neat, tall, louing, graue, iudicious, clothed in long white Calico, or Silke.

Cambaya hath bestowed the name on the whole Kingdome, which they called the Indian Cairo, for the excellencie therof: it standeth three miles from Indus. The Tides here encrease not, as with vs, at the full, but in the decrease of the Moone they are at the highest. Of this River Indus, *Ptolomy* and *Arrianus* in his *Periplus of the Erythrean Sea*, reckon seven Mouthes or Entrances into the Sea, and *Theut* (I know not with what Friar-like, and Lyar-like boldnesse) nameth seuen at this day: but *Arrianus* saith, in those times six of the seuen were ouergrowne, and but one nauigable. But *Dionysius Pomponius*, *Strabo* and the other *Arrianus*, which write the life of *Alexander*, ascribe but two vnto it; which is confirmed by the Portugals. *Arrianus* hath in his eighth Booke largely described the Voyage of *Nearchus* and *Onesicriius*, from this Riuer, about the Coast into the Persian Gulfe, employed by *Alexander* the Great. It is not 160 yeeres since *Machamuta* Moore expelled the Guzarat King.

This *Machamut* deserueth mention for one thing, wherein the Sunne hath scarce beheld his like. He so accustomed himselfe to poysons, that no day passed wherein hee tooke not some; for else hee himselfe had dyed, said *Barbosa*; as it fareth with *Amsian* or *Opium*, the vse whereof killeth such as neuer tooke it, and the disuse, such as haue. And beyond that which we reade of *Mithridates* in the like practice, his Nature was transformed into so venemous a habit, that if hee did meane to put any of his Nobles to death, hee would cause them to be set naked before him and chewing certaine fruits in his mouth, which they call *Chofolos* and *Tambolos*, with lime made of shells, by spitting vpon him, in one halfe houre depriue him of life: if a Fly sate vpon his hand, it would presently fall off dead. Neither was his loue to be preferred to his hatred, or with women was his dealing lesse deadly. For he had three or foure thousand Concubines of whom none liued to see a second Sunne, after hee had carnally knowne them. His Mustaches (or haire of his vpper lip) was so long, that he bound it vpon his head, as women doe with an haire-lace; and his beard was white, reaching to his Waste. Euere day when he arose, and when hee dined, fiftie Elephants were brought into the Palace, to doe him reuerence on their knees, accompanied with Trumpets and other Musicke.

Cœlius Rhodiginus mentions the like of a Maid, thus nourished with Poysons, her Spettle (and other Humours comming from her) being deadly: such also as lay with her carnally, presently dying. *Anicenna* hath also a like example of a Man, whose Nature, infected with a stronger Venome, poysoned other venomous Creatures, if any did bite him. And when a greater Serpent was brought for triall, he had by the biting thereof two-dayes Feuer; but the Serpent dyed: The other did not harme him.

Mamudius, the Successor, of King *Machamut*, was a great enemy to the Portugals; *Badurius* succeeded in state and affection, and exceeded in greatnesse and ambition. Hee inuaded Mandao, and Sanga, where hee besieged Citor :(*a*) then gouerned by a warlike woman: which not able to hold out longer against him, fled, and left the people in

(*a*) Chitpore. The memory of this famous siege is still preserved.

forlorne plight; who in a desparate resolution (like *Sardanapalus*) heaping vp their Treasures, set fire thereto, and then cast themselves therein. This fire continued three dayes, and comsumed three-score and ten thousand persons.

Hence *Badurius* triumphantly marched against the Mogor, whom *Masseus* calleth *Maramudius*, with an Army of an hundred and fiftie thousand Horse, whereof thirtie thousand were barded; and fiue hundred thousand Footmen; of great brazen Ordnance, a thousand; whereof foure Basiliskes were drawne (such was their weight) by so many hundred yokes of Oxen: with Shot and Powder hee laded fiue hundred Waynes, and as many with Gold and Siluer, to pay his Souldiers. These Forces, with this prouision, might rend the Ayre with Thunders, might make the Earth to shake with Terror, might dry and drinke vp Riuers of Water, might frame another fiery Element, of Arts inuention; but could not either terrifie the Mogor, or saue *Badurius* from a double overthrow; first, at Doceri; next, at Mandoa, where hee loseth his Tents and Treasures; and shauing his beard, flyeth disguised to Diu: in which, that the Portugalls might be engaged in the same warre, hee gaue them leaue to erect a Fortresse: A thing of such moment vnto them, that *Iohn Botelius* (confined before vnto India for crimes obiected) thought, by being the first Messenger thereof in Portugall, to purchase his liberitie: whereof he might well bee reputed worthy, who in a little Vessell, scarce eighteene foot long, and sixe wide, with vndaunted courage contemning that wide, long, and tempestuous Ocean, arriued with his small companie, great news, and greater admiration, at Lisbone. *Badurius* after altering his minde, and therein entertaining a treacherous Proiect against the Portugalls, coloured the same with kindnesse, and he (which feared all men, no lesse than hee was feared, as guiltie to his owne Tyranny, which sometime made *Dionysius* of a King, a Barbar, and now this, a

King of others, and his own Cooke, trusting no man to dresse his meat) aduentured to visit the Portugall Vice-Roy in his ships, professing great freindship, with great dissimulation, and by a meane Mariner, on his returne, was slaine; whereupon the whole Iland submitted itselfe to the Portugall yoke. And because we haue in this Chapter mentioned so many Wonders, let this also haue place among (if not aboue) the rest, which presently happened. Whiles the Portugalls were busie in their Buildings, a certaine Bengalan came to the Gouernour, which had liued, as hee affirmed three hundred thirtie fiue yeeres. The old men of the Countrey testified, That they had heard their Ancestors speake of his great age, and himselfe had a sonne foure score and tenne yeers old, and not at all Booke-learned, yet was a speaking Chronicle of those passed times. His teeth had sometimes fallen out, others growing in their places; and his beard, after it had beene very hoarie, by degrees returned into his former blacknesse. About an hundred yeeres before this time he had altered his Pagan Religion into the Arabian or Moorish. For this his miraculous age, the Sultans of Cambaya had allowed him a stipend to liue on; the continuance of which he now sought, and did obtaine of the Portugals. Friar *Ioano dos Santos* tells a long story of one yet aliue, *Ann* 1605, of whom the Bishop of *Cochin* had sent men to inquire, who by diligent search found that hee was then three hundred eightie yeeres old, and had married eight times, the father of many generations. They say his teeth had thrice fallen out, and thrice renewed: his haire thrice hoary, and as oft black againe. Hee could tell of nineteene successiue Kings, which reigned in *Horan* his Countrey in *Bengala*. He was also borne a Gentile, and after turned Moore, and hoped, he said, to dye a Christian, reioycing to see a picture of Saint *Francis*, saying, Such a man when he was twentie fiue yeeres old had foretold him this long life.

But to returne; *Mamudius*, successor to *Badurius*, sought

with all his forces to driue these new Lords out of Diu, as *Solyman* had done before, by a Nauie and Armie sent thither; but both in vaine: of which Wars, *Damianus à Goes* hath written diuers Commentaries. But this whole Countrey is now subiect to the Mogor. It was in *Alexander's* time, peopled by the Massani, Sodræ, or *Sabracæ*, Præstæ, and Sangadæ, as *Ortelius* hath placed them; where *Alexander* (as in diuers other places he had done) erected a Citie of his owne name, called Alexandria. Daman, another Key of this Bay, and entrance of the Riuer Indus into the Sea, fell to the Portugalls share.

The Land of Cambaya is the fruitfullest in all India; which causeth great traffique of Indians, Portugalls, Persians, Arabians, Armenians, &c. The Guzrates, or Cambayans, are the subtillest Merchants in all those parts. They haue amongst them many Histories of *Darius* and *Alexander*, which sometime were Lords of this Indian Prouince. The Portugals haue at diuers times conquered diuers of the chiefe Townes in this Kingdome, somewhere of they keepe still. The women in Diu, by Art dye their teeth black, esteeming themselues so much the more beautifull, and therefore go with their lips open, to shew the blacknesse of their teeth, drawing away the cover of their lips, as if they were lip-lesse, giuing the *prize of Beautie* to a double deformitie, Blacknesse, and a Mouth *O Hellish wide*. When a Cambayan dyeth, they burne his body, and distribute the ashes vnto the four Elements (of which man consisteth) part to the Fire, part to the Ayre, to the Water also and Earth their due portions, as *Bably*, hath obserued.

Mr Partike Copland (Minister in the *Dragon*, with Captaine *Best*) writes, that hee rode in this Countrey, from Medhaphrabadh to Surat, in a Coach drawne with Oxen, which is the most ordinary, though they haue goodly Horses. He saw at once the goodliest Spring and Haruest that euer he had seene: Fields joyning together, where one was greene as a meadow; the other yellow as gold, ready to be cut, of Wheat and Rice. All along, goodly Villages full of trees, yeelding Taddy (the Palme: of which after) a new sweet Wine, strengthening and fattening. A Smith which loved his liquor, said hee could wish no other wages, but a pot of this Taddy alway at his girdle.

CHAPTER X.

OF THE KINGDOMES OF DECAN.

Of the Decans we haue spoken before, in the Mogol conquests. Decan is the name of a Citie, sixe leagues from which is a Hill, out of which the Diamond is taken. This Hill is kept with a Garrison, and walled about. Of the Decan Kingdomes, *Barros* hath reported, That about the yeere 1300, *Sa Nosaradin* reigned in Delly, or Delin, inuaded the Kingdome of Canara (which reacheth from the Riuer Bate, North of Chaul, vnto the Cape Comori) and wonne much from the Ancestors of the King (now termed) of Bisnaga. At his returne, he left *Habedsa* his Lieutenant, who added to the former Conquests, gathering a Band of all mixtures, Gentiles, Moores, Christians. His sonne was confirmed in the Gouernment, therefore called *Decan*, and the people Decanins, because of this confusion of so many Nations, of which, his Fathers and His forces consisted: for *Decanins* signifies Bastards. He shooke off all allegeance to his Lord, and acknowledged none Superiour. Hee also much encreased his Dominions. His name was *Mamudsa.* He appointed eighteene Captaines or Commanders, allotting to each severall Prouinces. These Captaines hee made, were but slaues that so hee might the easier hold them in subjection. He commanded, that each of them should build a Palace at Bedir, his chief Citie, and there reside certaine moneths in the yeere, his sonne remayning there in perpetuall hostage. These, in processe of time, grew fewer, and therefore greater; the King holding nothing but his Royall Citie; all the Empire being in the hands of these slaues: which, when the Portugals came thither, were no more, but *Sabay, Niza Malucco, Madre Malucco, Melie Verida, Coge Mecadam*, the Abessine Eunuch, and *Cota Malucco*. The mightiest of them was *Sabay*, Lord of Goa: His sonne was *Hidalcam*. Thus *Barrius, Garcias ab Horto* writes, That the Mogors had possessed the Kingdome of Delly: but a certaine Bengalan (rebelling against his Master) slue him, vsurped his State, and by force of warre added this of Canara also to his Dominion; he was called *Xabolam*. This King made his sister's sonne his Successor, who was much addicted to Forreiners. He diuided his Kingdome into twelue parts, or Prouinces, ouer which, he set so many Captaines: *Idalcam*, from Angidaua to Cifarda: from thence to Negatona, *Nizamaluco*: Ouer Balaguate, or the vp-hill Country (for *Bala* in the Persian language signifieth The toppe, and *Guate* a Hill) *Imadmaluco*, and *Catalmaluco*, and *Verido*, &c. These all rebelled, and captiued *Daquem* their King at Beder, the chiefe Citie of Decan, and shared his kingdome amongst themselues, and some Gentiles, partners in the conspiracie. They were all forreiners, but *Nizamaluco*. This and the other names, before mentioned, were Titles of Honour, giuen them with their Offices, by the King, corrupted by the vulgar in pronouncing *Idalcam*, is *Adel-bam*; *Adel* in the Persian language, signifieth *Justice*; *Ham* is the Tartarian appellation, signifying a Prince, or King (which name might well be the Reliques of the Tartarian conquests in those parts) so *Adelham* is *King of Iustice*. *Neza* in the Persian (which *Scaliger* saith is of like extent in the East, as Latine in the West) is a Lance: *Maluco* signifieth the Kingdome. *Neza*, or *Nizamaluco*, the Speare or Lance of the kingdome. So *Cotamaluco* the Tower of the kingdome, *Imadmaluco* the Throne of the Kingdome, &c, *Nizamaluco* is also called *Nizamoxa*: which *Xa*, or *Scha*, is a Persian title (signifying as *Monsieur* in France, *Don* in Spaine) and giuen by *Ismael* the Sophi, and *Tamas* his sonne, to all those Kings that would communicate in their Sect, which *Nizamoza* only yeelded to. Other of them made shew, but soone recanted. Thus farre *Garcias*.

The Decan Kings being now ten or twelue, make joynt warre against the Mogoll, having one Lieutenant Generall, which is *Amber Chupu*, an Abassen slaue (before mentioned, out of Captaine *Hawkins*) who hath many Lacks of Rupias in ready money, and is Protector of the Kingdome of Amdanagar, the titular King being a childe. One *Robert Iohnson* an Englishman turned Moore, and was entertained with much respect of one of the Decan Kings, but died eight days after his Circumcision. So were *Robert Claxon* aud *Robert Trally*, voluntarily robbed of that which they neuer had (Faith and Religion) and turned Moores. The Decans dominions reach from the West Sea to that of Choromandel, or very neere there to. The chiefe reason of their Mahumedan Religion was that Conquest by *Nosaradin*, and his successors Moores that there are so many Kingdomes proceed from that diuision before mentioned.

CHAPTER XI.

OF THE BANIAN AND CAMBAYAN SUPERSTITIONS.

THE Religion in Cambaya is partly Moorish, partly Heathenish. The Banians are many, in Sinda and other Countries of the Mogol. There are some thirty Casts of them in Sinda (this is the Countrey which Indus last forsaketh, inhabited by Boloches, and Rasbooches, and Banians, the great Townes and Cities gouerned by Mogols.) These are of thirty different Sects, which may not eate with each other. They must also marry in their own Cast, Tribe, and Sect, and which is more, in the same trade, as the Sonne of a Barber with a Barber's Daughter. These marriages are made when they be young, sometime almost before they be. For when two women are pregnant, the Parents will make a match betweene their Children, if death or the sexe disappoint not. When they are three or foure yeeres old, the Parents which haue agreed on a match betweene their Children, make a great feast, and set this young couple on horsebacke (a man behind each of them to hold them) in their best clothes accompanied with the Bramenes or Priests, and many others according to their state, and so leade them vp and downe the Citie where they dwell, and then to the Pagode or Temple. After Ceremonies there done, they come home and make festiuall cheere certaine dayes, as they are able. At ten yeeres of age they lie together. The burning their dead is common to all their Sects. They are of the Pythagorean, or he was rather of their fancy, which he learned of the Indians. When the husband dies, the wife shaues her head, and weares her jewels no more, so continving till death. Thus farre Master *Withington*. M. *Couerte* relateth that they haue God in pictures of stone, hanging their Beades on the heads of the pictures, and then with their faces towards the Sunne doo worship it, saying all their comforts proceed from it. I saw a Cow, adorned with Iewels and a Vest of gold, her head bedecked with garlands & flowers, and then being brought to a burial place, where they vse to make Sermons, they kisse her feet and teats and worship her. I asking why they did so, they answered that she was the mother of beasts, and brought them milke, butter, cheese, and the Oxe to till the ground, and lastly, her Hide did make leather to make them shooes. Moreouer they say, she is blest by the Mother of God to be honored aboue all beasts.

Another writes that these Banians are the wisest Merchants in the East, exceeding the Iewes, very rich, some worth 2, or 300000 li. He addes that they pay a great summe to the Mogol to preuent killing of Oxen: and when our men had shot a Turtle doue through the wings, they will giue a Riall of eight to redeeme and preserue it. Generall *Downton* in his last Iournall writes, that when they would haue obtained a Bazar or Market by the shoare: answere was made that they might, but not for Bullocks. For the Mogol had granted his Firma to the Banians, for a mighty summe yeerly to save their liues. For Souldiery these are but shadowes of men, all their Fortitude smoking out in these superstitious speculations, and therefore an easie prey to any Inuader. So true a μεταμΨυχωσις haue they sustained, being metamorphosed and transanimated from men to blockes, and liuing statues, or to ghosts. *Beniamin Day* nameth one of their Sects called *Ash-men*, whose bodies being most part naked, are couered with ashes whereby they looke like ghosts or dead men. They liue idely on reliefe not so much as begging.

One of these was in great account, with haire hanging to his feet platted together, his nailes fiue or sixe inches long. *Vertomannus* is Author, that they worship, not Idols, or *Pagodes*. Others report, That this way, and others they are exceeding religiously deuoted. They obserue a strict kind of fasting, which lasteth with some eight dayes, with others fifteene, twenty or thirty dayes: in all which space they eate not a bit; onely, when they thirst, drinke water. One could not see when to make an end of this his penance, till his left eye fell out of his head, as both had done before out of his heart. In Cambaya they had one Bramene in such reputation of holinesse and honour, that they would salute him before they meddled with their worldly affaires. One affirmed to this Iesuite, That if his Bramene should command him to distribute all his goods to the poore, he would doe it, yea, he would lay downe his life at his command.

On the eight day of Ianuarie in that Citie, were giuen in almes twenty thousand Pardawes, (which is in value about a Flemish Dollar;) one man had giuen fiue thousand thereof, another three thousand, another fifteene hundred. The cause was, because that day (as their Bramenes affirmed) the Sunne departed from Sur to Horte. Of their Pilgrimages is spoken before; some Eastward to Ganges; some Westward to Mecca, to wit, the Moores; not men alone, but women also: and because *Mahomet* hath forbidden all vnmarried women this holy Iourney, they will marrie before they set forth, and dissolue the same marriage againe, after their return. Hereby they thinke to purchase merite with God.

I went one day (sayth *Pinnerus*) to the publike Hospitall, which the Citizens of Cambaya had founded for all kindes of Birds, to cure them in their sicknesse. Some Peacokes were there incurable, and therefore might have beene expelled the Hospitall. But (alacke for pitie of so rufull an accident) a Hawke had been admitted thither for the cure of his lame legge which being whole, hee inhospitably slue many of these co-hospitall weaker Fowles, and was therefore expelled this Bird-College by the Master thereof. For Men they had not an Hospitall, that were thus Hospitall to Fowles.

They have certaine Religious persons, called *Verteas* which liue in a Colledge together, and when I went to their House, they were about fiftie in number. They weare white cloth, were bare-headed, and shauen; if that word might bee applied to them; who pull off their haire on their heads and faces, leauing onely a little on their crowne. They liue on almes, nor receiue they but the surplusage of the daily food of him that giueth them. They are wivelesse. The Orders of their Sect are written in a booke of the Guzarates writing. They drinke their water hot, not for Physike, but deuotion, supposing that the water hath a Soule which they should slay, if they dranke the same vnsodden. For the same cause they beare in their hands certaine little brushes, with which they sweepe the floore, before they sit downe, or walk, lest they should kill the soule of some Worme, or other small creature. I saw their Prior thus doing.

The Generall of this Order is said to have an hundred thousand men vnder his canonicall obedience, and is newly chosen euery yeere. I saw amongst them little boyes, of eight or nine yeare old, resembling the countenances of Europe, rather than of India, by their parents consecrated to this Order. They had all in their mouth a cloth foure fingers broad, let thorow both their eares in a hole, and brought backe againe thorow their eares. They would not shew me the cause; but I perceiued it was, lest some Gnat or Flie should enter thither, and so bee slaine. They teach that the world was made many hundred thousand yeeres agoe: and that God did then send three and twentie Apostles, and now hath sent the foure and twentieth in this third age, two thousand yeeres since, from which time they haue had writing, which before they had not.(*a*)

The same Author in another Epistle saith, That the most of the Inhabitants of Cambaia are Banians. They eat no flesh nor kill anything, yea they redeem the beast and birds maymed or sicke, and carry them to their Hospitals to be cured. In Guzarat he had seene many *Gioghi*, a religious Order of Monks, which yeeld to none in Penance and Pouertie. They go naked in cold weather: they sleep on the dung-hils vpon an heape of ashes, with which they couer their head and face. I saw the place where one of these Gioghi kept in the middest of the Citie Amadeba, to whom, in conceit of holinesse, resorted more numbers of people then to the shoares of Lisbon at the returne of the Indian Fleet. This Gioghi was sent for by the Prince *Sultan Morad*, sonne of the *Mogor*, and refused to come, bidding that the Prince should come to him: *It is enough that I am holy*, or a Saint *to this end*. Whereupon, the Prince caused him to be apprehended, and (being soundly whipped) to bee banished.

This people killeth not their Kine, but nourisheth them as their mothers. I saw at Amadeba, when a Cow was ready to die, they offered her fresh grasse, and droue the Flies from her: and some of them gaue this attendance two or three dayes after till she was dead. A league and a halfe from this Citie, I saw a certaine *Cæmiterium* or burying-place, then which I had neuer seene a fairer sight, wherein had beene buried one *Cazis* the Master of a King of Guzarat, who had erected this fabrike, and three other were buried in another Chappell. The whole work and pauement was of Marble, contayning three Iles: in one whereof I told foure hundred and fortie pillars with their chapiters and bases of Corinthian worke, very royall and

(*a*) Our author is here referring to the Budhists, who were established in Central India, in opposition to the Brahmins, from about the fifth century, B. C., to the tenth century, A. D.

admirable. On one side was a Lake, greater then the *Rozzio* at Lisbon; and that building was curiously framed with faire windowes, to looke into the Lake.

Balbi telleth of a certaine Temple at Cape Bombain, not farre from Chaul, which is cut out of a Rocke: ouer the said Temple growe many Tamrinds, and vnder it is a Spring of running water, whereof they can finde no bottome. It is called *Alefante*, is adorned with many Images, a receptacle of Bats, and supposed the worke of *Alexander* the Great, at the period of his Peregrination. And hereto agreeth the report of *Arrianus* in his *Periplus* of many memorials and monuments of *Alexanders* Expedition to these Parts, as old Chappels, Altars, Camping-places, and great Pits. These hee mentioneth about Minnagara, which *Ortelius* in his Map placeth here-away.

Linschoten affirmeth the same things of their Pythagorean errour, and addeth that they sometimes buy Fowles or other beasts of the Portugals, which meant to haue dressed them and let them flie or runne away. In the High-wayes also and Woods they set pots with water, and cast Corne or other graine vpon the ground, to feed the Birds and Beasts, and (to omit their charitable Hospitals before mentioned) if they take a Flea or a Louse, they will not kill it, but put it in some hole or corner in the wall, and so let it goe: and you can doe them no greater iniurie, then to kill it in their presence, which with all intreatie they will resist, as being a hainous sin, to take away the life of that, to which God hath imparted both soule and body: and where words will not preuaile, they will offer money. They eate no Radishes, Onyous, Garlike, or any kind of Herbe, that hath red colour in it, not Egges, for they thinke there is bloud in them. They drink not Wine, nor use Vinegar, but only Water. They would rather starue, then eat, with any, but their countrey-men; as it happened when I sailed from Goa to Cochin with them in a Portugall Ship, when they had spent all their store, the time falling out longer then they made account of; they would not once touch our meat. They wash themselves euery time they eate or ease themselues, or make water. Vnder their haire they haue a star vpon their foreheads, which they rub euery morning with a little white Sanders tempered with water, and three or foure graines of Rice among it, which the *Bramenes* also do at a superstitious ceremony of their law. They sit on the ground in their houses, vpon Mats or Carpets, and so they eate, leauing their shooes (which are piked and hooked) at the doore: for the which cause the heeles of their shooes are seldome pulled vp, to saue labour of vndoing them.

The Moores amongst them will sometimes abuse the superstition of these Cambayans to their owne couetousnesse, bringing some Worme, Rat or Sparrow, and threatening to kill the same so to prouoke them to redeeme the life thereof at some high price. And likewise if a malefactor be condemned to death, they will purchase his life of the Magistrate, and sell him for a slaue. The Moores will sometimes make semblance, as if they would kill themselues, that these foolish *Guzzarates* may see them in like sort. They will go out of the path, if they light on an Ant-hill, lest they might happily treade on some of them: they sup by day light, lest their candle-light should occasion the death of some Gnat or Fly. And when they must vse a Candle they keepe it in a Lanthorne for that cause. If Lice doe much annoy them, they call to them certaine Religious and holy men, after their account: and these Obseruance will take vpon them all those Lice which the other can find, and put them on their head, there to nourish them. But yet for all this lousie scruple, they sticke not at coozenage by false weights, measures and coyne, nor at usury and lies.

Some are said to be so zealous in their idol-service, as to sacrifice their liues in their honour; whereunto they are perswaded by the preachings of their Priests, as the most acceptable deuotion. Many offer themselues, which being brought vpon a scaffold, after certaine ceremonies, put about his neck an Iron coller, round without, but within very sharpe: from which hangeth a chaine downe his brest, into which, sitting downe he putteth his feet, and whiles the Priest muttereth certaine words, the party before the people with all his force stretcheth out his feet, and cuts off his head: their reward is, that they are accounted Saints.

CHAPTER XII.

OF THE INDIAN NATIONS BETWIXT CAMBAIA AND MALABAR; AND THEIR RELIGIONS.

The mightie Riuers of *Indus* and *Ganges*, paying their fine to the *Lord of waters*, the Ocean, almost vnder the very Tropick of *Cancer*, do (as it were) betwixt their watery armes, present into that their *Mothers* bosome, this large *Chersonesus*; A Countrey, full of Kingdomes, riches, people, and (our dewest taske) *superstitious costomes*. As Italy is diuided by the *Appennine*, and bounded by the Alpes, so is this by the Hills which they call *Gate*(a) which goe from East to West (but not directly) and quite thorow to the *Cape Comori*, which not only haue entred league with many In-lets of the Sea, to diuide the soyle into many Signiories and Kingdomes, but with the Ayre and Natures higher officers, to dispence with the ordinary orders, and established Statutes of Nature, at the same time, vnder the same eleuation of the Sun, diuiding to Summer and Winter, their seasons and possessions. For where as cold is banished out of these Countries (except on the tops of some Hills) and altogether prohibited to approach so neere the Court and presence of the Sun; and therefore their Winter and Summer is not reckoned by heate and cold, but by the fairnesse and foulenesse of weather, which in those parts diuided the yeere by equall proportions; at

---

(a) Our author is here alluding to the Western Ghauts, which run in one continuous line from the South bank of the Taptee to Cape Comorin, forming a knot at the Nilgheries.

the same time, when on the West-part of this *Peninsula*, betweene that ridge of Mountaines and the Sea, it is after their appellation Summer, which is from September till April, in which time it is alwayes cleere skie, without once or very little raining ; on the other side the hills, which they call the coast of Choromandell, it is their Winter ; euery day and night yeelding abundance of raines, besides those terrible thunders which both begin and end their Winter. And from April till September in a contrary vicissitude; on the Westerne part, is Winter, and on the Easterne, Summer; insomuch that in little more then twentie leagues iourney in some place, as where they crosse the Hills to Saint *Thomas*, on the one side of the Hill you ascend with a faire Summer, on the other you descend attendant with a stormy Winter.(*a*) The like, saith *Linschoten*, hapneth at the *Cape Rosalgate*, in Arabia, and in many other places of the East.

Their Winter also is more fierce then ours,(*b*) every man prouiding against the same, as if he had a voyage of so

---

(*a*) Our author's description of the physical geography of the Dekhan, though somewhat obscure from the quaintness of the language, indicates the correctness of the observations made by the early travellers. The Dekhan may be described as a great tableland supported on the Malabar side by a great mountain chain known as the Western Ghauts, and on the Coromandel side by a low range of hills or mounds known as the Eastern Ghauts. Outside the mountain chains on either side, or rather between the mountain chains and the sea, is a plain country. The plain on the west is a narrow fertile strip known as Malabar and Canara ; that on the east is a much broader plain of sand, anciently known as Choromandel, but in the present day known as the Carnatic. The relative influence of the two monsoons upon the Western and Eastern Ghauts, may be thus described :—One sets in from the North-east about October, and blows more or less steadily for six months ; the other sets in from the South-west about April, and blows until the North-east begins. Thus the broad plain of the Carnatic enjoys the influence of the North-east monsoon ; whilst the narrow strip of Malabar and Canara is favoured by the South-west monsoon. Each of these monsoons bring a supply of rain. The North-east monsoon brings less water than the other, but then its influence is more generally felt, as the Eastern Ghauts are not sufficiently elevated to shut it out from Central table-land. Not so, however, with the South-west monsoon. That comes laden with a mass of waters from the Southern ocean, and pours a heavy torrent on the Western Ghauts ; but its influence is more or less shut out from the Central table-land by the abrupt and elevated wall of mountains.

(*b*) By Winter our author alludes to the rainy season, just as he alludes to the hot weather by the English term Summer.

many moneths to passe by Sea, their ships are brought into harbour, their houses can scarce harbour the Inhabitants against the violent stormes, which choake the Riuers with Sand, and make the Seas vnnauigable. I leaue the causes of these things to the further scanning of Philosophers; the effects and affects thereof are strange. The Sea roareth with a dreadfull noyse: the Windes blow with a certaine course from thence: the people haue a Melancholike season, which they passe away with play. In the Summer the Wind bloweth from the Land, beginning at Midnight, and continuing till Noone, neuer blowing aboue ten leagues into the Sea, and presently after one of the clock vntill midnight, the contrary winde bloweth, keeping their set-times, whereby they make the Land temperate, the heat otherwise would bee vnmeasurable.(a) But this change commonly causeth diseases, Fluxes, Feuers, Vomitings, in dangerous (and to very many, in deadly) manner, as appeareth at Goa, where, in the Kings Hospitall (which is onely for white men) there die fiue hundred in a yeere. Here you may see both the North and South Starres; and little difference or none is found in the length of day and night throughout the yeere.

Dely, is the next Kingdome to Cambaia, now not the next, but the same; the Mountaines which before diuided it, not prohibiting the Mogors Forces to annexe it to his Crowne. Of it is spoken before in the Chapter of Cambaya, as also of Decan, which lyeth along the Coast, betwixt the Riuers Bate and Aliga two hundred and fiftie miles. Here was, as is said, sometimes a Moore King; who leading a voluptuous and idle life, by his Captaines was dispossessed of his State: the one of these was called *Idalcan*: whose Seat Royall is Visapore, who in the yeare 1572, incamped before Goa, which the Portugals had taken from him, with an Army of seuenty thousand Foot, and

(a) The distinction between the land and sea breezes is here indicated.

fiue and thirty thousand Horse, two thousand Elephants, and two hundred and fiftie peeces of Artilerie. The other was *Nissamalucco*, which resideth in Danager, & besieged Chaul (now belonging to the Portugals) with not much lesse forces, against a Captaine of the Venazarie, which are a people that liue on spoyle, as the Resbuti in Cambaia, the Belemi in Delly. Canara or Concan, seemeth to haue beene a part of Decan, but is possessed by the King of Narsinga, whose state is on the East side of the Mountaines. It hath in it the Coast-townes of Onor, Batticalla, Mayander and Mangalor, famous for trafficke, but eclipsed by the Portugals neighbourhood.

The Religion of these parts is partly Mahumetan, partly Heathenish. These haue their proper Iolatries, as wee haue before noted, peculiar Idols and Sects to peculiar Tribes and Trades. They haue also more common Rites, worshipping the Images of diuers Beasts, Elephants, Kine, Apes, and the like, to which they dedicate Pagodes or Temples. They haue other common deuotions, & haue appropriated to War, to Seed, to Fortune, to Life, to Death, seuerall Deites. The Deuill they worship in horrible forme, as we shall after see ; for in this confusion the Reeder must pardon, if we do not keep exact order alway besides that in seuerall places the Rites somewhat differ in these which are accounted of one Sect. They paint him blacke, because to that colour they ascribe beauty : and in more solemne Festiuals with Oile, Suet, and fat Grease, and make them as lothsome to the Sent, as to the Eie. So senselesse is their Religion, and yet addicted the sense, and sensible Images (as they do their Temples, they call these Pagodes) and sacrifice thereto Goates, Sheep, and other Beasts, but not Kine, which they doe account sacred, and worship the same, esteeming that man most happy that dyeth in the presence of that beast or touching the same ; perswading themselues, that the departing soule passeth into one of these creatures. They will performe more pietie (let Piety pardon such abuse of the Name) to a Cow dying, then to their deceasing Parents: And would account it a hainous crime at vnawares to haue killed such a beast, seeking by sacrifices and offerings to turne away Diuine vengeance, after so Humane and accidentall error.

CHAPTER XIII.

OF GOA, THE HEATHENES AND CHRISTIANS LIUING THEREIN, AND THE COUNTRY ABOUT.*

GOA is the Seat of the Vice-Roy, and of the Arch-Bishop, and of the Kings Councell for the Indies, and the Staple of all Indian commodities. It standeth on a little Iland, in nineteene degrees, called *Tizzuarm*, nine miles long, and three broad, in circuit one and twentie. *Bardes* on the North, and *Salzette* are both in like subiection to the Portugalls; the King letting them to Farme, and employing the Rents to the payment of the Arch-bishop, Cloysters, Priests, Vice-Roy, and other his Officers. Salsette is nine miles from Goa, being a Peninsula twentie miles about, containing sixtie-six Villages or Townes, and about fourescore thousand inhabitants. *Antonius Norogna* the Vice-Roy, destroyed therein two hundred Temples, some of them sumptuous, 1567, and many *Pagodes*, which caused them to rebell, and afterwards they slew some of the Iesuites and their company.

Baross relates, that the King of Bisnaga, hauing warres with the Moores of Decan, and being then Lord of the Ports of Batecala and Onor, where he had store of Horses out of Arabia, and Persia, brought thither by Merchants, seruiceable for his Warres: the Moores in those parts forestalled the Market, and sold the Horses to the Decans his Enemies. Whereupon he commanded the King of Onor his Vassall, to kill all the Moores in the Countrey, which was affected to the death of ten thousand Moores.

The rest that escaped gate them to the Iland of Tizuarin, and first peopled this Citie of Goa, translating the Mart from Onor thither: but the King of Onor by a power at Sea forced the trade to be kept still at Onor till the Portugals came into those parts. This murther of the Moores was done, *An.* 1479. The Founders name was *Mellique Hocen.* This is to be vnderstood of this New Towne, for of the Ancient there is no memory. It seems by a Crosse there found, that it had beene inhabited by Christians. It stands in that part which is reckoned to the Kingdome of Canara *Sabaius* (one of those Decanine Captaines, which shared their Masters state, as before is deliuered) when he died, left his sonne *Idalcan* very young; hereupon his Subiects rebelled, and the King of Narsinga warred vpon him, to dispossesse him of his Dominion. *Abulquerke* taking that opportunitie, besieged, and vpon composition, tooke Goa with the Iland. Which was soone after recouered by *Idalcan*, comming with a strong Armie thither, the Portugals flying away by night. But when the King of Narsinga againe inuaded *Idalcan*, hee was forced to resist the more dangerous Enemy, leauing a strong Garrison at Goa, which yet *Albuquerk* ouercame, and sacked the Citie. Euer since, as a standing in the midst of that Tract of land, from Cambaia to Comori, it hath beene though the fittest Staple for Merchandize, and Seat for the Vice-Roy, the Chiefe of the foure chief Cities in the Indies. The three other, Ormus, Diu, and Malaca.

There dwell in Goa of all Nations and Religions. The Gouernment is as in Portugall. Onely publike vse of forraine Religion is forbidden them: but in their houses priuately, or on the maine land, they may practise the same. The Portugals many of them are married with Indian women, and their posteritie are called *Mesticos*, and in the third degree, differ nothing in colour and fashion from naturall Indians. Of the Portugals they reckon two sorts, married Men, and Souldiers, which is a generall name to all Batchellers, although they are at their owne command. Of these are many Knights, and are called *Cavalhiero Fidalgo:* for if a man doe any thing worth reckoning, presently his Captaine imparteth this honor to him; where of they much bost themselues, albeit that this Knight-hood hath descended to Cookes boyes. Many of the Portugals liue oneley by their slaues. They vse great Ceremony or Pride (whether you will call it) in their behauiour: the particulars whereof let *Lintchocen*, that there liued amongst them, teach you.

Besides both Abassine and Armenian Christians, Iewes, and Moores, here are many Heathens. The Moores eate all things but Swines flesh, and dying, are buried like the Iewes. The Heathens, as *Decanyns, Guzarates* and *Canaryns*, are burnt to ashes, and some women aliue are buried with the Gentlemen or Bramens, their husbands. Some will eate nothing that had life; some all but the flesh of Kine, or Buffles. Most of them pray to the Sunne and Moon: yet all acknowledge a God that made all things, ruleth them after this life, rendering to all according to their works. As for the Idols or *Pagodes*, they worship them, saith *Balby*.

But they haue *Pagodes*, which are Images cut and framed most vgly, and like monstrous Deuils, to whom they pray and offer: and to Saints which here haue liued holy, and are now Intercessours for them. The Deuill often answereth them out of those Images, to whom also they offer that he should not hurt them. They present their *Pagode* (when a marriage is to be solemnized) with the Brides mayden-head; but who can honestly name that which they dishonestly doe? They haue for the most part, a custome to pray vnto the first thing they meet withall in the morning, and all that day they pray vnto it; be it Hog, or any other thing. But if they first meet with a Crow (whereof there are great store) they will not for anything stirre out again that day, after so vnlucky a signe. They pray likewise to the New Moone, saluting her first appearance on their knees. They haue *Iogos* or Hermites, reputed very holy. Many juglers also and Witches, which shew deuilish tricks. They neuer goe forth without praying. Euery Hill, Cliffe, Hole, or Den, hath his *Pagodes* in it, with their Furnaces hard by them, and their Cisternes alwayes full of water, with which euery one that passeth by, washeth his feet, and then worshippeth and offereth Rice,*Egges, or what else their deuotion will affoord: which the Bramene eateth. When they are to goe to Sea, they will feast their *Pagode* with Trumpets, Fires, and hangings, fourteene dayes before they set forth, to obtaine a good voyage: and as long after their returne; which they vse to doe in all their Feasts, Marriages, Childbirths, and their Haruest and Seed-seasons.

The Indian women in Goa, when they goe forth, haue but one cloth about their bodies, which couereth their heads, and hangeth downe to the knees, otherwise naked. They haue rings thorow their noses, about their legs, toes, neckes, and armes, and seuen or eight bracelets vpon their hands (according to their abilitie) of glasse or other metall. When the woman is seuen yeeres old, and the man nine, they marry, but come not together till the woman is able to beare children. Mr. *Fitch* mentioneth the solemnitie of these marriages, and the cause to be the burning of the mother when the father is dead, that they might haue a father-in-law to bring them vp.

To leaue Goa with this Iland. The Canaras aud Decanijns weare their beards and haire long, without cutting, as the Bramens. They except from food, Kine, Hogs, and Buffles. They account the Oxe, Cow, or Buffle to be holy, which they haue commonly in the house with them, and they besmeere, stroke, and handle them with all friendship in the world; feed them with the same meat they eate themselues, aud when the beasts ease themselues, they hold vnder their hands, and throw the dung away: they sleepe with them in their houses, hereby thinking to doe God seruice. In other things they are as the Bramenes. For those are the Laitie, these are the Spiritualtie. When they take their oathes, they are set within a circle of ashes, on the pauement, and laying a few ashes on their heads, the other on their breasts, sweare by their *Pagodes* to tell the truth.

The Canarijns and the Corumijns are the rustickes, and Countrey-husbandmen, the most miserable people of all India: their Religion is much as the other. They couer onely their Priuities, and eate all things, except Kine, Oxen, Buffles, Hogs, and Hens flesh. Their women binde a cloth about their Nauell, which reacheth halfe way the thigh: they are deliuered alone by themselues, without other helpe: their children are brought vp naked, till they be seuen or eight yeeres old without any trouble about them, except washing them in a little cold water, and liue to be an hundred yeeres old, without head-ache or losse of teeth. They nourish a tuffe of haire on their crownes, cutting the rest. When the man is dead, the wife breaketh her glasse-jewels, and cutteth off her haire; his bodie is burnt. They eate so little, as if they liued by the ayre and for a penny would endure whipping.

In Salsette are two Temples, or holes rather of *Pagodes*, renowned in all India: one of which is cut from vnder a hill, of hard stone, and is of compasse within, about the bignesse of a Village of foure hundred Houses: with many Galleries or Chambers of these deformed shapes, one higher then another, cut out of the hard Rock. There are in all three hundred of these Galleries. The other is in another place, of like matter and forme. It would make a mans haire stand vpright to enter amongst them. In a little Iland called Pory, there standeth a high Hill, on the top whereof is a hole, that goeth downe on the Hill, digged and carued out of the hard Rocke; within, as large as a great Cloyster, round beset with shapes of Elephants,

Tygres, Amazons and other like worke, workemanly cut, supposed to be the Chinois handy-worke. But the Portugals haue now ouerthrowne these Idol-Temples. Would God they had not set new Idols in the roome: with like practice of offering and Pilgrimages, as did these to their *Pagode*.

I once went into a Temple of stone, in a Village, and found nothing in it, but a great Table that hung in the middle of the Church, with the Image of a *Pagode* thereon painted, hellishly disfigured with many hornes, long teeth out of the mouth downe to the knees, and beneath his nauell with such another tusked and horned face. Vpon the head stood a triple crowne, not much vnlike the Popes. It hung before a wall, which made a partition from another Chamber, like a Quire, close without any light: in the middle whereof was a little doore, and on each side of it a furnace within the wall, with certaine holes, thereby to let the smoake or sauour of the fire to enter into that place, when any offering should bee made. Whereof wee found there some Rice, Corne, Fruits, Hens, and such like. There issued thence such a filthy smoake and stinke, that it made the place black, and almost choaked such as entered. We desired the Bramenee to open the doore, which with much entreatie he did, offering first to throw ashes on our fore-heads, which wee refused, so that before hee would open vs the doore, we were forced to promise him not to enter beyond the doore. It shewed within like a lime-kill, being close vaulted, without hole or window: neither had the Church it selfe any light but the doore. Within the said Cell hung an hundred burning Lampes, and in the middle stood a little Altar couered with Cotton Cloth, and ouer that with Gold; vnder which, as the Bramene told vs, sate the *Pagode* all of Gold, of the bignesse of a Puppet.

Hard by the Church without the great doore, stood within the earth a great foure square Cistern, hewed out of freestone, with staires on each side to goe downe into it, full of greene, filthy, and stinking water, wherein they wash themselues, when they meane to enter into the Church to pray. In the euening they carried their *Pagode* on Procession, first Ringing a Bell, wherewith the people assembled, and tooke the ' *Pagode* out of his Cell with great reuerence and set it in a *Palamkin*, which was borne by the chiefe men of the Towne; the rest following with great deuotion, with their vsuall noise and sound of Trumpets, and other Instruments; and hauing carried him a prettie circuit, brought him to the stone Cisterne, washed him and placed him againe in his Cell, making a foule smoake and stinke, and euery man leauing his offering behind him, intended to the *Pagode*, but consumed by the Bramene and his family. As we went along by the wayes, we found many such shapes vnder certaine couertures, with a small Cisterne of water hard by, and halfe an Indian Nut hanging thereby, to take vp water withall, for the Trauellers to wash and pray. By the said *Pagodes* doe stand commonly a Calfe of stone, and two little Furnaces; before which they present their offerings. My fellow leaping on one of those Calues in the Church, the Bramane called out, and the people came running, but we stayed their fury, by gentle perswasion of the Bramene before. And thus much of these deformed formes, and misshapen shapes, with their worshippings and worshippers suitable. Like lips, like lettice. Vaine Rites, stinking sinks and smoakes, vgly Idols, conspiring with Internall *Darkenesse* of the Mindes, and External *Darkenesse* of their Temples, to bring an Eternall *Darknesse* to the Followers, that all may shut vp (as they are begun) in an hellish period.

I haue seene in Mr. *Hakluites* hands a large Treatise, written by *Don Duart de Menezes* of the Customes, Courts, Officers, Expences, and other remarkable obseruations, for knowledge of the Portugall State and affaires, in the East Indies. He saith, that the Iland Tisoare (so he writeth it) in which Goa standeth, hath thirtie two Townes and Villages therein. The Iesuits Colledge in Salsete enioyeth the Rents before belonging to the *Pagodes*, being two hundred and fiftie pound yeerely, besides their Gleb-lands of Rice grounds, and other commodities: also the Parishes subiect to them are worth two hundred ninetie eight pounds, and sixteen shillings. In Goa they receiue seuen hundred and fifteene pounds, twelue shillings and sixe pence *per Annum*, and their yeerely Presents amount to three hundred seuentie fiue pound. In Cochin also they haue three hundred thirtie seuen pound. The Monastery of Saint *Francis* in Goa hath Rents sixe hundred and thirteene pound and ten shillings, and one hundred fortie three pound twelue shillings and sixe pence in other duties. The Dominicans reçeiue fiue hundred pound, and fourescore and ten pound in other rights. The Friars of Saint *Augustine* foure score pound twelue shillings and sixe pence. The Inquisition one hundred three pound and ten shillings (besides the Rents of the Hospitall, one thousand eight hundred seuenty five pound, and an Almeshouse for Widowes and Orphans two hundred and fiftie pound.) These things I thought worthy relation, not so much to satisfie the curious, as to answere the ordinary brags of that *World-wandring Generation*, pretending Mortification to the World, strictnesse of their Vow, loue to Religion, and compassion to the poore Pagans, when as they haue such *Golden chaines* to draw them thither. Whereunto if wee add the bountie of Christians in those parts vnto these pretended holy Fathers, their gaines from the pearle-fishings, the vowes of such as become of their Societie, and many other wayes accruing to their Coffers, together with those nouelties and rarities, wherewith euery sense in varietie is here presented; wee may see the *World* a sufficient argument to lead them about the world, whatsoeuer other pretences notwithstanding. But this hath beene learnedly handled against them by others already:

amongst others and before others, Our most Reuerend and Learned Metropolitan, in *vnmasking the reasons* of *Hill* for Popery, hath shewed both this our *Hill* to be an ignorant Mountebanke, and our Iesuites in India rather enrichers of their owne Societie in Europe with Gold, Pearle, Spice, and other Indian wares, then of those Asian Proselites with sound Europæan Christianitie; besides that, they seeme necessary to their Nation for the establishing of their Trading and ciuill affaires, vnder colour of Religion, winning estimation with the Pagans, and remaining there as well for Intelligencers, and as it were Leeger Embassadours with their Kings, as for Conuersion of the Heathens. For me, what I can shew against this their allegation, belongeth to another taske.

CHAPTER XIV.

OF THE INDIAN BRAMENES, BOTH SECULAR AND RELIGIOUS.

THE Indian Wise men may be diuided into two Sects, the Banianes, of whom is already spoken ; and the Bramenes. These obserue the Indian Heathen custome, that no man may change his fathers trade, but must succeed in the same, and marry a wife also of the same Tribe. The Brachmanni, or, as they are at this day called, the Bramenes (who haue their shops, as well as other Merchants, throughout the Cities) are the chiefe Tribe, and of best reputation, and weare in signe of their profession (from the shoulder, crosse vnder the arme, vpon their naked body, downe to the girdle) three strings like sealing threds : which for their liues they will not, nor may by their vow put off. They are naked, sauing that about their middles they haue a cloth bound to hide their priuities. And sometime when they goe abroad, they cast a thin Gowne ouer them.. Vpon their heads they ware a white cloth, wound twice or thrice about therewith, to hide their haire, which they neuer cut off, but weare it long, and turned vp as the women doe. They haue commonly hanging at their eares, Gold-rings. They are very subtill in writing and accounts, making other simple Indians beleeue what they will. Whatsoeuer they meet first with in the streets, they pray to all day after.

When the Bramenes die, all their friends assemble together, and make a hole in the ground, in which they throw much sweet Wood, Spices, Rice, Corne, and Oyle. Then lay therein the dead body ; his wife followeth with

Musicke, and many of her neerest friends, singing praises in commendation of her husbands life, encouraging her to follow him, which accordingly she doth. For parting her jewels among her friends, with a cheerefull countenance she leapes into the fire, and is presently couered with Wood, and Oyle, whereby shee is quickly dead, and with her husbands body burned to ashes. And if it chanceth (which is seldome) that any woman refuseth this *Fiery Coniunction*, they cut the haire cleane off from her head; neither may shee after that weare a Iewell, but is accounted a dishonest woman. This custome is (as may appeare) very ancient, and supposed to haue beene ordained because of the libidinous disposition of the Indian women, which for their lusts would poyson their husbands.

The Bramenes obserue Fasting-dayes with so great abstinence, that they eat nothing that day, and sometime not in three or foure dayes together. They tell many miracles of their *Pagodes*. They hold the immortalitie of the Soule, both of Beasts and Men, and that so often mentioned Pythagorean succession, and reuuing of mens soules in beasts; and contrariwise. They by the direction of the Deuill (the author of their miracles) frame such deformed Statues to their Idols.

Botero saith, the Bramenes also worship one *Parabramma*, and his three sonnes, and in honour of them weare those three threeds aforesaid. He affirmeth that the *Iogki* wander vp and downe through India, abstaining from all carnall pleasure, but a certaine time; which being expired, they are past possibilitie of further sinning, and are then called *Abduti*, as the *Illuminate Elders of the Familists*, polluting themselues in all filthinesse. The Bramenes haue Images of the *Trinitie*, and haue in religious estimation the number of *Three*. They acknowledge and pray to the *Trinite Vnitie*, but affirme many Demigods, which are his Deputies in gouerning the World. They honour the Portugals Images also, as approaching to their owne superstition. They marry but one wife, and admit no second succeeding marriage. The Bramenes must descend of the Bramene Tribe, and others cannot aspire to that Priesthood: but some are of higher account than other. For some serve for messengers, which in time of warre, and among theeues may passe safely, and are called *Fathers.* They will not put a Bramene to death for any crime. *Heurnius* reporteth that they haue bookes and Prophets, which they alledge for confirmation of their opinions; that they thinke God to be of blacke colour: that they worship the herbe *Amaracus* or *Marioram* with many supertitious Ceremonies: that they haue in their writings the Decalogue, with the explanation thereof: that they adjure all of their Society vnto silence touching their mysteries: that they haue a peculiar language(*a*) (as Latine in these parts) wherein they teach the same in their Schools: that their Doctors hallow the Sundayes in diuine worship, adoring the God which created heauen and earth, often repeating the sentence, *I adore thee O God, with thy grace and aide for euer*: to take food from the hands of a Christian, they account as sacrilege.

When they are seuen yeeres old, they put about their necke a string two fingers broad, made of the skinne of a beast called *Cressuamengan*, like a wilde Asse, together with the haire: which he weareth till he is fourteen yeeres old, all which time he may not eate *Betelle.* The time expired, the said string is taken away, and another of three threeds put on, in signe that hee is become a Bramene which hee weartho all his life. They haue a Principall amongst them, which is their Bishop, which correcteth them if they doo amisse. They marrie but once, as is said, and that not all, but onely the eldest of the brethen, to continue the Succession, who is also heir of the fathers substance, and keepeth his wife straitly, killing her, if he finde her adulterous, with poison. The yonger

(*a*) Sanscrit.

breathren lie with other mens wiues, which account the same as a singular honour done vnto them; hauing liberite, as *Balby* affirmeth, to enter into any mans house, yes of the Kings no lesse then of the Subjects, of that Religion: the husbands leauing the wiues, and the brethren their sisters vnto their pleasures, and therefore departing out of the house when they come in. And hence it is that no mans sonne inheriteth his fathers goods, and I knowe not whether they may inherite that name of father or sonne) but the sisters sonne succeedeth, as being most certaine of the blood. They eate but once a day, and wash before and after meate, as also when they make water and go to stoole.(*a*)

They haue great reuenues belonging to their Churches, besides offerings, and at set houres of the day resort thither to sing, and doe other their holy Rites. Twice in the day, and as often in the night, their *Payode* is taken out of the Altar, and set on the Bramenes head, looking backward, and is carried in Procession three times about the Church; the Bramenes wiues carrying lights burning euery time they come to the principall doore of the Church, which is on the West side thereof (some Churches haue two doores on a side) they set it downe on their offering-stone, and worship it. Twice a day they bring it to eate of their sod Rice, as often (it seemeth) as the Bramene is hungry. When they wash them (which is often) they lay a little ashes on their heads, foreheads, and breasts, saying that they shall returne into ashes. When the Bramenes wife is with childe, as soone as he knoweth it, he cleanseth his teeth, and abstaineth from *Betele*, and obserueth fasting till shee bee deliuered. The Kings of Malabar will scarce eate meate but of their dressing. They are of such estimation, that if Merchants trauell among theeues and robbers, one Bramene in the companie

(*a*) Our author is here referring to the peculiar customs of Malabar.

secureth them all: which Bramene will eate nothing of another mans dressing; and would not become a Moore for a Kingdome. *Nic. di Conti* saith, he saw a Bramene three hundred yeeres old; hee addeth that they are studious in Astrologie, Geomancie, and Philosophie. To be short, they are the Masters of Ceremonies and the Indian Religion, in whose precepts the Kings are trained up.

The Bramenes haue (it seemeth) much familiaritie with the Deuill, so strangely doe they foretell things to come, though they bee contingent. They also interpret Prodigies, Lots, Auguries, and thereby growe into great credit, the people depending on them, and the Kings becomming of their Order. They perswade the people that their *Pagodes* doe often feast together, and therefore would haue such dainties offered, which they and theirs deuoure: threatning if they be sparing and niggardly, plenty of Plagues and diuine wrath.

Besides these, Secular, There are other Religious or Monastical Bramenes, which are called *Iogues*; anciently called by the Greekes, Gymnosophists, because they went naked; and so they still doe, professing much austeritie of life, at least for a time, with long Pilgrimages, and much *bodily exercise little profitting* the soule, possessing nothing but want and beggarie, seeking thereby to winne credite to themselues and their Sect. The Verteas I take to bee another Sect, the religious Votaries of the Banians or Pythagoreans. Both those and these are kindes of Ethnike Monkes, which professe by strict penance and regular obseruations, to expiate their sinnes, and procure saluation to their soules. There are also some that liue as Heremites in Desarts, some in Colledges, some wander from place to place begging: some (an vnlearned kind) are called *Sanasses*: some contrary to the rest, nothing esteeme Idols, obserue chastitie twenty or fiue and twenty yeeres, and feed daily on the pith of a fruit called *Caruza*, to preserue in them that cold humour, neither doe they abstaine from flesh, fish, or wine, and when they passe along the way, one goeth before them crying *Poo, Poo,* that is, way way, that women especially may auoid: for their vow will not permit the sight of a woman. These weare not three threads which the other Bramenese weare, neither are their bodies burned after death, as of the rest, yea, the King himself honoreth them, and not they the King: some liue enclosed in iron Cages all filthie with ashes, which they strew on their heads and garments: some burne some part of their body voluntarily. All are vain-glorious, and seeke rather the shell, then the kernell, the shew, then the substance of holinesse.

Xauerius once in conference with the Bramenes, demanding of them what their God commanded to those that would come to Heauen, was answered; Two precepts, one to abstaine from killing of Kine in whose shape the Gods were worshipped: and the other to obserue the Bramenes, the Ministers of their Gods. But they haue more mysticall learning, which one of them secretly disclosed to the Iesuite. This was of a famous Schoole, College or Vniuersity of those Bramenes, all the Students whereof at their first Admission, he said were sworne by solemn Oath vnto their Doctors, neuer to reueale any of their secrets: First, that there was one God, maker of Heauen & Earth, who alone, & not the *Pagodes,* ought to be worshipped: after that, they were instructed in precepts necessary to saluation. *Xauerius* asking what? he repeated the Ten Comandements in order as we do, and that in a mystical language known to few, which their Doctors obserue in their holy things. But the Bramene pronounced and explained them in the vulgar. Further, that the eight day, or Sunday is to be kept holy, & then often to repeat the prayer *Oncery Naraina Noma* (the same which before is related and interpreted out of *Heurnius*) this to be spoken with a lowe voice that they breake not their Oath likewise that their old bookes foretell of a time when all shall be of one Religion.

Fenicim another Iesuite learned of one of their Doctors, other their mysteries contained in their Bookes, that God produced all this world out of an Egge: out of one part thereof the Land, Sea, and inferiour creatures: out of the other, the Heauens for habitation to the Gods; that this World was founded on the end of a Buffels horne, and be cause this beast leaned on one side ready to fall, a huge Rocke was placed vnder him to support him. But as before, so here also followed some notice of better things. For there was a Malabar Poet which writ 900 epigrams against their *Pagodes*, each consisting of eight verses, wherein he speakes many things elegantly of the Diuine Prouidence, of Heauen, and the torments of Hell, and other thing agreeing to the Christian Faith; that God is present euerywhere, and giues to euery one according to his estate, that Celestiall blessednesse consists in the vision of God, that the damned in Hell shall be tormented 400 millions of years in flames and shall neuer die; The Bramenes he calls fooles and blockes. By this booke, and by Mathematicall doctrine of the Sphere, which they had scarcely euer heard of, he made way for conuerting the people.

I haue thought good to say thus much together of them, as in one view representing the Bramenes; a name so ancient, so vniuersally communicated to the Indian Priests, although some particulars before haue beene, or hereafter may be said touching some of them in other places, according to the singularitie of each Nation in this so manifold a profession, which they all demonstrate in their singular Superstitions.

CHAPTER XV.

THE KINGDOME OF CALICUT.

Malabar extendeth it selfe from the Riuer Congeraco to the Cape Comori; which some take to be the Promontory *Cory* in *Ptolomey*. *Maginus* doubteth, whether it be that which he call *Commaria Extrema*. In the length it containeth little lesse then three hundred miles, in bredth from that ridge of *Gate* to the Sea, in some places, fifty. From Cangerecora to Puripatan are 60 miles of Coast; therein Cota, Colan, Nilichilan, Marabia, Bolepatan, Cananor, where the Portugals haue a Fort, in 12 degrees I Tramapatan, Chomba, Main, and Perepatan. From thence; to Chatua is the Kingdome of Calicut fourescore miles in coast: therein Pandarane, Colete, Capocate, Calecut in II. I5. Chale a Portugall Fortresse, Patangale. Tanor at Citie Royall, Panane, Baleaneor and Chatua. Then followes the Kingdome of Cranganor. Next to that the Kingdome of Cochin: then that of Porca without a good Port in her foure and fortie miles coast. Coulan is next, and then that of Trauancor, which the Portugals called the Great King, as being greater in State then the former, subiect to the King of Narsinga. It is full of people, diuided into many States, by variety of Riuers, which cause Horses to be vnseruiceable in their Warres, and nourish many Crocodies, enrich the soyle, and yeeld easie transportation of commodities, which are spices of diuers kinds. They haue Bats, in shape resembling Foxes, in bignesse Kites. The chiefe Kingdomes in this tract are Kanonor, Calicut, Cranganor, Cochin, Carcolam, and Trananor. About seuen hundred yeeres since it was one Kingdome, gouerned by *Soma* or *Sarama Perimal*, who by perswasion of the Arabian Merchants became of their Sect, in which he proued so deuout, that he would end his dayes at Mecca. But before his departure he diuided his estate into these pety Signiories, among his principall Nobles and kindred: leauing vnto *Coulam* the spirituall preeminence, and the Imperiall Title vnto his Nephew of Calicut, who onely enjoyed the title of *Zamori*, or Emperour, and had prerogatiue of stamping coine. Som e exempt from this Zamorin Empire and Allegeance, both Coulam the Papal See of the high Bramene, and Cananor: and some haue since by their owne force exempted themselues. This *Perimal* died in his holy Voyage: and the Indians of Malabar reckon from this diuision, their computation of yeers, as we doe from the blessed *Natiuitie of our Lord*. He left saith (*Castaneda*) to himselfe but twelue leagues of his Countrie, which lay neere to the shoare, where he meant to embarque himselfe, neuer before inhabited: this he gaue to a Cousin of his then his page, commanding that in memorie of his embarquing there it should be inhabited, and the rest to take Him for their Emperour (except the Kings of Coulan and Cananor) whom yet with the rest he commanded not to coine money, but onely the King of Calicut. For Calicut was therefore here built: and the Moores for the embarquing tooke such deuotion to the place, that they would no more frequent the Port of Coulan, as before (which therefore grew to ruine) but made Calicut the Staple of their Merchandise.

Calicut, the first in order with them, shall be so with vs. The Citie is not walled nor faire built, the ground not yeelding firme foundation, by reason of the water which issueth if it be digged. This Kingdome hath not aboue fiue and twenty leagues of Sea-coast, yet rich both by the fertilitie of the soyle, which yeeldeth Corne, Spices, Cocos, Iaceros, and many other fruits: and by the situation; as the Staple especially before the Portugals vnfriendly neighbourhood, of Indian merchandise, and therefore in her uarietie of Merchants, being a Map (as it were) of all that Easterne World. The Egyptians, Persian, Syrians, Arabians, Indians; yea euen from Catay (a) the space of six thousand miles journey, here had their trade and traffique. The Palace also contained foure Halls of Audience, according to their Religions, for the Indians, Moores, Iewes, Christains. Of their Bramenes or Priests we haue already said. They yeeld diuine honours to diuers of their deceased Saints, and build Temples vnto beasts. One of which (dedicated to an Ape) hath a large Porch for cattell, to the vse of Sacrifice, in which are (saith *Massæus*) seuen hundred marble Pillars, not inferiour to those of *Agrippa* in the Roman *Pantheon*. It seemeth that the ground in that place is not of so greasy and watery a stomacke, but that it can digest deepe foundations. To Elephants they attribute like Diuinitie: but most of all to Kine, supposing that the soules of Men departed doe most of all enter into these beasts. They haue many bookes of their superstition, neere the *Augurall* discipline of the Hetrurians, and fond fables of the Græcians: and diligently conceale the same from vulgar knowledge, except some Bramene Proselyte doe detect those mysteries. They beleeue *one God, maker of Heauen and Earth,* but adde that he could haue no pleasure in so weighty a charge of gouerning the world, and therefore hath delegated the same to the Deuill, to reward euery man according to his workes; Him they call *Deumo*: they name GOD *Tamerani*. The King hath in his Palace the Chappell of *Deumo*, carued full of Deuils, and in the middest sitteth this Image of metall in a Throne of the same matter, with a triple Crowne, like the Pope's, and foure hornes, with teeth, eyes, and mouth wide and terrible, hooked hands, and feet like a Cocke. In each

(a) China

corner of this square Chappell is a Deuill set in a fiery Throne, wherein are many Soules, the Deuill putting one with his right hand into his mouth, and taking another from vnder him with his left hand. This Idoll is washed by the Bramenes with sweet water, incensed, and worshipped euery morning. Sometime in the weeke they sacrifice on this manner: They haue an Altar strewed with flowers, on which they put the bloud of a Cocke, and coales of fire in a siluer Chafing-dish, with much perfumes incensing about the Altar, and often ringing with a little Bell of siluer. They hold in their hands a siluer Knife with which the Cocke was killed, which they dip in the bloud, and put into the fire with many Apish gesture. All the bloud is thus burned, many Waxe-candles burning meane-while. The Priest hath on his wrists and legs as it were Morrice-bells, which make a great noise, a certaine Table hanging at his necke: and when he hath ended his Sacrifice, he taketh his hands full of Wheat, goeth backward from the Altar (on which hee alwaies fixeth his eies) to a certaine Tree, and then hurleth the Corne vp ouer his head as high as he can: after which he returneth and vnfurnished the Altar. The King of Calicut eateth no meate, before foure principall Bramens haue first offered thereof to the Deuill, which they do lifting both their hands ouer their heads, and shutting their fists draw back the same with their thumbe, presenting of that meate to the Idoll, and then carrie it to the King on a great Leafe, in a Treene Platter. The King sitteeth on the ground at his meate, without any thing vnder him, attended with Bramenes, standing four paces off, with their hands before their mouthes in great reuerence. And after the King hath eaten, those Priests carry the Relikes into the Court, where they clap thrice with their hands, whereat presently certaine Crowes resort thither to eate the Kings leauings, which crowes are hereunto accustomed, and may not bee hurt of any.

When the King marrieth a wife, one of the principall Bramenes hath the first nights lodging with her, for which he hath assigned him by the King foure hundred or fiue hundred Ducats. The King and his Gentlemen, or Nayros, eate not flesh without license of the Bramenes. The King committeth the custodie of his Wife to the Bramenes when he trauelleth any whither, and taketh in too honest part their dishonest familaritie. But for this cause, the Kings Sonne succeedeth not in the Crowne, but his sisters Sonne, as being certainly of his blood. These sisters of the King choose what Gentleman they please, on whom to bestow their Virginitie, and if they proue not in a certaine time to be with child, they betake them to these Bramenes.

The Gentlemen and Merchants haue a custome to exchange Wiues, in token of great friendship. Some women amongst them haue sixe or seuen Husbands, fathering her children on which of them shee best pleaseth. The Men when they marry, get others to vse them (if they be Virgins) fifteene or twentie days before they themselues will bed them. This Author affirmeth, that there were a thousand Families of Christians in Calicut, at the time of his being there, a hundred and twentie yeeres since.

If a Debtor breake day without his Creditor, and often disappoint him, hee goeth to the principall of the Bramenes, and receiueth of him a Rod, with which he approcheth to the Debtor, and making a Circle about him chargeth him in the name of the King, and the said Bramene, not to depart thence till he hath satisfied the Debt, which if he do not, he must starue in the place, for if he depart, the King will cause him to be executed. The new King for one yeeres space eateth neither Fish nor Flesh, nor cutteth his Haire or Nailes, vseth certaine Prayers daily, eateth but one meale, and that after he hath washed, neither may hee looke on any man till he hath ended his repast. At the yeeres end hee maketh a great Feast, to which resort aboue tenn thousand persons to confirme the Prince and his Officers: and then much Almes is giuen. Hee entertaineth twelue thousand Women in diuers Offices in his Palace. These make to the King (after his fasting yeere is out) a Candlemasse Feast, each of them carrying diuers lights from the Temple (where they first obserue many Idoll Ceremonies) vnto the Palace with great Musicke and other iollitie.

CHAPTER XVI.

THE KING OF CALICUT.

Of the election and erection of the Zamoryn, we haue spoken in the beginning of the Chapter; let vs here add out of *Castaneda* concerning his deuotion. Hee saith, that this King of Calicut is a Bramene, as his Predecessors also. And for that it is a custome that all the Kings die in one *Pagode*, or Idoll Temple, hee is elected for that cause. For alwaies there is and must be in that House a King to serue those Idols; and when hee that serueth there dieth, then must the King that then raigneth leaue his Empire, and goe serue in that place as the other did; another being elected to succeed him in the Kingdome. And if any refuseth to forsake his Court for the *Pagode*, they enforce him thereunto.

The Kings of Malabar be browne men, and goe naked from the girdle vpward, and from thence downward they are couered with cloth of Silke and of Cotton adorned with Iewels. For their Children; the Sonnes inherit not, but the Brother, or if there bee none the Sisters Sonne. When their Daughters are ten yeeres old, they send out of the Kingdome for a Nayro, and presenting him with gifts, request him to take her Virginitie: which hauing done, hee tieth a Iewell about her necke, which she weareth during her life, as a token that from thenceforth she hath free power of her bodie to doe what she will, which before she might not. After their death these Kings are carried forth into a plaine Field, and their burned with sweet wood very costly, their kindred and all the Nobilitie of the Country being present: which done, and the ashes buried, they shaue themselues, without leauing any haire except on the browes and eye-lids, euen on the least child; and for the space of thirteene dayes cease to eate *Betele* (his lips are cut that doth it) and all that time is an *Inter-regnum*, wherein they obserue if any will come in to obiect any thing against the new future King. After this hee is sworne to the Lawes of his Predecessor, to pay his debts, to recover whatsoeuer belonged to his Kingdome being lost; which Oath he taketh, hauing his Sword in his left hand, and in the right a Candle burning, which hath a Ring of Gold vpon it, which he toucheth with two of his fingers, and taketh his Oath. This being done, they throw or powre vpon him a few graines of Rice, with many other Ceremonies and Prayers, and he worshippeth the Sune three times; after which, all the *Caymailes* or principall Nobles sweare their fealtie to him handling also the same Candle. The thirteene dayes ended, they eate their *Betele* againe and Flesh as before; the King except, who then taketh thought for his Predecessor, and for the space of one whole yeere (as is before obserued in part out of *Carbasa* eates no *Betele*, or shaueth his beard, nor cutteth his nailes: eateth but once a day, and before hee doth it, washeth all his bodie, and obserueth certaine houres of Prayer daily. These yeere being ended, he obserueth a kind of *Dirige* for his Predecessor's soule, whereat are assembled 100,000 persons, at which time hee giueth great Almes, and then is confirmed. All these Malabar Kings haue one speciall Man, which is the chiefe Administrator of Iustice, who in matters of gouernment is obeyed no lesse then the King himselfe. The Souldiers are *Nayros*, none of which can be imprisoned or put to death by ordinarie Iustice: but if one of them kill a Cow, or sleepe with a Countrie-woman, or speake euill of the King, the King after information giues his Warrant to another *Nayro*, who with his Associaters kill him wheresoeuer they find him, hewing him with their

Swords, and then hang on him his Warrant, to testifie the cause of his death. These *Nayros* may not weare their Weapons, nor enter into combate, till they be armed Knights, although that from the Age of seuen yeeres they are trayned vp in Feates and practice of Armes. He is dubbed or created by the King, who commandeth to gird him with a Sword, and laying his right hand vpon his head, muttereth certaine words softly, and afterward dubbeth him, saying, *Haue a regard to keep these Bramenes, and their Kine.* These are the two Great Commandements, of the Bramene Law. The King sometimes commits this Ceremonie to their Panicall or Master in the Feats of Armes whom they euer honour as their Father, and next to the King most reuerence. They teach them to Run, Leape, Fencing, and managing of Weapons, and anoint them with Oyle of *Gergelin*, to make their sinewes pliant for all winding and tumbling gestures. They begin to go Schoole at seuen yeeres olde. In fight they are valorous, and account it no shame to flee, but will doe it in policie, and yet when they yeeld themselues to any, bind themselues to die with him, and for him, which they faithfully performe, fighting till they bee killed. They are great Southsayers, haue their good and bad Dayes, worship the Sun, the Moone, the Fire, and the Kine, and the first they meet in the morning. The Deuill is often in them (they say it is one of their *Pagodes*) which causeth them to vtter terrible wordes; and then hee goeth before the King with a naked Sword, quaking and cutting his flesh, saying with great cries, I am such a god, and I am come to tell thee such a thing; and if the King doubteth, he roreth lowder, and cutteth himselfe deeper till he be credited. The Portugals haue much eclipsed the greatnesse of the King of Calicut, and caused many other alterations in all the East in this last Age of the World. Of whose exploits, *Castaneda*, *Barrius*, *Massæus*, *Osorius*, and others haue written at large. Our *English-Indian* Societie haue setled a Factory at Calicut, touching the conditions and condition whereof you may reade at large in *Roger Hawes* his Iournall. He telleth of the perfidiousnesse of this people, how hardly they could get in debts, they chusing rather to spend much in bribes then to pay debts. Ours made vse of their Superstition to Iustice: for vnderstanding that they would neither eate nor wash whiles the English were in their houses, they would threaten not to depart till they were payed, hauing meane while Nayros for their Guard. Thus Iniustice made them just, and vncharitableness charitable. For rather then be long troubled with their company, most of them would pay part of their debts. So that they got fifty *Fanos* (kind of Coine) of one, 100 of another, but one notwithstanding their three days abode, would pay nothing: it seemes, equally prophpane, superstitious and vniust.

CHAPTER XVII.

OF THEIR DIFFERING SECTS.

Barbosa reckoneth eighteene Sects that haue no mutuall conuersation, nor may marrie, but in their owne rankes or order. Next to the King and Bramenes, he placeth the Nayros, which are Gentlemen and Souldiers, and are not professed Nayros (notwithstanding their bloud) till they be by their Lords or by the King made Knights or Souldiers. And then hee must neuer from that time goe without his Weapons, which commonly are a Rapier and a Target, and sometimes Peeces or Bowes. They neuer marry but lye with such of the Nayros Women or Daughters as like them, leaving his Weapons meanwhile at the doore, which forbid any man else, although it be the goodman himselfe, to enter, till he hath ended his businesse and be gone. And if one of the common people once touch a Nayro, it is lawful for the Nayro to kill him: and he is also vncleane, and must be purified by certaine washings. And for this cause they cry as they goe in the streets, *Po*, *Po*, that the baser Raskality may giue place. They haue a Pit of standing Water at their doores, hallowed by the Bramenes, wherein euery morning they wash themselues, although it bee greene, slimie, and stinking, imagining thus to be cleansed of their sinnes. They are brought vp altogether to Feats of Armes and Actiuitie, from their Child-hood, admirably able to wind and turne themselues, and are very resolute and desperate, binding themselues by oath to liue and die with their King or Lord. No Nayro's women may enter into Calicut but one night in the yeere, when the Citie is full of Lightes: and then they goe with the Nayros, to behold and gaze their fill. They intend nothing but their lust, and thinke that if they die Virgins, they shall neuer enter into Paradise.

The Biabari are another sort, and are Merchants Gentiles, and enioy great priuiledges. The King cannot put them to death, but by sentence of the principall of themseues. They were the only Merchants before the Moores traded there, and still enioy many possessions. These marry one Wife, and their Children inherit, and they may touch the Nayros. The Cugianem are a Sect of the Nayros, hauing a Law and Idols by themselues, which they may neuer alter. They make Tiles to couer the Temples and the Kings Palace. The Nayro's may lie with their women, but must wash themselues before they goe home.

Another Sect is called *Manantamar*, which are Landerers, nor may they or their Posteritie be of other function; nor may they mingle themselues with any other Generation. They haue Idol-ceremonies and Temples by themselues. The Nayros may vse their Wiues (or Women rather.) Their Brethren or Nephewes are their Heires. The *Calien* are Weauers, and haue a distinct Idolatrous Sect, otherwise are as the former.

Besides these of better condition, there are of baser sort eleuen Sects, which may not marrie nor meddle with others. The first of these are called *Tiberi*, Husbandmen; the second *Moger*, and are Mariners; both hauing their proper Superstitions, and vse their women in common: the third are *Astrologers*, whom they called *Caniun*. Great men aske their counsell, but may not touch their persons. The *Aggeri* are Masons and Workers in Metals. The *Muchoa* or *Mechoe* are Fishers, dwelling in Villages by themselues; the men Theeues, the women Harlots, with whom they please. The *Be ua* are Salt-makers: the *Parian* are Iugglers, Inchanters, and Physicians (if such damnable Deuillish practices may deserue so honourable Name) which, when any are sicke and require their helpe, vse Coniuration to cause the Deuill to enter into some of them, and then by his suggestion declare the euent of the Disease, and what Sacrifices or other things are to be performed. They may not touch or bee touched of other men.

The *Reuolet* are a baser sort of Gentiles, which carry wood into the Citie to sell, and herbs. The *Puler* are as excommunicate persons, and liue in Desarts, where the Nayros haue no occasion to passe, and when they goe neere any of these Nayros, or any of the better sort, they cry as lowd as they can (as the Lepers among the Iewes) that others may auoid them. For if any touch them, their Kindred may for such action or passion slay them, and as many of these *Puler* also, as may make satisfaction for such disparagement. Some nights they will go of purpose, seeking to touch some of the Nayro women with hand, sticke or hurling of a stone: which if they effect, there is no remedie for the woman but to get her forth and liue with these Villaines, or to be sold, to escape killing by the hands of her Kindred. These *Puler* are Theeues and Sorcerers. The *Pareas* are of worse esteeme, and liue in Desarts without commerce of any, reputed worse then the Deuill. These ten sorts, (or eleuen, if you reckon two sorts of the *Tiberi*, as our Author doth ; where of one are Warriors, distinguished by a certaine cudgell, which they must cary in their hands from the Nayros,) are as well differing in Religions, as matters of common life; though for their seuerall Rites, it were wrong to the Reader at large to recite them, if we had the particulars to deliuer. But this is common in India, that each Trade and Tribe distinguish a new Sect.

There are besides these Gentiles, Naturall of Malabar, many strangers of Indians, Moores, and Christians. But in other Kingdomes of Malabar, the Heathenish Religion is little differing from that in Calicut.

Cranganor is a small Kingdome; the Inhabitants of the Citie, which giueth name to the Region, are Christians of Saint *Thomas* profession, about seuentie thousand in number. Cochin is now growne great by the Portugals traffique and friendship. Of the rest there is not much worth the recitall. The Papall honour among the Bramenes, was by ordination of *Perimal*, which placed there the Supremacie of the Bramens, because He to whom he gaue *Coulam*, was a greater Man then the rest. This Papall title was *Cobritin*, a dignity which the King of Cochin still retayneth to be supreme Head of the Bramenes. For the ancient Kings of Coulan remoued their seate to Cochin, which was then in their Territories. But Warres haue since much altered the face of things in those parts. In these parts are now many Christian Proselites of the Iesuites Conuersion, besides many of the olde *Thomas Christians*. Both Men and Women in Cochin, account it a great Gallantry to haue wide Eares, which therefore they stretch by Art, hanging Weights on them till they reach to their shoulders.

Porca is a Kingdome Southwards from Cochin, but little we can say of it. In *Trauancor* betweene Coulan and the Cape were many Christains, if they may be so called, which want Sacraments. For in fifty yeeres together they had not seene a Priest, only they had the priuiledges and name of *Thomæan-Christians*. These *Thomæans* are now, as the Iesuites report, reduced to their Catholicisime.

The King of *Trauancors* Dominion stretcheth beyond the Cape *Comori*, (where *Malabar* endeth) on the East-side fourescore and ten miles, as farre as *Cael*: which diuers great Lords hold vnder him. Among the rest is the Signiory of *Quilacare*. In the City of *Quilacare* is an Idoll of high account, to which they solemnize a Feast euery twelfth yere, where the Gentiles resort as the Popish Christians in the Romish Iubilee. The Temple sacred to this

Idoll hath exceeding great reuenue. The King (for so he is called) at this Feast erecteth a Scaffold couered with silke, and hauing washed himselfe with great solemnity, he prayeth before this Idoll: and then ascendeth the Scaffold, and there in presence of all the people cutteth off his Nose, and after that his Eares, Lips, and other parts, which he casts towards the Idoll, and at last he cutteth his throate making a butcherly sacrifice of himselfe to his Idoll. He that is to be his successor, must be present hereat: for he must vndergoe the same Martyrdome, when his twelue yeares Iubilee is come: Along this Coast dwell the *Paraui*, simple people, and Christians, which liue by fishing of Pearles. The *Nayros* make such holes in their Eares, that *Cæsar Frederike* sayth, hee thrust his arme vp to the shoulders in one of them. They are prodigal of their liues in the honour of their King. *Osorius* telleth of some, which like the renowned *Decij*, had vowed themselues to death, and not to returne from the enemy without victory. *Aloiisius Goueanus* numbreth in the Sea Coast of Coulam three and twenty townes, of which nineteene had Christian Churches.

The *Malabars* are generally of one Language, and one kind of writing. This their writing was in leaues of Palme, which they call Olla, two fingers broad, and long as the matter they intended, written on both sides with a stile of Iron, which they binde vp in Bookes betweene two boords in greater or lesser forme as they please. Their writing is from the left hand to the right. They reckoned their times before the *Portugals* came into the *Indies*, from the departure of *Perimal*. There are two sorts of Moores, one Mesticos of mixed seed of Moore-fathers and Ethnike-mothers, called *Naiteani*, Mungrels also in their Religion: the other Forreiners, which come thither in trading. There are also many Iewes which haue almost lost their Iudaisme, minding more their merchandize then superstition.

Besides those former Sects, *Stephanus de Brito* speaks of the *Maleas* which inhabit small Villages in the Mountaynes, which are Hunters of Elephants: amongst whom are no thefts or robberies, and therefore they leaue their doores open when they goe abroad. They haue no Idoll, amongst them: only they obserue their Ancestours Sepulchres. These haue no Commerce with their Neighbours nor are much subiect to Kings, only pay them a kinde of tribute, hauing *Arelli* set ouer them as Iudges or Magistrates, vnder each of them fiue or sixe thousand men. Their houses are made of *Indian* Canes dawbed with earth, and some liue on trees laying beames from one tree to another, and so building them lofty Cottages free from Tygres and wilde Elephants whereof the Montaynes are full, which they take in Pits couered ouer with leaues. They haue fertile fields and Valleyes, but not diligently husbanded. They are content with one Wife, which they carry with them whithersoeuer they goe, though but a Hunting-voyage. They are as other Malabars naked from the waste vpwards, a long garment hangs thence to the ankles, and on their heads a Turbant as the Mores. Their necke, ears and nostrils, are laden with gold. For the Malabars weare gold as well for nose-rings, as earrings. These Maleas are of better estimation then the base vulgar, nor is it accounted pollution to touch them, no more then other Nayros or Thomæan Christians. They haue their Pipes and Tabors on their Feasts. They are also Sorcerers and diuine by familiar Spirits, but vse not to kill or hurt men by Witchcraft, as other Indians and Malabars doe. A witty, docible, honest people, perhaps descended of those Malliani, which *Plutarch* and *Curtius* mention in the life of *Alexander*.

Of the Feast which all the Malabar Kings hold every twelfth yeare in honour of the Riuer Ganges, we haue there spoken of where we haue discoursed of the Riuer. This Feast lasteth eight and twentie or thirtie dayes with grea solemnitie: the Samorin euery day washing himselfe and offering Sacrifices to Ganges: after which hee returnes to his Palace with innumerable troupes of men, riding vpon an Elephant in great pompe: and three dayes after in the morning and euening with greatest Royaltie, makes shew of himselfe in a high Throne, many Lampes of gold and siluer burning about him, many Peeces discharged, with other ceremonie of State. The King prostrates himselfe on the ground, and three times doth reuerence to the People, and they to Him, the Kings Vassals then doing him homage. After this many Champions exercise their Fencing-skill before him, and at the sound of Instruments, the Chiefe Nobles by two and two in a ranke, with their faces to the ground, doe reuerence: the Elephants are likewise to honour him. Twentie thousand Crownes are spent on this solemnitie by the King. Another more diuelish rite followes. About the yeere 1520, the Zamorin slue a certaine King. In memorie whereof the Sucessors of that King send a certayne number of their Soldiers to reuenge his death, themselues being sure to be slaine: these are called Amocæ, which are Clients to that King, and are either to come themselues, or to send so many Souldiers, to the number of thirtie, which rush among the People, and kill as many as they can; themelues certayne to be killed of the Kings Shouldiers.

CHAPTER XVIII.

KINGDOME OF NARSINGA AND BISNAGAR, FUNERALL AND IDOLATROUS RITES.

FROM those places where our feet last rested (or touched rather) vnto the Cape Guadauerin, betwixt that ridge of Mountaines called Gate, and the Ocean (which is there named the Gulfe of Bengala) trendeth the Kingdome of Narsinga, or Bisnagar; those two Royall Cities contending which shall giue name to this mightie Empire, containing two hundred leagues of Sea coast. The King hath in continuall pay forty thousand Nairos. But as occasion serueth, he can bring into the field very many thousands more; as in that Expedition against *Idalkan*, specified by *Barrius* and *Boterus*; in which, was a world of people (seuen hundred thousand foot, fortie thousand horse, seuen hundred Elephants, twentie thousand harlots.) Hee sacrificed also vnto Idols twentie thousand seuen hundred and threescore head of Beasts and Fowles in nine dayes space, which in Idoll-deuotion were all bestowed after on the poore.

In the yeare of our Lord 1565, Biznagar was sacked by foure Kings of the Mores (as saith *Frederike*) naming them *Dialkan*, *Zamaluc*, *Cotamaluc*, and *Viridy*, through treason of two More Captaines, which had seuen or eight score thousand Souldiers vnder them; but being of the same Religion with the Kings of Decan, betrayed their owne King, forsaking him in the midst of the battaile. This was a iust reward of treason to the true King of Biznagar. For three Captaines had kept the King thirtie yeares as prisoner, once a yeare shewing him to the people, themselues ruling the State. When he dyed, then *Ramaragio* exalted himselfe to the Throne. *Temiragio*, the second, swayed the gouernment, and the third *Bengahe* was General of the Armie. Onely *Temiragio* escaped and returned (when the Decans had sacked the Citie, and were gone) to Biznagar, and sent to Goa great promises for Horses, if any Merchants would bring any. Whereupon *Frederike* went with other Merchants, which carried store of them, but brought no store of money in payment; the Tyrant accepting the Horses, but paying nothing. *Temiragio* remoued his Court from Biznagar to Penegorde, eight dayes journey within Land. And his sonne put to death the sonne of that King before mentioned, which had beene imprisoned, as this also had beene, till Death by a murthering hand freed him. Hence grew many broyles, the Nobles, refusing to acknowledge this New King; and thus Biznagar being forsaken, remained after this an Habitation for Tygres and wild Beasts, containing in circuit foure and twentie myles as our Author (that stayed there seuen moneths) affirmeth. He neuer saw Palace exceeding that of Biznagar. It had nine Gates with guards of Souldiers. Here hee obserued their Rites in burning the women, so often mentioned, which after his and *Balby* his relations are thus. (I haue declared the like for substance before; this as in some Rites differing, I adde also.)

The woman taketh two or three moneths respite after her husband's death: The day being come, she goeth earely out of her house, mounted on a Horse or Elephant, or else on a Stage, carried by eight men: apparelled like to a Bride, adorned with Iewels, and her haire about her shoulders; holding in her left hand a Looking-glasse; in the right an Arrow: and joyeth as shee passeth through the Citie, saying, That she goeth to sleepe with her husband. She is accompanied with her friends, vntill it be one or two of the clocke in the afternoone: then they goe out of the Citie, passing by the Riuers side to the burning-place, where is prepared a great square Caue, full of Wood. Here is made a great Banquet, the woman eating with ioy, as if it where her wedding-day; and after, they sing and daunce, till the woman bid to kindle the fire in the Caue: then she leaueth the Feast, and taketh her husbands neerest kinsman by the hand, and goeth with him to the banke of the Riuer where she strippeth her of her cloathes and iewels bestowing them at her pleasure, and couering herselfe with a cloth, throweth herselfe into the Riuer, saying '*O wretches, wash away your sinnes.*' Comming out of the Water, shee rowleth herselfe into a yellow cloth; and againe taking her husbands kinsman by the hand, goeth to the said Caue, by which is erected a little Pinnacle on which she mounteth, and there recommendeth her children and kindred to the people. After this, another woman taketh a pot with oyle, and sprinkleth it ouer her head, and therewith annoynteth all her bodie, and then throweth it into the Furnace, the woman going together with the same. Presently after the woman, the people throw great pieces of Wood into the Caue, so that with those blowes and the fire she is quickly dead, and their great mirth is on a suddaine turned into great lamentation and howling.

When a Great man dyeth, all the women of his house, both his wife and slaues, with whom hee hath had carnall copulation, burne themselues together with him. Amongst the baser sort, I haue seene (saith Master *Frederike*) the dead man carried to the place of buriall, and there set vpright: the woman comming before him on her knees, casteth her armes about his necke, while a mason maketh a wall round about them: and when the wall is as high as their necks; one comming behind the woman, strangleth her; the workeman presently finishing the wall ouer them: and this is their buriall.

Ludonicus Vertomannus relateth the same Funerall Rites

of Tarnasseri (as in other parts of India) sauing that there fifteene or twentie men, in their idolatrous habit, like Diuels, doe attend on the fire wherein the husband is burned, all the Musicians of the Citie solemnizing the Funerall pompe: and fifteene dayes after, they haue the like solemnitie, at the burning of the woman; those diuellish fellowes holding fire in their mouthes, and sacrificing to *Deumo*, and are her intercessors to that Diuell for her good entertainment.

The cause of burning their wiues, is by some ascribed to their wonted poysonings of their husbands, before this Law; by others, that the husband might haue her helpe and comfort in the other world.

Odoricus telleth of a strange and vncouth Idoll, as bigge as Saint *Christopher*, of pure Gold, with a new band about the necke, full of precious stones, some one whereof was of value (if he valued iustly) more then a whole Kingdome: The roofe, pauement, and seeling of the walls, within and without the Temple, was all Gold. The Indians went thither on pilgrimage, some with halters about their neckes, some with their hands bound behind them, some with kniues sticking on their armes and legges; and if, after their pilgrimage, the wounded flesh festered, they esteemed that limbe holy, and a signe of their Gods fauour. Neere to the Temple was a Lake, whereinto the Pilgrims cast Gold, Siluer, and Gemmes, for honour of the Idoll, and reparation of his Temple. At euery yearely Feast, the King and Queene, with the Pilgrims and People, assembling, placed the said Idoll in a rich Chariot, and with a solemne procession of Virgins, two in a ranke, singing before him, and with Musicall Instruments carrie him forth. Many Pilgrims put themselues vnder the Chariot wheeles, where they are crushed in pieces. More then fiue hundred persons vsed thus to doe, whose carkasses were burned, and ashes kept for holy Reliques. Otherwise also they will deuote themselues to such a martyrdome in this manner: The parents and friends assemble and make a Feast to this Votarie, and after that hang fiue sharpe kniues about his necke, and so carrie him before the Idoll; where he taketh one of his kniues, and cryeth, '*For the worship of my God I cut this my flesh*;' and cutting a piece, casteth it at the face of the Idoll; and so proceeding, at the last sayth, '*Now doe I yeeld myselfe to death in the behalfe of my God*;' and being dead, is burned as before.

Our Country-man Sir *Iohn Mandeuile* reporteth the same Historie of their Idoll-Procession, and the ashes of those voluntary Martyrs; which they keepe, to defend them against tempests and misfortunes. He also sayth, That some Pilgrims, in all their peregrinations, not once lifted vp their eye-lids; some, at euery third or fourth pace fell downe on their knees, to worship; some whipped; others wounded themselues; yea, killed themselues (as is before said.) *Nicolo de Conti* reporteth the same in his time.

Neither is this bloudy custome yet left, as *Lincsholen* affirmeth, by report of one of his chamber-fellowes that had seene it. They haue (sayth he) a Waggon, or Cart, so heauie, that three or foure Elephants can hardly draw it, which is brought forth at Faires, Feasts, and Processions. At this Cart hang many Cables or Ropes, whereat all the people hale and pull, of deuotion. In the vpper part of the Cart standeth a Tabernacle, and therein the Idoll: vnder it sit the Kings wiues, playing on Instruments. And while the Procession passeth, some cut pieces of their flesh, and throwe at the *Pagode*; some lay themselues vnder the wheeles of the Cart, with such euent as you haue heard.

Gasparo Balby relateth the same, and addeth, That the Priests, which haue care of this Idoll, and certaine women, are consecrated to these deuotions from their Cradles, by their *Zeale-blind* parents. And the women prostitute their bodies, to gaine for the Idoll whatsoeuer they can get ouer and aboue their owne maintenance. This filleth the Citie with Strumpets; there being of this *Sacred* (you may interpret it *Cursed*) crue, foure hundred in one place of the Citie. These haue their place in the Idoll-procession, some of them in the Chariot which is drawne by men; euery one accounting himselfe happy, that can touch or draw the same. This he sayth was at Negapatan.

He further affirmeth, That not farre from the Citie of Saint *Thomas* is the Towne Casta: where the Wife is not buried (as at Negapatan) but a great Graue being made for the deceased Husband, they place the liuing Wife by the dead corps, and their neerest kindred cast earth vpon them both, and stampe thereon. They which marry, wed in their owne degree, as a Smith to a Smiths daughter: and they powre out their prayers at the Image of some Cow, or a Serpent, called *Bittia di Capella*. Their Bramenes burne Cowes dung; and if they intend any warres with other Nations, they anoint their Nose and Forehead with those ashes, not washing themselues till the euening. They which sacrifice themselues to the *Pagode*, when they haue wallowed a long time in lustfull pleasures, shoot into the aire pieces of their flesh tyed to Arrowes, and diuersly mangle themselves; at last, cut their owne throats, so sacrificing themselues to the *Pagode*.

There are also certaine people called *Amouchi*, otherwise *Chiani* which perceiuing the end of their life approach, lay hold on their weapons, which they call *Chisse*, and going forth, kill euery man they meet with, till some body (by killing them) make an end of their killing. They are loth (it seemes) to come into the Deuils presence empty-handed, or to goe to Hell alone. Some of them worship God in the likenesse of a Man; some in the images of Kine and Serpents: some inuoke the Sunne and Moone; others, some Tree or Riuer.

Among many Feasts which they celebrate in the yeere,

one in Autumne is most solemne, in which they take some great tree, and fasten it in the ground, hauing first fashioned it like a mast of a Ship, with a crosse-yard, whereon they hang two hookes of iron. And when any one by sicknesse, or other miserie, hath made a vow to their Idoll or *Pagode*, hee commeth thither, and being first admonished by the Priests to offer his sacrifice, they lift him with those hookes by both the shoulders, and there hold him to the Idoll, till he hath three times saluted the same, with clapping his folded hands to his breast, and hath made some sport thereto with weapons which be hath in his hand. After this he is let downe, and the bloud which issueth from his shoulders is sprinkled on the Tree, in testimonie of his deuotion. Then they draw him vp againe by the middle, to giue thankes to the Idoll: and then giue him leaue to heale himselfe, if he can. They which are in great miserie, or seeke some great matter at the hand of their Idoll, doe this. They haue another Feast, celebrated in the night, continuing eight nights: in which many Candles were seene burning thorow the Citie. Three or foure runne from one end of street to the other, and hurling Rice, and other meats after them, say, they offer it to the Deuill which followes them; not daring to looke behind, lest he should slay them. In other places also they haue those Idol-chariots, like vnto Towers, to the drawing whereof, many thousands of deuout persons put their helping-hand.

Anno 1598. there was a great contention, whether the signe of *Perimal* should bee erected in the Temple of *Cidambacham*. This signe was a gilded Mast, with an Ape at the foot thereof. Many Embassadors were there about this quarrell; some vrging, some resisting this deed. But the Prince (called the *Naicho* of Gingi) would haue it set up, notwithstanding the Priests greatest vnwillingnesse. The Priests therefore, both regular (which are the *Iogues*) and secular *Bramenes* ascended vp the roofe of the

Church, and thence threatned to hurle downe themselues, which twenty of the *Iogues* did, and the rest threatned to follow. But the *Naicho* caused Gunnes to be discharged at them, which slue two, and caused the rest to retire and breake their couenant (rather then their necks) with their fellowes. A woman also of this faction cut her owne throat for zeale of this new superstition.

CHAPTER XIX.

OF THE KINGS AND BRAMENES IN THIS KINGDOME.

THE swelling stile of this King of Bisnagar, I thought worthie to be here inserted, which is this—"The Husband of good fortune, the God of great Prouinces, King of the greatest Kings, and God of Kings, the Lord of horsemen, the Master of them which cannot speake, Emperour of three Emperours, Conquerour of all he sees, and Keeper of all he conquers, Dreadfull to the eight coasts of the world, Vanquisher of the Mahumetans, &c. Lord of the East, West, North, and South, and of the Sea, &c. Vencapadinus Ragiu Denamaganus Ragel, which now ruleth, and gouerneth this world."

These Kings of Bisnagar haue, as sayth *Barrius*, a great part of the Westerne coast subiect vnto them, all betweene the riuers of Aliga and Cangerecora : in which space are these coast Townes, Ancola, Agorapan, Mergeu, Onor, a Royall Citie, Baticala, Bendor, Bracelor, Bacanor, Carara, Carnate, Mangalor, Mangliran, Cumlata, and Cangerecora. From this Citie standing on a Riuer of the same name, Southwards vnto the Cape Comori is reckoned the Malabar coast. And although Goa and Calicut much hinder those his Ports, yet to salute and shake hands, with both Seas, argues a great State, specially where the adioyning are so small. There are three Naichi or Tributary Kings subiect to Him ; such in power, but in title Naichi, that is, Deputies or Presidents, of Madurat Gingi, and Tanaior. The Naicho of Madura is Lord of the Fishing coast. The people are called Badagæ, and despise the Portugals, because they drinke Wine, eate Beefe, and suffer themselues to be touched of the Parese, and carried on their shoulders. For these in their Bramene zeale, would not endure to touch or talke with the baser vulgar, and their Bramenes would die rather then eate that which a Bramene had not dressed. And therefore *Robert Sforce* a Iesuite comming amongst them, professed himselfe of the Bramene of Rape bloud, that is of Noble race, procured a Bramene to dresse his meate, abstained from Flesh, Fish, Wine, and Egges, after their Countrey manner, and attired himselfe in the habite of a Sanasse (one of their votaries) and in pretence of chastity stirred not out of his house in a whole yeere, nor would be spoken with by euery one, alleaging somtimes his deuouter conference with God, so to winne credite with these Ethnikes. He learned by conference with a Bramene, that they maintayned that Philosophicall axiome, that *Nothing could be made of nothing*, and held three *Beginnings* or Vniuersall Causes, the first *Padi*, that is God, the second *Paiu*, the Matter of which they say the Soules are made, the third *Passan*, the Corporall matter. They maintayned also the μετεμψύχωσις or Pythagorean passage of Soules out of one body into another: for else (say they) how could there be such diuersite of Men, one a King, another a Seruant; one a Bramene, an other a Parea? They are also Platonikes, holding the Soule not to be the forme of the Body, but enclosed therein as a Bird in a Cage.

The Bramenes weare ashes on their heads. It seemes they are zealous *Baneanes*. Their Saneasses are Asses indeed for literreature, only as Hermites, they vow chastitie. The Gorupi or Gorusi are Doctors of their Law. The Iesuites professed the Doctorship of these, in the habite of the former; which is a white Garment to the ankle with another of the same colour but thinner ouer it, a red cloth ouer the shoulders, one like a Cap or Hat on the head: from his necke hangs downe a corde of fiue threeds, three of gold, and two of white silke; they eate but once a day.

Their Bramenes haue a proper language and mysticall (as Roman for the Romish holies) called Gueredan, which the Iesuite learned, and thereby out of their books, that there had beene in these parts foure Lawes or Sects, three of which the Bramenes still obserued, to wit, of Veshnu, of Brama, of Rubren; the fourth meerely spirituall, partly mixed with others, and partly lost, tending to the saluation of the Soule, which he said that He brought now vnto them; their Almes and Bodily chastisements, without this, not being effectuall to their saluation. Any might learne and choose a Doctor for any of the other three, but none was able to teach this. When they be come Schollers to such Doctors, they doe a triple reuerence vnto the ground, lifting vp their hands aloft, then letting them downe to their heads; and must (like the Pythagoreans of old, which was learned of the Indians) rest satisfied with his Masters bare assertion, without questioning or further disputing. He was once brought before a Consistorie of the Bramenes, and accused for his new Doctrine. Some articles were, That he should affirme that the washing in *Remanancor* and *Ganges* were to no effect; That the Bramenes are inferior to the *Raij* or Princes; That they should be all damned, notwithstanding there were of them many *Nhanisij* and *Sanasses* (the *Nhanisij* also vow chastitie and to forsake the World.) The President of this Councell cleered the Iesuite vpon the Apologie of another Bramene. For that of *Remanancor*, it is a corner of the Fishing Region, wherein is a Temple famous through all the East, which hee that shall visit and wash himselfe in the Sea iust by, shall bee cleered from all his sinnes as well as if it were done in *Ganges*.

In Madura and the Territorie thereof are numbred a hundred thousand Bramenes, the chiefe of which is *Choca-*

nada, as their Bishop or Pope: He would haue this Iesuite expelled the Countrie, for that this Franke (so euer since the Expedition to Ierusalem vnder Duke *Godfrey* of Bullen, all Westerne Christians are called in all the East, a name, it seemes which the Saracens communicated to the Ethnikes) had eaten with another Franke. He meant *Fernandes*, another Iesuite, that had not thus acted the *Sanasse* and *Gurupi* amongst them. He alleadged also that His Temple was built in the ground of His *Pagode*. But this Iesuite with Gold stopped this Bramenes mouth, and had the soyle of the Church granted him in peace, with promise of all fauour. One thing that holds them intangled in this errour, is, that they hold it vnlawfull to copie out their Lawes and Religion in writing, so that they which wil learne them, must (like the *Druydes*) from their youth learne them of some Doctour, and commit them to memorie: in which they spend tenne yeeres and more And if any should write them, they would pull out his eyes.

Emanuel Leitanus, another Iesuite, comming to Madura in the like *Sanassian* Habit, obserued the Gorupian order, and fell downe before *Sforce* to the ground, Hee sitting in a Chaire couered with red; because some of the *Madurians* were present. The Bramenes in the Kingdome of Bisnagar are of such power, that nothing is done without them; and of the fiue Counsellours of State, foure are Bramenes: yea, with their face to the earth, all men, and the King himselfe, adore the Bramen-Pope: nor doth the King admit any to conference in the morning, before hee hath seene two Bramenes. In Chandegrin is a Clocke that strikes not foure and twentie houres, but sixtie and foure, according to their diuision of the Night and Day, each into foure parts, and those subdiuided into eight. The Iesuites conceiue that these Bramenes are of the dispersion of the Israelites, and their Bookes (called *Sameseretan*) doe somewhat agree with the Scriptures, but that they vnderstand them not. They haue some propheticall phrases, and some of them affirme that God made *Adam* the first man, and being pressed acknowledge one God. The King and his Nobles speak the learned and sacred tongue of the Bramenes.

Anno 1609. One of his Great men rebelling against him, and fortifying the Castle of Vellur, the King besieged him, and on his submission pardoned him; but so as hee turned his Fort (which had stood the Rebell in a hundred thousand Crownes) into a Palace besides twentie Fannes, each worth an hundred thousand Pardowes, and innumerable Horses and Elephants. The same yeere did the King write to the King of Spaine in commendation of the Iesuites, with promise to assist the Vice-roy against the Moores and Hollanders, which had obtained to build a Fortresse of the Naichus of Tanauapatan, desiring the same friendship, that since the King of Narsingas dayes had beene betwixt both their Ancestors, subscribed *King Ventacaxa.*

Thus you see the same King diuersly entituled according to the Citie Royall, yea I finde him called (of the Castle before named) King of Vellur; for *Floris* stiles him, saying that in Iune 1614, he granted trade to the English, as likewise did *Obiana* Queene of Paleacatte, one of his Wiues which (it seemes) gouerned that Citie: On Iuly the nine and twentieth, his *Abeskian* was sent, being a white cloth where his owne hand is printed in Sandall or Saffron, and another the like from the Queene of Paleacatte. The Kings Letter was written vpon a leafe of Gold, wherein hee made excuse of former wrongs, gaue them libertie to build a House or Fort, with other priuiledges. He gaue *Floris* the English Merchant a Towne of foure hundred Pardawes yeerely reuenue, notwithstanding the Hollanders (his Countrimen) did what they could to hinder it. *Wengali (Floris* his man) had beene in the Kings presence, who laid his hand vpon his head. But on the eight and twentieth of October following, newes came that this King was dead, hauing raigned aboue fiftie yeeres. His three wiues, of which *Obiana* Queen of Paleacatte was one, burned themselues with his corpse, and great troubles were expected. The Hollanders had presented this King with two Elephants of Seilan. *Cotabaxa* the King of Badaya and Lellengana his Neighbour, died not long before. *Mahumed Vmin Cotabaxa* his Brothers Sonne succeeded. *Musulipatan* is in his Dominion. Golconda is the Metropolitan Citie. But hee is a Moore of the Sophi his Sect. Golconda is the Citie Royall.

With the *Naicho* or King of Gingi (vassall to the King or Emperour of Bisnagar) the Iesuites found good entertainment. Heere some of the *Iogues* distributed the water of Ganges out of certaine vessels couered with foule and filthie clothes, which yet the people for deuotion kissed. These *Iogues* with admirable patience endured the Sunne heate: and one among the rest enclosed himselfe in an Iron Cage, with his head & feet onely out of the Cage, that he could neither sit nor lie downe at any time: and on the Cage were hanged an hundred Lampes, which foure other *Iogues* his companions lighted at certaine times. And thus walked he in this his perpetuall Prison, as a *Light vnto the World*, in his vaine glorious opinion. They reasoned with certaine Bramenes; some of which held the Sunne for God, and yet sometime to haue beene a man, and for his merits so promoted. Some denied a multitude of Gods, onely allowing that priuiledge to *Pyrama*, *Vidbun*, and *Vuitir*, one of which maketh, another keepeth the third destroyeth all things.

Neere to Madure is an Idoll calle *Chocanda:* which by night appeared in a vision to a Priest, and bade him goe say to the *Naicho* of Madure, that hee or I must abide in this house: wherevpon he would not be corriuall with his Idoll, but resigned the Palace to him. His deuotion is such, that euery day, while hee sitteth in judgement, a

Bramene euer and anon soundeth the name of *Arrangan-assi* in his eares : and when one is wearie, another succeedeth in the same Office, neuer ceasing this Idols remembrance, although hee there sitteth fiue or sixe houres.

I thought meete to mention one custome which some report of the *Brama*, or Popelike *Bramene* in these parts, who by his authority dispenseth with many of their Lawes, and dissolueth Marriages: giuing libertie at his pleasure to the woman to marrie another ; which his Dispensation is sealed on her right shoulder, with a marke of a hote Iron.

CHAPTER XX.

MANY OTHER STRANGE RITES: AND OF SAINT THOMEE.

CHANDARIN is the Royall Seat of the great King of Bisnagar. The chiefest Families therein are the *Bramenes*, *Raias*, and *Cretius*. They affirme that their Idoll *Perimal* did bring forth the *Bramenez* out of his head (as the Poets tell of *Minerua*) the second out of his brest; third out of his belly: and all other inferiour Families out of his feet. The *Bramenes* haue some opinions, not altogether dissonant from the Scriptures. They say, That God onely by his thought made a man, which they call *Adam*.

On the tenth day of Iuly, *Anno* 1600 happened an Eclipse of the Sunne, which the *Bramenes* said was by meanes of the *Dragon* (which they make a Celestiall Signe) his byting of the Sunne and Moone: whereupon the King and others neither ate nor dranke that day; deploring their misery, because the Dragon deuoured the Sunne. In the Citie Prepeti, three miles from Chandagrin, is the Feast of *Perimal*, in remembrance of his Marriage: at which the Offerings amounted to two hundred thousand Crownes: and the Chariot of the Idoll was drawne forth a mile and a halfe in Procession by ten thousand men. They haue another Feast of the Kine, because they suppose *Perimal* to bee the Sonne of a Cow, and then the wayes and streets are full of all that cattle. They haue a Feast in honour of the Sunne, which lasteth eight dayes, solemnized by the Emperour himselfe, and he is iudged a Traytor which is not present thereat. Then they cast lots, the King first, and after the rest, diuining by Arrowes the next yeeres destinie. If an Arrow light on a Tree, and being plucked out, causeth a red liquor to follow, it prognosticateth Warres; if white, Peace. Not farre hence is an Idoll called *Tripiti*, to which are great Pilgrimages and Offering; alwayes they goe, some begin, and the rest answere, and so all continue to resound the name of the Idol *Goia*. Before they enter into the Temple, they shaue and wash themselues. The Heremites, which they call *Sanasses*, liue in Deserts, and at sometimes appeare before the people naked. The *Gurups* beare a great port, and neuer goe forth on foot. The Idoll *Tripiti* is seated on a Mountaine, about which are fertile Valleyes, stored with Fruites, which none may touch, as being consecrated.

There are in the Woods great abundance of Apes so tame, that they will take meate out of mens hands : the people esteeme them a diuine Race, and of the samiliaritie of *Perimal* the chiefe God, whom they worship in many colours and shapes, as of a Man, Oxe, Horse, Lion, Hogge, Ducke, Cocke, &c. *Francis Fernandes* saith, that Cidambaram is the Mother-citie of their Pagan Rites, wherein are many stately Temples, and the reuenue of the *Bramens* amounted to 30,000 Ducats, but now they are payd 12000 yeerely.

Here happened a strange accident, the same day the Iesuits departed, the occasion of which was this: There is in this Citie a Temple of *Perimal*, wherein they worship an Ape called *Hanimant* whom they report to have beene a God, and (for I know not what) together with many thousands of other Gods, to haue remained there, being all transformed into Apes. Now when this principall Ape was forced to passe into the Iland Zeilan, and wanted a ship, he leaped, and at euery leape left an Iland or heape of Land behind him, so making way for his Apish traine to Zeilan. The tooth of this Ape was kept for a great relike in that Iland, with great resort of Pilgrims thereunto:

and in the yeere 1554 was by the Portugals (who made a roade thither, in hope of great bootie) taken away. The *Indian* Princes offered the Vice-roy three hundred thousand (or as *Linschoten* telleth, seuen hundred thousand) Ducats, for the ransome of this Apes tooth, but the Archbishop disswaded the Vice-roy; who thereupon burnt the same before those Indian Embassadors, and threw the ashes into the Sea. Not long after, a *Beniane* of Cambay perswaded the *Indians*, that hee by Diuine Power had taken away that holy Tooth, beeing inuisibly present, and had left another in the roome which was burnt. Superstition is credulous, and the King of Bisnagar gaue him a great summe of Gold for that Apes Tooth, wherewith hee thus Apishly had bitten and mocked them, which was after holden in like veneration as the former. But to returne to our Cidambaran Historie.

They tell, That an holy man, in great penance, had many yeeres held his foot pierced thorow with a piece of Iron, and when he was often by God commanded to leaue that selfe rigour, he flatly refused, vnlesse that hee might see God dancing about him, which also Hee condescended vnto; and with the Sunne, Moone and Starres, which played the Musicians, he appeared dancing: And as he danced, a Chaine of Gold fell from his foot, whereof this Towne tooke name. For *Cidambaran* signifieth *Golden Chaine.*

As *Viega* and *Ricius*, two Iesuites, trauelled to Chandegrin, they came to Trauilur, where they say their Idoll, with a white Banner on his back, and after him three sacred Kine, with Drummers on their backes, and after them Trumpetters and many Musicians of other sorts. Then followed twentie women dancing, which were also consecrated to the Idols seruice, and might not marry, but yet prostitute their bodies: these were richly attired, and carried Lights. The Priests followed with the Idoll, and were followed by the people with Lights. At their return they set downe the Idoll and set sodden Rice before him to eate; others meanwhile driuing away the flies, and others couering him that hee should not bee seene eating, and at last, one maketh a long Oration of the worthy acts of their God, and then set him againe in his place. This lasted foure hours and in the meane space many reasoned with the Iesuits, and some held vaine Discourses of the Creation: as that there were seuen Seas; one of Salt-water, the second of fresh, the third of Honey, the fourth of Milke, the fifth of *Tair* (which is Creame beginning to sowre), the sixth of Sugar, the seuenth of Butter, that the Earth had nine corners, whereby it was borne up by the Heauen. Others dissented, and said, that the Earth was borne up by seuen Elephants; the Elephants feete stood on Tortoises, and they were borne by they know not what.

When the *Naicho* of Tangaor died, 375 of his Concubines willingly offered themselues to the fire, to honour his Funerall, so much can Custome harden so delicate and soft-hearted a nature.

The Temples in the Countrey haue great reuenues, which in some places are encreased by the deuotion of women, which prostitute themselues to gaine for their Idols; and many young Girles are brought vp for this purpose. Many are in these parts, of the Sect of the *Guzzarates*, which kill no quicke thing, as is spoken. Some haue a stone hanging about their necks, as bigge as an Egge with certaine lines drawne thorow the middle thereof; and this they worship, and call it *Tambarane:* they keepe euery Friday holiday.

The Kingdome of Orissa hath on the Sea-coast 350 miles, betwixt the richer Kingdomes of Bengala and Bisnagar, poore of Ports and Traffique. *Frederike* writes that before the King of Patane had conquered Orissa, there was great Trade for Oile of Zerzeline, Lacca, Long Pepper, Ginger, Mirabolans, and cloth made of herbs, which grow with a bowle as bigge as an Orange, yeelding silke. The Countrey was so safe, that a man might haue trauelled with his Gold in his hand. The King was a Gentile, and resided in the Citie Catecha, sixe days Iourney within Land. The King of Patane was soone after subdued by the Mogoll. The Inhabitants (except a few Moores) are Gentiles, little or nothing (that I can learne) differings in Rites from their Neighbours, of which ye haue heard. Some ascribe to the Cittie Orissa, as the name, to the Principalitie of the other Cities of the Kingdome.

In these parts is the Citie of Saint *Thomas* or *Malepur*, where they say Saint *Thomas* (after be had preached the Gospell to the Indians) was martyred and burned. The Legend which some report of his death, were too tedious to recite: and as little likelihood of truth is in that long tale of the miraculous Crucifixes heere found, related by *Osorius*, who likewise declareth the Rites of those Saint *Thomas* Christians, of their Chaldean-Pope, Cardinals, Patriarches and Bishops; of which in another place we shall more fitly speake. On the first day of Iuly Saint *Thomas* Holiday is celebrated, as well by the Pagans as Christians: and his Sepulchre is had in deuout estimation, both of the Moores, Gentiles, and Christians; each pretending the right of his owne Religion to the Church, where this Saint lieth interred, to which the Indian Christians goe on Pilgrimage, carrying with them a little of that earth for a great Relique. A Moore had the keeping of the Church which was built after our fashion, and begged of the commers for maintenance of it, and of a light continually burning therein.

The Portugals now inhabit this Towne almost desolate; the Iesuites also have heere a Residence. The Church doores (by the Superstition of some) are almost cut in pieces, and carried away to set in Gold and Siluer, and to weare about their neckes, as a holy relike; the Portugals herein being exceedingly vaine, and attributing here unto many Miracles, veryfying that Prouerbe which the Spaniards vse, affirming the Portugals to be *Pocos fotos deuotos*. One sent *Linschoten* a whole Bead-roll or paire of Beads, thereof the bringer affirming that those Beades had calmed a Tempest miraculously by the way. The Inhabitants in this respect haue driuen their Church-doores full of nails: but Saint *Thomas* bones are new remoued to Goa. Those doores are of such renowned holinesse, because they were made of that wood which Saint *Thomas* drew with his girdle out of the Hauen (which it choaked) and could not before this Miracle by any means be remoued.

One thing I thought not to omit, that there bee whole Villages and Kindreds of people, in other things like to other men, but are borne with one of their legs and one foot from the knee downwards, as thicke as an Elephants legge; which the common people imagine to be a curse by Diuine Iustice, inflicted vpon the whole Generation, for that their Progenitors Murthered Saint *Thomas*. *Linschoten* saith, he hath seene and spoken with them, and could learne no other cause thereof. It is to them a deformitie, but no let or impediment otherwise.

The Gouernour of Musulipatan being of *Mahomet's* posteritie, had agreed for custome to take foure *per centum*, and exacted twelue, offering the English there diuers wrongs. Here the Gentiles haue in those parts a Feast when the New Moone comes vpon Munday, and then both Sexes wash themselues in the Sea, as a matter of much Indulgence for their sinnes. And then after much indignitie the Cape-Merchant *Floris*, performed a worthy exploit, deseruing still to flourish, though he be dead. The Gouernours Sonne being set ouer the Custome, and at the Costome-house guarded with his Souldiers, *Floris* enterd lone as it were for businesse, and as he had plotted, a few English followed by diuers wayes, which seized on the weapons of the Guard, at the Custome-house door, and *Floris* laid hold of the Gouernours Sonne *Wucatadera* by name, which was suddenly conueyed into their Boat, three thousand people presently running to the shoare. But being vnder their ships protection, they both secured themselues, and for redemption of his Sonne, forced the Father to pay all debts by him detained, with satisfaction for wrongs offered. Yet such was his Superstition, that he almost first starued a shipboord rather then he would eate or drinke with the English. Thus from the foure and twentieth of Nouember till the thirtieth, he kept a strict *Bramens* Fast, the English pittying his misery, and willing therefore to take pledges in his roome. But after that weeke of cleane Lent without eating or drinking, he was redeemed, the debts being paid by his Father. And hence let the Reader iudge of bodily exercise and *opus operatum* without true faith, how little it auaileth.

In Narsapur Peta (a place not faire hence, where they Careened the *Globe*) happened in August that yeare such ouer flowings of water, that many thousands of men and cattell were drowned, Townes, Fields of Rice and Salt-hils ouerflowne, foure thousand houses washed away, and two Stone Bridges ouer the Riuer, one of nineteene, the other of fifteene Arches, comparable to Rochester Bridge, standing three fathome aboue water. Many Portugals also liue in the parts of Bengala adioyning like Wildmen; and *Iaric* speakes of I200 which thus obserue not Christianitie, and therefore many be reckoned amongst these Heathens.

And thus haue we finished our perambulation. Now let vs ship ourselues ouer (for wee are not skilfull of *Hanimants* leaps) vnto other lands.

TRAVELLS IN INDIA

BY

VAN LINSCHOTEN.

OBSERVATIONS OF THE EAST INDIES

BY

IOHN HVIOHEN VAN LINSCHOTEN.

CHAPTER I.

HIS VOYAGE TO GOA.

VPON the eight of Aprill, being Good-friday, in the yeere of our word 1583, which commonly is the time when their ships set sayle within foure or fiue dayes vnder or ouer, wee all together issued out of the Riuer of *Lisbon* and put to Sea, setting our course for the Ilands of *Madera*.

The ships are commonly charged with foure or fiue hundred men at the least, sometimes more, sometimes lesse, as there are Souldiers and Saylers to be found. When they goe out they are but lightly laden, onely with certaine pipes of Wine and Oyle, and some small quantitie of merchandise, other thing they haue not in, but balast, and victuals for the companie, for that the most and greatest ware that is sent into *India*, are Rials of eight, because the principall Factors for Pepper doe euery yeere send a great quantitie of money, wherewith to buy Pepper, as also diuers particular Merchants, as being the least ware that men can carrie into *India*: for that in these Rials of eight they gaine at the least forty *per cento*: when the ships are out of the Riuer, and enter into the Sea, all their men are mustered, as well Saylers as Souldiers, and such as are found absent and left on land, being registred in the Bookes, are marked by the Purser, that at their returne they may talke with their Sureties, (for that euery man putteth in Sureties); and the goods of such as are absent, being found in the ship are presently brought forth and prised, and an Inuentorie being made, it is left to be disposed at the Captaines pleasure. The like is done with their goods that die in the ship, but little of it commeth to the owners hands, imbeseled and priuily made away.

The Master and Pilot haue for their whole Voyage forth and home againe, each man an hundredand twenty Milreyes, euery Milrey being worth in *Dutch* money seuen Gilders, and receiue before hand each man foure and twenty Milreyes, besides that they haue Chambers both vnder in the ship, and Cabbins aboue the hatches, as also Primage, and certaine tunnes fraight. The like haue all the other Officers in the ship according to their degrees, and although they receiue money in hand, yet it costeth them more in gifts before they get their places, which are giuen by fauour and good will of the *Proueador*.

The chiefe Boat-swain hath for his whole pay 50 Milreyes, and receiueth 10 in ready money. The Guardian, that is the quarter master, hath 1400 Reyes the moneth, and for fraught 2800, and receiueth 7 Milreyes in ready money. The *Seto Pilito*, which is the Masters mate, hath 1200 Reyes, which is three Duckets the moneth, and as much fraught as the quarter Master. Two Carpenters, and two Callafaren which helpe them, haue each man foure Ducats a moneth, and 3900 Milreyes fraught. The Steward that giueth out their meate and drinke, and the *Merinho*, which is he that imprisoneth men aboord, and hath charge of all the Munition and Powder, with the deliuering forth of the same, hath each man a Milreye the moneth, and 2340 Reyes fraught, besides their Chambers and freedome of Custome, as also all other Officers, Saylers, Pikemen, Shot, &c. haue euery man after the rate, and every one that serueth in the ship. The Cooper hath three Duckets a moneth, and 3900 Reyes fraught. Two *Strinceros*, those are they which hoise vp the Main-yard by a wheele, and let it downe againe with a wheele as neede is, haue each man one Milrey the moneth, and 2800 Reyes fraught. Three and thirty Saylers haue each man one Milrey the moneth, and 2800 Reyes fraught. Seuen and thirty Rowers haue each man 660 Reyes the moneth, and 1860 Reyes fraught. Foure Pageants, which are Boyes, haue with their fraught 443 Reyes the moneth, one master Gunner, and eight vnder him, haue each man a different pay, some more, some lesse. The Surgeon likewise hath no certaine pay. The Factor and Purser haue no pay but onely their Chambers, that is belowe vnder hatches, a Chamber of twenty pipes, for each man ten pipes, and aboue hatches each man his Cabbin to sleepe in, whereof they make great profit. These are all the Officers and other persons which sayle in the ship, which haue for their portion euery day in victuals, each man alike, as well the greatest as the least, a pound and three quarters of Bisket, halfe a Can of wine, a Can of water, an Aroba which is 32 pound of salt flesh the moneth. Some dried Fish, Onions and Garleeke are eaten in the begining of the Voyage, as being of small value; other prouisions, as Sugar, Honie, Raisins, Prunes, Rice, and such like, are kept for those which are sicke: yet they get but little thereof, for that the Officers keepe it for themselues, and spend it at their pleasures, not letting much goe out of their fingers: as for the dressing of their meate, Weede, Pots, and Pannes, euery man must make his owne prouision: besides all this there is a Clarke and Steward for the Kings Souldiers that haue their parts by themselues, as the Saylers haue.

This is the order and manner of their Voyage when sayle they vnto the *Indies*, but when they returne againe they haue no more but each man a portion of Bisket and Water vntill they come to the Cape *de Bona Esperance*, and from thence home they must make their owne prouisions. The Souldiers that are passengers haue nothing else but free passage, that is roome for a Chest vnder hatches, and place for their Bed in the Orloope, and may not come away without the Viceroyes pasport, and yet they must haue beene fiue yeeres Souldiers in the *Indies* before they can haue licence, but the Slaues must pay fraught for their bodies, and custome to the King. The one and twentieth of September wee entred the Riuer into the Road vnder the Land of *Bardes*.

CHAPTER II.

OF THE TOWNE AND ISLAND OF GOA, CHIEFE CITY OF INDIA.

The Citie of *Goa*, is the Metropolitan or chiefe Citie of all the Orientall *Indies*, where the *Portugals* haue their traffique, where also the Vice-roy, the Arch-bishop, the Kings Counsell, and Chancerie haue their residence, and from thence are all places in the Orientall *Indies*, gouerned and ruled. There is likewise the staple for all *Indian* commodities, whither all sorts of Merchants doe resort, comming thither both to buy and sell, and out of *Arabia*, *Armenia*, *Persia*, *Cambaia*, *Bengala*, *Pegu*, *Sian*, *Malacca*, *Iaua*, *Molucca*, *China*, &c. The Citie and Iland of *Goa* lieth vnder 15 degrees, on the North side, and is distant from the Equinoctial, (by the way that the *Portugals* ships, doe come thither from *Mossambique*) foure hundred miles. It is an Iland wholly compassed about with a Riuer, and is aboue three miles great, it lieth within the Coast of the Firme Land, so that the Iland, with the Sea coast of the Firme Land, doe both reach as farre as each other into the Sea. It is onely separated from the firme Land by an arme of the Sea, or of the Riuer, that runneth in by the North side of the Towne, and so round about the Iland to the South side, where it entreth againe into the Sea, and is in forme almost like a Halfe-moone. The Riuer runneth euen vnto the Towne, and is indifferent broad, there are betweene the Firme Land and the Iland, certaine small Ilands that are all inhabited by the natural borne Countrimen, and on the other side of the towne the Riuer is there so small, that in Summer time, by wading to the knees in water, a man may passe it ouer on foot. On the which side the Iland hath a wall with certaine Bulwarkes, which the *Portugals* of late yeeres haue caused to be made, to defend them from the Firme Land in time of warre, as it often hapneth, for it hath diuers time beene besieged by *Dialcan* or *Hidalcam*, at the mouth and the entrie of the Riuer. On the North side lieth the Land of *Bardes*, which is high Land, vnder which Land the *Portugals* doe anchor safely out of all danger, and there they haue a place to lade and vnlade their wares. This Land of *Bardes* is also vnder the *Portugall* subiection, and is full of Villages inhabited with people that are of the Firme Land, lying aboue it, called *Canarign* who for the most part are *Christians*, but obserue their owne manner of apparell, which is to goe all naked, their priuie members onely couered. This Land is full of *Indian* Palme trees, whereon the *Indian* Nuts called *Cocos* doe growe, as also on all the Ilands lying in the Riuer. This Iland of *Bardes* is separated from the Firme Land by a small Riuer, which is so little, that it cannot almost be discerned from the Firme Land. On the South side by the Iland of *Goa*, where the Riuer runneth againe into the Sea, there commeth euen out with the coast a Land called *Salsette*, which is also vnder the subiection of the *Portugals*, and is inhabited, and planted both with people and fruit, like the Land of *Bardes*, and is likewise parted with a little Riuer from the Firme Land. Betweene this Land of *Salsette*, and the Iland of *Goa*, lie also some small Ilands, all full of *Indian* Palme trees, and by the mouth or issue of the Riuer, lieth an Iland which is called *Goa Valha*, that is old *Goa*, from whence there commeth no speciall thing, neither is it much inhabited. Those Lands of *Bardes* and *Salsette*, are by the Kings of *Portugall* let out to farme, and the rents thereof are employed to the payment of the Arch-Bishop, Cloisters, Priests, and other the Kings Officers, yeerely stipends, which is granted them by speciall Priuiledges and Patents from the King. The Iland is very hilly, and in some places so desart and rough, that on some sides men can hardly trauell ouer land (but with great labour) to the Towne of *Goa*. The Iland euen to the Sea sides is full of Villages, and inhabited by the *Canarijns* which are the naturall borne people of the Land, and doe altogether liue by working vpon the Land, and by their Palme trees. The Villages and dwellings of these *Canarijns* are most round aboue the Iland, and on the water sides, or by small Lakes, whereof there are some few within the Iland; and the cause why they dwell thus, is for that the Palme trees will not growe in any other place but on lowe ground by the waters, specially in sandy ground: so that there are no Palme trees to bee found on the high land within the Countrie vnlesse it bee vpon sandy grounds on the Sea coast, or Riuers sides. On the East side of the Towne of *Goa* vpwards, into the Riuer, about three miles from Towne of *Bardes*, lieth a place where the *Portugals* ships doe anchor. The Riuer hath some creekes, and a ship of two hundred tunnes or there abouts, may easily discharge before the Towne, but the *Portugals* great ships must discharge themselues at *Bardes*: which being done, they may if they will freely goe and lie before the Towne. The Towne is well built with faire houses and streets, after the *Portugall* manner, but because of the heate there somewhat lower. They commonly haue their Gardens and Orchards at the back-side of their houses, full of all kind of *Indian* fruits: as also the whole Iland through, they have many pleasant Gardens and Farmes, with houses to play in, and trees of *Indian* fruits, whither they goe to sport themselues, and wherein the *Indian* women take great delight. The Towne hath in it all sorts of Cloysters and Churches as *Lisbon* hath, onely it wanteth Nunnes, for the men cannot get the women to trauell so farre, where they should bee shut vp, and forsake *Venus*.

Touching the *Portugals* ivstice and ordinances, as well

in worldly as spirituall causes, they are all one as they are in *Portugall.* They dwell in the Towne among all sorts of Nations, as *Indians, Heathens, Moores, Iewes, Armenians, Guesartes, Benianes, Bramenes,* and of all *Indian* Nations and People, which doe all dwell and traffique therein; euery man holding his owne Religion, without constraining any man to doe against his conscience, onely touching their ceremonies of burning the dead, and the liuing, of marrying and other supperstions and deuillish inuentions, they are forbidden by the Arch-bishop to vse them openly, or in the Iland, but they may freely vse them vpon the Firme Land, and secretly in their houses, thereby to shun and auoide all occasions of dislike that might be giuen to *Christians,* which are but newly baptised: but touching the worldly policy or good gouernment of the Countrie, and executing of iustice, as also for the ruling of the Townsmen in the Citie: it is common to them all, and they are vnder the *Portugals* law, and hee that is once christned, and is after found to vse any heathenish superstitions, is subiect to the Inquisition, whatsoever he be, or for any point of Religion whatsoeuer.

The Iland hath nothing of itselfe to nourish withall, but only some Cattell, Hennes, Goats, Doges, &c. but very few, because of the barrennesse and euill situation of the place, which is a most hilly, barren, and wilde Countrie, and full of waste ground; all their necessaries, as Beasts, Hennes, Hogges, Egges, Milke, &c., come from *Salsette* and *Bardes,* but most part out of the Firme Land, Corne, Rice and other Graine: also Oyle, and all other necessaries come from other Countries, and are brought in by the River, as from *Cambaia* on the North side, and from the coast of *Malabar,* and other places, as in the description of the coast we have in part declared: of Wine called Wine of Palme trees, they haue enough, and so much that they haue to spare for other places. The haue but little fresh water, but onely one Well, called *Banganijn,* which standeth about a quarter of a mile without the Citie, wherewith the whole Towne is serued, which the slaues fetch in Pots and sell it in the Towne, and is very good to drinke: for water to dresse meate, wash, and doe other things withall, they commonly haue Wells within their houses: the Land of itselfe is very stony and drie, hauing a kind of red earth, so that some *Italian* Alchimists haue promised to get Copper and Gold out of some, which neither the King nor Viceroy would ever consent unto, fearing lest the report of such treasure would be the occasion of greater trouble.

The *Portugals* in *India*, are many of them married with the natural born women of the Countrie, and the children proceeding of them are called *Mestiços*, that is, *half-countrimen*. These *Mestiços* are commonly of yellowish colour, notwithstanding there are many women among them that are faire and well formed. The children of the *Portugals*, both boyes and girles, which are borne in *India*, are called *Castiços*, and are in all things like unto the *Portugals*, only somewhat differing in colour, for they draw toward a yellow colour: the children of those *Castiços* are yellow, and altogether like the *Mestiços*, and the children of *Mestiços* are of colour and fashion like the natural borne Countrimen or *Decanijns* of the Countrie, so that the posteritie of the *Portugals*, both men and women being in the third degree do seeme to be naturall *Indians*, both in colour and fashion. Their liuings and daily traffiques are to *Bengala*, *Pegu*, *Malacca*, *Cambaia*, *China*, and euery way, both North and South: also in *Goa* there is holden a daily assemblie or meeting together, as well of the Citizens and Inhabitants, as of all Nations throughout *India*, and of the Countries bordering on the same, which is like the meeting vpon the *Burse* in *Antwerpe*, yet differeth much from that, for that hither in *Goa* there come as well Gentlemen, as Merchants and others, and there are all kindes of *Indian* commodities to sell, so that in a manner it is like a Faire.

This meeting is onely before noone, euery day in the yeere, except Sundayes and Holidayes : it beginneth in the morning at seuen of the clocke, and continueth till nine of the clocke, but not in the heate of the day, nor after noone, in the principall street of the Citie named the *Straight street*, and is called the *Leylon*, which is as much to say, as an outroop : there are certaine Criers appointed by the Citie for the purpose, which haue of all things to be cried and sold : these goe all the time of the *Leylon* or Outroop, all behangd about with all sorts of gold chaines, all kinds of costly Iewels, Pearles, Rings, and Precious stones: likewise they haue, running about them, many sorts of Captiues and Slaues, both men and women, young and old, which are daily sold there, as beasts are sold with vs, where euery one may chuse which liketh him best, euery one at a certaine price. There are also *Arabian* Horses, all kind of Spices and dried Drugs, sweet Gummes, and such like things, fine and softly Couerlets, and many curious things, out of *Cambaia, Sinde, Bengala, China*, &c. and it is wonderfull to see in what sort many of them get their liuings, which every day come thither to buy wares, and at another time sell them again. And when any man dieth, all his goods are brought thither and sold to the last peniworth, in the same outroop, whosoeuer they be, yea, although they were the Vice-royes goods : and this is done to doe right and iustice vnto Orphans and Widows ; and that it may bee sold with the first, where euery man may see it, so that euery yeere there is great quantitie of ware sold within that Citie, for that there die many men within the Towne, by meanes of their disorded liuing, together with the hotnesse of the Countrie : the like assemblie his holden in all places of *India* where the *Portugals* inabite. There are some married *Portugals* that get their liuings by their slaues, both men and women, whereof some haue 10 some 20 and some 30, for it costeth them but little to keep them. These slaues for money do labor for such as haue need of their helpe, some fetch fresh water, and sell it for money about the streets: the women slaues make all sorts of confectures and conserues of *Indian* fruits, much fine needle-worke, both cut and wrought workes, and then their masters send the fairest and the youngest of them well drest vp with their wares about the streets to sell the same, that by the neatnesse and beauty of the said women slaues, men might be moued to buy, which hapneth more for the affection they haue to the slaues, & to fulfill their pleasure with them, then for any desire to the conserues or needle-workes: for these slaues do never refuse them, but make their daily liuing thereby, and with the gaines that they by that meanes bring home, their masters may well keepe and maintayne them. There are others that vse exchanging of moneys, and to buy money when it commeth, as time serueth to sell it again, for they buy the Rials of eight, when the ships come from *Portugall*, whereof some buy at the least ten or twelve hundred, and keepe them till the moneth of April, which is the time when ships sayle to *China*, for then are Rials of eight sought for to carrie thither, & are commonly worth fiue and twenty or thirty in the hundred profit, and then they receiue for them a certaine money, which at the same time is brought from *Ormus*, called *Larryns*, that come out of *Persia*, which they buy for eight or ten in the hundred profit, and keep them till the *Portugals* on the moneth of September come thither, and so deliuer them againe for twenty or fiue and twenty in the hundred profit, in exchange for Rials of eight, as I said before, for they must haue these *Larryns* with them to *Cochin*, to buy Pepper and other wares, for that is the best and most profitable money. There are yet other sorts of money called *Pagods*, *Venetianerss*, and *Santbone* which are gold, all which they doe likewise buy and sell, so that there are many that doe nothing else, and become rich, specially he that hath a good stocke. This exchange commeth most commonly from the Spiritualtie, who doe secretly vse it, by other mens meanes, without any let or hinderance. Some there are that liue vpon their rents which they haue by their Palme trees.

There are among them but two manner of people, that is, Married men, and Souldiers, for that all Young men vnmarried are named Souldiers, which is the best name that a man can haue ; not that the Souldiers are any wayes bound or vnder the commandement and Regiment of any Captaine, which throughout *India* is not vsed, but when the *Portugals* come into *India* out of *Portugall*, and are arriued there, euery man goeth where he thinketh best, although in *Portugall* euery mans name that goeth in the ship is written and registred, which is done in this sort: euery man is written vp, both his name and sirname, with a note what pay they receiue of the King, whereof some beare the title of *Fidalgo da Caza del Rey nossas Senor*, that is, a Gentleman of the Kings House, which is the chiefest title : there are others named *Mozos Fidalgos*, which is also an Honourable title, and they are commonly Gentlemens Sonnes, or by the Kings fauour aduanced thereunto : There are yet others that are named *Caualhiero Fidalgo*, which is not so much as the other two, yet it is an Honourable title, and is the title of a Knight, who for some Valiant act by him done is made Knight, which they doe for a small matter : for that if he doe any Act to be accounted of, or be in a manner of such an action doing, presently he is of a Captaine or a Gentleman made a Knight, whereof they much boast themselues : and it is now growne so common among them, that very Cookes Boyes and others as meane as they, are made Knights: there are others also that are named *Mosos da Camara, do Numero, e do Seruiço*, which is seruants to the King, some of his Chamber, some of his Accounts, and some for his Seruice, this is the first Title or Degree of credite, whereby through their good seruice they attaine vnto better, and are more glorious of their Titles, then of all the riches in the world. There are also that are named *Escuderos Fidalgos*, that is Esquires, which is likewise a degree of credit: Others are named *Hommes honorados*, which is men of Honour, and the poorest among them (which are not named by any title) are set downe for Souldiers, which are the common and Rascall sort: these are euery man paied their wages according to their Titles, and may each man in his qualitie (by long seruice, or some good action, but most by fauour) rise to higher degree; for that according to their Titles their seruice is rewarded. The *Portugals* which sayle for *India* being thus registred and written downe, the said Register at their arriuall there, is deliuered to be kept by one of the Kings Officers thereunto appointed, which euery three yeeres is likewise changed, as other Officers are, and is called the chiefe Clerke of the *Matricola* Gallener.

The *Portugals*, *Mesticos* and *Christians*, keeps Worshipfull and bountifull Houses, hauing commonly (as it is said before) fiue, sixe, ten, twentie, some more, some lesse Slaues, both men and women, in their houses euery man according to his estate and qualitie. I meane Married men. They are very cleanly and sweet in all things belonging to their Houses, specially in their Linnen, for that euery day they change Shirts and Smockes both men and women, and their Slaues and Seruants likewise, with other things that they weare, which they doe because of the great heat in that Land. The *Portugals* are commonly serued with great grauitie without any difference betweene the Gentleman and the common Citizen, Townesman or Souldier, and in their going, curtesies, and conuersations, common in all things: when they goe in the Streets they step very softly and slowly forwards with a great pride and vaine-glorious maiestie, with a Slaue that carrieth a great Hat or vayle ouer their heads to keepe the Sunne and Raine from them. Also when it raineth they commonly haue a Boy that beareth a Cloake of Scarlet or of some other Cloth after them, to cast ouer them: and if it bee before Noone, he carrieth a Cushion for his Master to kneele on when he heareth Masse, and their Rapier is most commonly carried after them by a Boy, that it may not trouble them as they walke, nor hinder their Grauities. When they meet in the streets a good space before they come together, they begin with a great *Besolas maos*, to stoope with their bodies, and to thrust forth their foot to salute each other, with their Hats in their hands, almost touching the ground: likewise when they come into the Church where they haue Stooles readie, which their Slaues haue prepared for them: all that are by him that commeth in, doe stand vp, and with the same manner of bowing their bodies doe him great Reuerence, and if it chanceth that any doth him reuerence (as the manner is) and that hee to whom it is done doth not greatly esteeme thereof, so that he doth him not the like curtesie, they doe altogether for that cause goe after him, and cut his Hat in peeces, saying that he had disgraced the partie, wherein it is not for them to aske wherefore they should so doe, for it would bee the greatest shame and reproach in the world vnto them, if they should not reuenge so great an iniurie: and when they seeke to be reuenged of any man that hath shewen them discurtesie, or for any other cause whatsoever it bee, they assemble ten or twelue of their Friends, acquaintance or companions, and take him wheresoeuer they find him, and beat him so long together, that they leaue him for dead, or verie neare dead, or else cause him to be stabbed by their Slaues. But if they desire not to kill him, they baste him well about the ribbes and all his bodie ouer with a thicke Reed, as big as a mans legge, which is called *Bambus*, whereby for eight daies after and more he hath enough to doe to keepe his Bed, and sometime in that manner they leaue him for dead. This is their common Custome, and is neuer looked vnto or once corrected. Also they vse long bagges full of Sand, wherewith they will giue such blowes each vpon the other, that therewith they will breake each others limbes, and for euer after make them lame.

When any man goeth to visit another in his House, although he which is visited bee one of the principall Gentlemen of the Citie, and the visitor but a simple Souldier, or some other man, it is the manner that hee which is visited commeth vnto the doore of his House, with his Hat in his hand, and with great curtesie to receiue him that commeth to visit him, and so leadeth him vp into his Hall or Chamber, wherein hee will speake with him, where he offereth him a Chaire to sit downe, and then he himselfe sitteth by him, then he asketh him what he would haue, which hauing vnderstood hee bringeth him downe againe to the doore in the like sort, and so with a *Besolas manos*, biddeth him farewell, and if he should not doe so, or when he giueth him a Stoole, should giue him one vnlined, or one that is lesse or lower than that he taketh for himselfe, hee that visiteth him would take it in euill part, esteeming it a great scorne, and seeke to be reuenged on him for the same.

When they haue any Weddings and are married, whosoeuer they bee if they haue any wealth, all the Friends and Neighbours come together, euery man on Horsebacke and hee that hath not a Horse will borrow one, and are euery man very costly Apparelled, at the least some fiftie or a hundreth Horses little more or lesse, as the person is of qualitie, and so they ride altogether in good order vnto the Church with their Seruants, and euery man his Hat for the Sunne, the Parents and Friends in the hinder part, and in the last row the Bridegroome betweene two of them, whom they call Gossops: after them followeth the Bride betweene two *Commeres* each in their *Pallamkin*, which is most costly made, and after follow the Slaues both men and women going in Troupes, as if they ranne to Hunt, and so coming to the Church, and being Married according to the order vsed in the Church of *Rome*; they are in the same order brought home againe, and passing through the streets, the neighbours leaning vpon *Indian* Carpets looke out of the windowes, and throw Rose water vpon the Bride and Bridegroome, and other sweet smelling waters, with Roses and Sugar Comfets, or Corne. In the meane time their Slaues play vpon Shalmes and Trumpets most pleasant and melodious to heare, and comming to the House where the Bride and Bridegroome dwell with great reuerence and courtesie bowing down their bodies, they take their leaues of all the Companie, which are all on Horsebacke about the doore. And so the Bride the Bridegroome and the *Commeres*, goe vp and sit with great grauitie in a Window, and then begin the Horsemen that led them to Church, in honour of the Married couple, one after the other to runne a course, the Gossops beginning first, and the rest following twice or thrice one after the other, with continuall playing on Shalmes, which are very common in *India*, for that he which is of any wealth hath them of his owne within his House. This being ended, they all passe before the window where the Bride & Bridegroome sit with a great reuerence, and so passe on all sauing the Gossops, for they goe vp to the Bride and Bridegroome, and bid *God giue them Ioy*; then is there some Comfets and Marchpane brought forth, to drinke a Cup of water withall, and after some curteous salutations and congratulations to the new Married couple, they take their leaues and depart: so there remaineth with the Bride and Bridegroome but three or foure of their nearest friends and kinsmen, for whom there is a Dinner prepared, with litle meat, yet very costly, which they passe ouer very lightly, and not many words, which done they presently bring the Bride to Bed, without any other Ceremonies or Charges, wherewith the Marriage is done and ended. Oftentimes it chanceth, that they goe to bed at the least two houres before Sun-setting, not hauing the patience to stay so long as wee doe in these Countries.

When a Child is to bee Christened, it is likewise in the same sort led to Church with Horses, and last of all commeth the Father alone, after whom followeth two men on Foot, the one with a great Siluer or Gilt vessell full of Bread baked like Cracklings, which in *Portugall* are called *Rosquilhos*, and in the middle a great Waxe candle, well made and gilded, thrust through with some peeces of money of Gold and Siluer, for an Offering to the Priest that baptiseth the Child, and all ouer strowed and couered with Roses; the other carrieth a great Siluer or gilt Saltseller in one of his hands, and a Lampe of the same stuffe in his other hand, each with rich and costly Towels on their shoulders: after that followeth two *Pallamkins*, on the one side the *Commere*, on the other side the Midwife with the Child, couered with a costly Mantle, made for the purpose, and so the ceremonies of Baptisme being ended in the Church, it is againe in the like sort brought home, and being there, they haue the like manner of Musicke & Shalmes, running and leaping with their Horses before the window where the *Commere* sitteth, with the same Ceremonies as at the Wedding. This is the manner and custome of those that are Married and keepe House.

But concerning the Souldier that is vnmarried, thus it is. They goe in the Summer time into the *Armado* lying on the water, and being within the Townes and on the Land, they are verie stately apparelled and goe verie grauelie along the streets with their Slaues or men hired for the purpose, that beare Hat ouer them for the Sunne and Raine: for there are many *Indians* that are daily hired for the purpose, and haue twelue *Basarucos* the day which is as much as two Stiuers or a Stoter, and they serue such as haue no slaues, and that will not keepe any to that end. The Soudiers dwell at least ten or twelue in a house, where they haue among them a slaue or hired *Indian* or two which serueth them and washeth their Shirts, and haue foure or fiue Stooles with a Table, and euerie man a Bed. Their meat is Rice sodden in water, with some salt Fish, or some other thing of small value (without Bread) and cleare Fountaine water for their drinke, wherewith they are well pleased. They haue amongst them all one or two good suites of Apparell, all of Silke as the manner is there, and when one goeth abroad, the other stay at home, for in the house they haue no need of Clothes (but sit whoseuer they be) in their Shirts and a paire of linnen Breeches, and so as it were naked by reason of the great heat, for if some of them haue occasion to goe out twentie times in one day, they must so often lend him their Apparell, and he must likewise put off his clothes, as often as he commeth home againe. Some Souldiers haue a Gentleman or Captaine to their friends which lendeth them money to apparell themselues withall, to the end when Summer time commeth, they may bee readie to goe with them in Fleet to Sea, as also to haue their friendship, by night and at other times to beare them companie, or to helpe them to be reuenged of any iniurie by them receiued as I said before: for that he which in *India* hath most Souldiers to his friends, is most regarded and feared. So that to be short, in this manner they doe maintaine themselues in common, whereby they are able to come in presence of the best of the Countrey. Many and most of them haue their chiefe maintainance from the *Portugals* and *Mestiços* wiues, as also the *Indian Christians* wiues, which doe alwaies bestow liberall rewards and gifts vpon them to fulfill their unchaste desires, which they know very well how to accomplish, and secretly bring to passe. There are some likewise that get their liuing by their Friends, trauelling for them from place to place with some wares and Merchandizes, and they are called *Chattijns.* These doe giue ouer and leaue the office of a Souldier in the Fleet, and the Kings seruice: and now likewise they are all giuen to scraping and catching, as well the Vice-roy, Gouernours, and others, as also the Church-men and Spiritualtie, little passing or esteeming the common profit or the seruice of the King, but onely their particular profites, making their account, that the time of their abode is but three yeeres : wherefore they say they will not doe otherwise then those that were before them did, but say that others which come after them shall take care for all: for that the King (say they) gaue them their Offices, thereby to pay them for their seruices in times past.

The *Portugals*, *Mesticos*, and *Indian Christian* women in *India* are little seene broad, but for the most part sit still within the house, and goe but seldome forth, unlesse it bee to Church, or to visit their friends, which is likewise but verie little, and when they goe abroad, they are well prouided not to be seene, for they are carried in a *Pallamkin* couered with a Mat or other cloth, so that they cannot be seene.

When they goe to Church, or to visit any friend, they put on very costly apparell, whith bracelets of Gold, and Rings vpon their armes, all beset with costly Iewels & Pearles, & at their eares hang laces full of Iewels. Their clothes are of Damaske, Veluet, and cloth of Gold, for Silke is the worst thing they doe weare. Within the house they goe bare headed, with a Wastcoate called *Bain*, that from their shoulders couereth their nauels and is so fine that you may see all their body through it, and downwards they haue nothing but a painted cloth wrapped three or foure times about their bodies. These clothes are very faire some of them being verie costly wrought with Loome-worke, and diuers figures and flowers of all colours, all the rest of the body is naked without any hose, but onely bare-footed in a paire of Moiles or Pantofles, and the men in like sort. This is their manner in the House both old and young, rich and poore, none excepted, for they goe forth but very little, and then they are both couered and carried, and what they need abroad, that the Slaues both men and women doe fetch in. The Women eate no Bread or very little, nor yet the Slaues, not that they refuse it for the dearenesse or waut of bread, (for they haue enough and great abundance) but they are so vsed to eate Rice, that they desire no other, which they seeth with water and eate it with some salt Fish or a kind of salt fruit called *Mangas*, or with some other composition both of Fish and Flesh, with Pottage which they powre vpon it, and so eate it with their hands: for there they eate nothing with Spoones, and if they should see any man doe so, they would laugh at him. When they drinke they haue certaine pots made of blacke earth verie fine and thinne, much like those that wee vse in *Holland* for Flower-pots, hauing in the necke thereof a partition full of holes with a spout, (and these Cruses are called *Gorgoletta*,) to this end, that when they drinke, they may hold the pot on high, and touch it not with their mouthes, but the water running from the spout falleth into their mouthes, neuer spilling drop which they doe for cleanlinesse, because no man should put it to his mouth, and when any man commeth out of *Portugall*, and then beginneth to drinke after their manner, because he is not vsed to that kind of drinking, hee spilleth it in his bosome, wherein they take great pleasure and laugh at him, calling him *Reynol*, which is a name giuen in iest to such as newlie come for *Portugall*, and know not how to behaue themselues in such graue manner, and with such ceremonies as the *Portugals* vse there in *India* : so that at the first they are much whooped and cried at in the streets, vntill by use and practice they haue learned the *Indian* manner, which they quicklie doe. The men are very iealous of their Wiues, for they will neuer bring any man into their houses, how speciall a friend soeuer hee be, that shall see their Wiues or their Daughters, vnlesse it be some gossip or other married man with his wife in companie. When they will goe together to some place to sport and solace themselues, they are alwaies well guarded by their Slaues, both men and woman for their safetie and seruice. If any man commeth to the doore to aske for the Master of the House, presently their Wiues and their Daughters runne to hide them, and so leaue the man to answer him that standeth at the doore : likewise they suffer no man to dwell within their houses, where the Women and Daughters be, how neere kinsman souer he been unto them, being once fifteene yeeres of age, nor their owne Sonnes, but haue certaine Chambers and places beneath, or besides their house where they lie, and may in no sort come among the women, and thither they send them their meat and other prouisions, for it hath oftentimes beene seene in those Countries, that the Nephew hath layne by his Aunt, and the Brother by the Brothers wife, and the Brother with his Sister : whereof I haue knowne some that haue been taken in the manner, and that both they and the woman haue been slaine by the Husbands. The women are very Luxurious and vnchaste, for there are very few among them, although they be married, but they haue besides their husbands one or two of those that are called Souldiers, with whom they take their pleasures : which to effect, they vse all the flights and practises they can deuise, by sending out their slaues and Baudes by night, and at extraordinary times, ouer Walls, Hedges, and Ditches, how narrowly soeuer they are kept and looked vnto. They haue likewise an Hearbe alled *Deutroa* which beareth a seed, whereof bruising out the sap, they put it into a Cup or other vessell, and give it to their Husbands, either in meat or drinke, and presently therewith, the man is as though he were halfe out of his wits, and without feeling, or else drunke, doing nothing but laugh, and sometime it taketh him sleeping, whereby he lyeth like a dead man, so that in his presence they may doe what they will, and take their pleasure with their friends, and the husband neuer know of it. In which sort he continueth foure and twentie houres long, but if they wash his feet with cold water hee presently reuiueth, and knoweth nothing thereof, but thinketh he had slept.

There are many men poysoned by their wiues, if once they be moued: for they know how to make a certaine Poyson or Venome, which shall kill the person that drinketh it, at what time or houre it pleaseth them: which poyson being prepared, they make it in such sort, that it will lie sixe yeeres in a mans body, and neuer doe him hurt, and then kill him, without missing halfe an houres time. They make it also for one, two or three yeeres, monethe or dayes, as it pleaseth them best, as I haue seene it in many,and there it is very common. There are likewise many women brought to their ends by meanes of their Husbands, and slaine when soeuer they take them in Adulterie, or that they doe but once suspect them; which if they doe, presently they cut their throats, and bring three or foure witnesses to testifie that strange men entred into their houses by night, at vnaccustomed times, or else by day, and had their pleasures of their Wiues, or in other sort as they will deuise it; whereby they are presently discharged of the crime, according to the Lawes and Ordinances both of *Spain* and *Portugall* and presently may marrie with another wife. This notwithstanding is no meanes to make the Women feare, or once to leaue their pleasures, although there are euery yeere many women without number so dispatched and made away by their husbands, and it is so common with them, that no man thinketh it strange, or once wondereth there at, because of the Custome. The Women also for their part say and flatly affirme, that there can be no better death then to die in that manner, saying that so they are sacrificed for Loue, which they thinke to be a great Honour vnto them.

The women are by nature very cleanly and neat, as well in their Houses as in Apparell, for that although all whatsoeuer shee putteth on her bodie euery day, is both white, cleane and fresh: yet they haue a manner euery day to wash themselues all the bodie ouer, from head to foot, and sometimes twice a day, in the morning and at euening. They are no great workers, but much de lighted in sweet Herbes, and in perfumes and Frankincense, and to rub their bodies and their foreheads with Sweet Sanders and such like woods, which with water they doe steepe or breake in peeces: also the whole day long they doe nothing, but sit and chaw Leaues or Herbes, called *Bettele* with Chaulke and a certaine Fruit called *Arrequa*, whereof in another place among Fruits and Herbes I will speake more. This *Arrequa*, some of it is so strong, that it maketh men almost drunke, and wholly out of sence, although in shew and in taste it is almost like Wood or Rootes: these three things they sit all the whole day chawing in their mouthes, like Oxen or Kine chawing the cudde: they let the sap goe downe into their throats, and spit the rest out of their mouthes, whereby they make their mouthes so red and blackish, that to such as know it not it is strange to see: all which, with their washing, Frankinsence, and rubbing with Sanders, they haue learned and receiued of the Indian Heathens, which haue had those Customes of long time, and yet till this day vse them: they say it preserueth the Teeth, and keepeth them sound, good for the mawe, and against a stinking mouth and euill breath, insomuch as they are so vsed to chaw it, that wheresoeuer they goe or stand, they must alwaies haue of those Leaues caried with them, and the women Slaues doe likewise goe alwaies chawing, and are so vsed thereunto, that they verilie thinke, that without it they can not liue, for their common works is to sit all day, when their Husbands are out of doores, behind the Mat which hangeth at the window, alwaies chawing the herbe *Bettele*, seeing those that passe by in the streets, and no man seeth them: but as any man passeth by which liketh them, and they will let them haue a sight, they lift vp the Mat, where by they doe the passenger a great fauour, and with that manner of shewing themselues and casting looks, they make their beginnings of Loue, which by their slauish women they bring to effect: to the which end they haue all diuellish deuises that possible may bee inuented, for that both night and day they doe practise no thing else, but it make their onely worke, and to make nature more liuely to abound and moue them thereunto, they doe vse to eate those *Betteles*, *Arrequas* and Chaulke, and in the night it standeth by their bed sides, thus they eate, whole handfuls of Cloues, Pepper, Ginger, and a baked kind of meat called *Chachunde*, which is mixed and made of all kinds of Spices and Herbes, and such like meates.

And they are not content therewith, but giue their Husbands a thousand herbes for the same purpose to eate, they not knowing thereof, thereby to fulfill their pleasures, and to satisfie their desires, which can not by any means bee satisfied. They are likewise much vsed to take their pleasures in Bathes, by swimming therein, which they can verie well doe, for there are verie few of them, but they would easilie swim ouer a Riuer of halfe a mile broad.

Everie three yeeres there is a new Vice-roy sent into *India*, and sometime they stay longer, as it pleaseth the King, but verie few of them, he continueth in *Goa*. In the Hall of his Palace stand the Guard, and in the great Hall, where his Councell sit, are painted all the Viceroyes, that haue gouerned in *India*, since the first Discouerie and Conquest thereof, and as they new come, their Pictures are likewise placed there. These Viceroyes haue great reuenues, they may spend, giue, and keepe the Kings treasure, which is verie much, and doe with it what pleaseth them, for it is in their choice, hauing full and absolute power from the King, in such sort, that they gather and hoord vp a mightie quantitie of Treasure, for that besides their great allowance from the King, they haue great Presents and Gifts, bestowed vpon them. For it is the custome in those Countries, when any Viceroy commeth newly ouer, that all the Kings bordering about *Goa*, and that haue peace and friendship with the *Portugals*, doe then send their Ambassadours vnto him, to confirme their Leagues with great and rich Presents, therewith likewise to bid the Viceroy welcome, which amounteth to a great masse of Treasure: these Presents in this sort giuen the *Iesuites*, by their practises had obtained of the King, and for a time enioyed them at their pleasure (looking verie narrowly vnto them, that they might not be deceiued) vntill long time since, a Viceroy named *Don Lois de Taide* Earle of *Atougia* came thither, and refused to let them haue them, saying that the King being in *Portugall* knew not what was giuen him in *India*, and that those Presents were giuen vnto the Viceroy and not to the King, and said the King had no power to giue them to the *Iesuites*: so that hee kept them for himselfe, which the *Iesuites* tooke in euill part, and said, the Viceroy was an Hereticke. Yet from his time euer since the Viceroyes have vsed to keepe them for themselues. They say, and it is found to bee most true, that the first yeere of the Viceroyes time, he hath enough to doe to repaire and furnish his House, and to know the manners and customes of the Countries, without any further troubling of himself. The second yeere to gather Treasure, and to looke vnto his particular profits, for the which cause he came into *India*. The third and last yeere to prepare himself and set all things in order, that he bee not ouertaken or surprised by the new Viceroy when hee commeth, but that he may returne into *Portugall* with the goods which he had scraped together. The same is to bee vnderstood of all the Captaines in the Fortes, and of all other Officers in *India*.

In the Towne and Iland of *Goa*, are resident manie *Heathens*, *Moores*, (which are *Mahumetans*) *Jewes*, and all strange Nations bordering thereabout, euerie one of them vsing seuerall customes and superstions in Religion. The *Moores* eate all things except Swines flesh, and dying are buried like the *Iewes*; but the *Heathens* as *Decanijns*, *Gusarates*, and *Canaras*, and other *Indians* being dead, are burnt to ashes, and some Women being aliue are burned with them, that is, such as are Gentlemen or Noblemen, and the Wiues of the *Bramenes*, which are their Idolatrous Priests. Also for the Merchants, some of them eate all things except Kowes, or Buffles flesh, which they esteeme to be Holy. Others eate not any thing whatsoeuer, that hath either life or bloud in it, as those of *Gusarata*, and the *Banianes* of *Cambaia*, which obserue *Pythagras* Law: most of them pray vnto the Sunne and Moone yet they doe all acknowledge God that made, created and ruleth all things, and that after this life there is another, where in men shall be rewarded according to their workes. But they haue Idols and Images, which they call *Pagodes*, cut and formed most vglie, and like monstrous Diuels, to whom daily they offer, and say, that those Holy men haue been liuing among them, where of they tell so many Miracles as it is wonderfull, and say, that they are intercessours betweene them and God. The Diuell often times answereth them out of those Images, whom they likewise know, and doe him great honour by offering vnto him, to keeph friendship with him, and that hee should not hurt them. They haue a Custome, when any Maide is to be married, and that they will honour their *Pagode*, for the more credit to the Bridegroome, they bring the Bride with great Triumph and Musicke before their *Pagode*, to whom the nearest friends and kinswomen of the Bride, together with the Bride doe goe * * * * * * * and then after other diuellish superstitions and Ceremonies, hauing made their Offerings, they bring the Bride home, where shee is deliuered to the Bridegroome, hee being very ioyfull and proud, that *Pagode* hath honoured him so much. They haue for the most part a custome to Pray vnto the first thing they meet with all in the Morning, and all that day after they pray vnto it, bee it Hog, or any other thing. And if in the morning they goe out, they chance at the first sight to see a Crow (whereof there are great numbers in *India*) they will not goe forth of their doors all that day no not for all the goods in the world, for they esteeme it an euill signe, and an *vnluckie* day. They pray likewise to the *New Moonie*, and when she first appeareth, they fall upon their knees, and salute her with great Deuotion. There are among them, certaine people called *Iogos*, which are such as we call Hermits, & those doe they esteem for Holie men; these men liue a verie strict life with great Abstinence, and make the common people beleeue many strange things. They haue likewise many Southsaiers and Witches, which vse Iugling, and trauell throughout the Countrie, hauing about them many liue Snakes, which they know how to bewitch, and being shut vp in little Baskets, they pull them out and make them dance, turne, and winde at the sound of a certaine Instrument, whereon they play, and speake vnto them. They wind them about their neckes, armes, and legges, kissing them, with a thousand other deuises, onely to get money. They are all for the most part verie skilfull in preparing of Poysons, wherewith they doe many strange things, and easilie poyson each other; their dwellings and Houses are verie little and low, couered with Straw without windowes, and verie low and narrow doores, so that a man must almost creepe vpon his knees to go in: their Houshold stuffe is Mats of straw, both to sit and lie vpon, their Tableclothes, and Napkins, are made of the great *Indian* Fig-leaues, they serue them not onely for Tables, Sheetes, and other Linnen, but also for Dishes, wherein they put their meat, which you shall likewise see in the Grocers, and Pothecaries shops, to put and wrap in all things whatsoever they haue within their shops, (as wee doe in Paper.) They likewise joyne them together in such sort, that they can put both Butter, Oyle, and much liquid stuffes therein, and also whatsoever came to hand. To dresse their meat they haue certaine Earthen pots wherein they seeth Rice, and make a hole in the ground, wherein they stampe it or beat it with a woodden Pestell made for the purpose, and they live so miserable, that they buy the Rice in the Huskes, as they groweth on the ground, and some of them haue Rice growing behind their House to serue their necessarie vse. They vse to drinke out of a Copper kanne with a spout, whereby they let the water fall downe into their mouthes and neuer touch the Pot with their lippes. Their Houses are commonly strawed with Kow-dung, which they say killeth Fleas. They are verie cleane on their Bodies, for euerie day they wash themselues all their bodie ouer. They wash themselues with the left hand, because they eate with the right hand, and use no Spoones. They doe keepe and obserue their Ceremonies and Superstitions with great deuotion, for they neuer goe forth without praying when they trauell by the way. They haue on euery Hill, Cliffe, Hole, or Denne their *Pagodes* and Idols in most deuilish and deformed shapes cut and hewed out of the stones and rockes, with their Furnaces hard by them, and a Cisterne not farre from them, which is alwaies full of water, and euery one that passeth by, washeth their feet therein, and so fall downe before their Idoll, some setting before him for an offering Fruits, Rice, Egges, Hennes, &c., as their deuotions serue, and then commeth the *Bramene* their Priest and taketh it away and eateth it, making the common people beleeue that the *Pagode* hath eaten it.

When they will make a voyage to Sea, they vse at the least fourteene daies before they enter into their

Ships, to make so great a noise with founding of Trumpets, and to make Fires, that it may bee heard and seene both by night and day, the Ship being hanged about with Flagges, wherewith (they say) they feast their *Pagode*, that they may haue a good Voyage. The like doe they at their returne for a Thanksgiuing fourteene daies long & thus they vse to doe in all their Feasts, Affaires, Mariages, Childbirths,& at other times of the yeere, as Sowing, & Mowing, &c.

The Heathenish *Indians* that dwell in *Goa* are very rich Merchants, and traffique much : there is one street within the Towne, that is full of shops kept by those Heathenish *Indians* that not only sell all kinds of Silkes, Sattins, Damaskes, and curious workes of Porceline from *China* and other places, but all manner of wares, Veluet, Silke, Sattin and such like, brought out of *Portugals* which by means of their Brokers they buy by the great, and sell them againe by the piece or elles wherein they are very cunning, and naturally subtile. There is also another street, where the *Benianes* of *Cambaia* dwell that haue all kinds of wares out of *Cambaia*, and all sorts of precious stones, and are very subtile and cunning to bore and make holes in all kinds of stones, Pearls, and Corrals: on the other side of the same street dwell other Heathens which sell all sorts of Bedsteads, Stooles, and such like stuffe very cunningly couered ouer with Lacke, most pleasant to behold, and they can turne the Lacke into any colour that you will desire. There is also a street full of Gold and Siluer Smiths that are Heathens, which make all kind of workes, also diuers other Handicrafts men, as Coppersmiths, Carpenters, and such like Occupations, which are all Heathens, and euery one a street by themselues. There are likewise other Merchants that deale all by great, with Corne, Rice, and other *Indian* wares and merchandises, as Wood and such like. Some of them farme the Kings Rents and reuenues, so that they are skilfull euery way to make their profits. There are also many Heathen Brokers very cunning and subtile in buying and selling, and with their tongues to pleade on both sides.

There are in *Goa* many Heathen Physicians which obserue their grauities with Hats carried ouer them for the Sunne, like the *Portugalls*, which no other Heathens doe, but onely Ambassadors, or some rich Merchants. These Heathen Physicians doe not onely cure their owne Nations and Countrimen, but the *Portugalls* also, for the Vice-roy himselfe, the Arch-bishop, and all the Monkes and Friers doe put more trust in them then in their owne Countrimen, whereby they get great store of money, and are much honoured and esteemed. The countrimen in the Villages round about *Goa*, and such as labour and till the land are most *Christians*: but there is not much difference among them from the other Heathens, for that they can hardly leaue their Heathenish superstitions, which in part are permitted them, and is done to draw the other Heathens to bee christened, as also that otherwise they would hardly bee parswaded to continue in the *Christian* Faith. There is in euery place of the street Exchangers of money by them called *Xaraffos*, which are all *Christian Iewes*. They are very ready and expert in all manner of accounts, and in knowing of all sorts of money, without whose helpe men dare not receive any money, because there is much counterfeit money abroad, which is hard to be knowne from the good, were it not for these *Xaraffos*, which can discerne it with half an eye. The *Indian* Heathens, have a custome, that no man may change nor alter his *Trade* or *Occupation*, but must use his fathers Trade, and marrie mens daughters of the same Occupation, Trade, or dealing, which is so neerely looked unto, that they are devided and set apart, each Occupation by it selfe, as Countries and Nations are, and so they call one another: for if they speake to a man, they aske him of what Trade he is whether he be a Goldsmith, Barber, Merchant, Grocer, Fisherman, or such like. They give no house-hold-stuff with their daughters, but only Iewels, and pay the charges of the Wedding. The Sonnes inherite all their goods.

The times and seasons of the yeeres are as followeth. Winter beginneth on the last of April, throughout the whole coast which is called *India*, from *Cambaia* to the Cape *de Comorin*, and commeth with a Western winde, which bloweth out of the Sea upon the Coast : the beginning thereof is with thunder and lightning, and after that a stedfast and continuall rains, which lasteth night and day till the moneth of September, and then Winter endeth with thunder and lightning: and by reason of that continuall raine, it is called Winter, as also because at that time they cannot travel on the Seas. But in warm weather, when fruit time commeth on, it is then right Summer: for the time, which in *India* is called Summer, because of the clearenesse and drinesse of the weather, is the colder and the wholsomer, and then there blowe East windes, so that the nights are then very coole, and somewhat sharp; and then there are no speciall kindes of fruits in season, but such as growe continually all the yeere. Against the Winter commeth, euery man maketh his prouision of victuals, and all other necessaries, like as in a ship that is to make a Voyage of fiue or sixe moneths : also all their ships are brought into the Riuer, and vnfurnished of tacklings, and euery thing being taken out of them they are couered with Mats, otherwise they would rot with the raine, which is so stedfast and continuall all the Winter, that many times diuers houses by reason of the great moistnesse doe fall vnto the ground and as soone as Winter beginneth, there driueth into the mouth of the Hauen great bankes and shoales of sands, which stop it vp, so that neither Ship nor Boat can either goe out or in: and the Sea both there and along the coast maketh so great a roaring and noise, that men can neither heare nor see : also the water of the Riuer of

Goa which runneth about the land in Winter, by meanes of the land-waters that by the continuall raine falleth from the Hills, is cleane fresh water, and of a red colour, which in Summer is cleane contrarie and like sea-water by reason of the concours it hath with the Sea. In the Moneth of September when Winter endeth, the bankes of sand doe fleet and vade away out of the Riuer, so that not onely small ships may come in and goe out, but also the great *Portugall* ships of sixteene hundred tunnes may freely enter without Pilot for it is deepe enough, and without danger. In Winter it is a heauy and melancholike being there, for there is no other exercise to be vsed, but onely to sit in their shirts, with a paire of linnen breeches, and goe and passe the time away with their neighbours, in playing and such exercises, for that throughout the whole Towne there is no other doing. The women and *Mesticos* take great pleasure in the Winter time when it raineth, with their husbands and slaues to goe into the fields, or some Garden, whether they carrie good store of victuals, and there in their Garden haue many Cesternes or Ponds of water, wherein they take their delights to swimme and to bathe themselues. In this time most of their *Indian* fruit is in season.

The Summer beginneth in September, and continueth till the last of April, and is alwaies cleare skie and faire weather, without once or very little raining: Then all the ships are rigged and made ready to sayle for all places; as also the Kings Armie to keepe the Coast, and to convoy Merchants, and the East windes beginne to blowe from off the Land into the Seas, whereby they are called *Terreinhos*, that is to say, the *Land windes*. They blowe very pleasantly and cooly, although at the first, by hanging of the weather they are very dangerous, and cause many great deseases, which doe commonly fall in *India*, by the changing of the time. These winds blowe alwaies in Summer, beginning at midnight, and continue till noone, but they never blowe above ten miles into the Sea, from off the coast, and presently after one of the clocke until midnight the West winde bloweth, which commeth out of the Sea into the Land and is called *Virason*. These winds are so sure and certain at their times, as though men held them in their hands, where they make the Land very temperate, otherwise the heate would be unmeasurable.

It is likewise a strange thing that when it is Winter upon the coast of *India*, that is from *Diu* to the Cape *de Comorin*, on the other side of the Cape *de Comorin*, on the coast called *Choramandel*, it is clean contrary, so that there it is Summer, and yet they lie all under one height or degrees, and there is but seventy miles by land betweene both coasts, and in some places, but twenty miles, which is more, as men travel over land from *Cochin* to Saint *Thomas* (which lieth on the same coast of *Choromandel)* and comming by the Hill of *Ballagatte*, where men must pass over to go from the one coast unto the other : on the one side of the Hill to the top thereof it is pleasant clear sunne shinning weather, and going downe on the other side there is raine, winde, thunder and lightning, as if the world should end and be consumed : which is to be understood, that it changeth from the one side to the other, as the time falleth out, so that on the one side of the Hills it is Winter, and on the other side Summer : and it is not only so in that place and Countrie, but also at Ormus, the coast of *Arabia Felix* by the Cape of *Rosatgatte*, where the ships lie, it is very still, cleare, and pleasant water, and faire Summer time ; and turning about the Cape on the other side, it is raine and wind with great stormes and tempests, which with the times of the yeere doe likewise change on the other side, and so it is in many other places on the Orientall Countries.

The sicknesses aud diseases in *Goa*, and throughout

India, which are common, come most with the changing of the times and the weather, as it is said before: there raigneth a sickness called *Mordexin*, which stealeth vpon men, and handleth them in such sort, that it weakneth a man, and maketh him cast out all that he hath in his body, and many times his life withall. This sickness is very common, and killeth many a man, whereof they hardly or neuer escape. The bloudy Fluxe is there likewise very common and dangerous, as the Plague with vs. They haue many continuall Feuers, which are burning Agues, and consume mens bodies with extreme heate, whereby within foure or fiue dayes they are either whole or dead. This sicknesse is common and very dangerous, and hath no remedie for the *Portugals* but letting bloud: but the *Indians* and Heathens doe cure themselues with herbes, as Sanders, and other such like ointments, wherewith they ease themselues. This sicknesse consumeth many *Portugals* euery yeere, some because they haue little to eat and lesse to drinke of any meate or drinke that is nourishing, and vse much company of women, because that Land is naturall to prouoke them thereunto, as also the most part of the Souldiers by such means haue their liuing and their maintenance, which oftentimes costeth them both life and limme, for although men were of Iron or Steele, the vnchaste life of a woman, were able to grind him to powder, and sweepe him away like dust, which costeth many a man's life, as the Kings Hospitall can well beare witnesse, wherein they lodge, when soeuer they are sicke, where euery yeere at the least there entred fiue hundred liue men, and neuer come forth till they are dead, and they are onely *Portugals*, for no other sicke person may lodge therein, I mean such as are called white men, for the other *Indians* haue a Hospitall by themselues. In this Hospitall they are very well looked vnto by the *Iesuites*, and Gentlemen; where of euery moneth one of the best is chosen and appointed, who personally is there by them, and giueth the sicke persons whatsoeuer they will desire, and sometimes spend more by foure or fiue hundred Duckets of their owne purses, then the Kings allowance reached vnto.

But returning to our matter of sicknesse, Pockes and Piles, with other secret diseases, they are in those Countries very common, and not hidden or concealed, for they thinke it no shame, more then to haue any other disease. They heale them with the root China: there are some that haue had them at the least three or foure times, and are not any things at all shunned or disliked for the same, but dare both boast and bragge thereof. It is not any thing perilous for the body, insomuch that they had rather haue them, and feare them lesse then any of the foresaid diseases. The Plague hath neuer been in *India*, neither is it knowne vnto the *Indians*, but poisoning, witchcraft, and such like, whereby some lose their healths, and some their liues, is their daily exercise and very common with them. The stone, grauell, and rupture raigneth much among them, especially among married men, by reason of the great quantitie of water that they drink; being giuen to all pleasure and riotousnesse, enjoying all what their hearts desire sitting alwaies with their bellies open in their shirts in a Gallerie, recreating themselues with the wind which cooleth them, sometimes hauing a slaue to scratch and pare their nayles and feet, another the head, the third holds a Fanne to driue away the Flies. This is the common vse for two houres after noone, where likewise they take an after noones sleepe, and euer as they haue thirst, they bring him a dish of Conserues or other Comfets, that the water should not worke too much in his body, but taste the better. With such and the like exercises they doe passe the day till night comes on, so that commonly they haue all swollen bellies like *Bacchus* whereby the Souldiers and other *Indians* call them *Barrigois*, that it is, *Bellies*, or *Great bellies*.

The day both Summer and Winter is there all of length, not much difference, onely in the change they have about an houres difference. The Sun riseth at sixe, and setteth at sixe. When it is noone, commonly they have the Sunne in the middle of the element just over their heads, and it giveth no shadow, although it stretcheth somewhat out as the Sunne taketh his course. In *Goa* you may see both the Poles of the world, the North and South Starres stand not farre above the Horizon.

The *Bramenes* are the honestest and most esteemed Nation among all the *Indian* Heathens: for they doe alwaies serue in the chiefest places about the King, as Receivers, Stewards, Ambassadors, and such like Offices. They are likewise the Priests and Ministers of the *Pagods* or deuilish Idols. They are of great authoritie among the *Indian* people, for that the King doth nothing without their counsell and consent, and that they may bee knowne from other men, they weare vpon their naked bodie, from the shoulder crosse under the arm over their bodie downe to the girdle, or the cloth that is wrapped about their middle, three or foure strings like sealing thread, whereby they are knowne: which they neuer put off although it should cost them their liues, for their Profession and Religion will not permit it. They goe naked, sauing onely that they haue a cloth bound about their middles. They weare sometimes when they goe abroad, a thinne cotton linnen Gowne called *Cabaia*, lightly cast ouer their shoulders, and hanging downe to the ground like some other *Indians*, as *Benianes Gusarates*, and *Decanyns*. Vpon their heads they weare a white cloth, wound twice or thrice about, therewith to hide their haire, which they neuer cut off, but weare it long and turned vp as the women doe. They haue most commonly round rings of gold hanging at their eares, as most of the *Indians* haue. They eate not any thing that hath life, but feed themselues with herbes and Rice, neither yet when they are sick will for any thing be let bloud, but heale themselues by herbes and ointments, and by rubbing their bodies with Sanders, and such like sweet woods. In Goa and on the Sea coasts there are many *Bramenes*, which commonly doe maintayne themselues with selling of Spices and other Apothecarie ware, but it is not so cleane as others, but full of garbish and dust. They are very subtile in writing and casting accounts, whereby they make other simple *Indians* beleeue what they will.

Touching the points of their Religion, wherein the common people beleeue them to bee Prophets: whatsoeuer they first meet withall in the streets at their going forth, that doe they all the day after pray vnto. The women when they goe forth haue but one cloth about their bodies; which couereth their heads, and hangeth downe vnto their knees: all the rest of the body is naked. They haue rings through their noses, about their legs, toes, neckes and armes, and vpon each hand seuen or eight rings or bracelets, some of siluer and gilt, if they be of wealth and abilitie: but the common people of glasse, which is the common wearing of all the *Indian* women. When the woman is seuen yeeres old, and the man nine yeeres, they doe marrie, but they come not together before the woman be strong enough to beare children. When the *Bramenes* die, all their friends assemble together, and make a hole in the ground, wherein they throwe much wood and other things: and if the man bee of any account, they cast in sweet Saunders, and other Spices, with Rice, Corne, and such like, and much Oyle, because the fire should burne the stronger. Which done, they lay the dead *Bramenes* in it: then commeth his wife with musike and many of her neerest friends all singing certaine praises in commendation of her husbands life, putting her in comfort, and encouraging her to follow her husband, and goe with him into the other world. Then she taketh all her Jewels, and parteth them among her freinds, and so with a cheerful countenance, she leapeth into the fire, and is presently couered with Wood and Oyle: so shee is quickly dead, and with her Husbands body burned to ashes :: and if it chance, as not very often it doth, that any woman refuseth to be burnt with her Husband, then they cut the haire cleane off from her head: and while she liveth she must never after weare any Jewels more, and from that time shee is despised, and accounted for a dishonest woman. These *Bramenes* observe certaine Fasting dayes in the yeere, and that with so great abstinence, that they eate nothing all the day, and sometimes in three or four dayes together. They have their *Pagodes* and Idols, whose Ministers they are, whereof they tell and shew many Miracles, and say that those *Pagodes* have beene men living upon earth, and because of their Holie lives, and good Workes done here in this world, are for a reward thereof, become Holie men in the other world, as by their miracles, by the Divell performed, hath beene manifested unto them, and by their commandements their formes all shapes are made in the most ugly and deformed manner that possible may be devised. Such they Pray and Offer vnto, with many divelish Superstitions, and steadfastly beleeue also that they are their Advocates and Intercessors vnto God. They beleeue also that there is a supreame God aboue, which ruleth all things and that mens soules are Immortall, and that they goe out of this world into the other, both Beasts and Men, and receive reward according to their workes, as *Pythagoras* teacheth, whose Disciples they are.

The *Gusarates* and *Banianes*, are of the Countrey of *Cambaia*: many of them dwell in *Goa, Diu, Chaul, Cochin*, and other places of *India*, because of their trade and traffique in Merchandise, which they use much with all kindes of wares, as Corne, Cotton, Linen, Anil Rice, and other wares, specially and kind of precious Stones wherein they have great skill. They are most subtill and expert in casting of Accounts and Writing, so that they doe not onely surpasse and goe beyond all Jewes and other Nations thereabouts, but also the *Portugals*: and in this respect they have no advantage, for that they are very perfect in the trade of Merchandise, and very readie to deceive men. They eate not anything that hath Life or Blood in it, neither would they kill it for all the goods in the world, how small or unnecessarie soever it were, for that they steadfastly beleeue, that euery living thing hath a Soule, and are next after men to be accounted of, according to *Pythagoras* law, and now it must die: and sometimes they doe buy certain Fowles or other Beasts of the *Christians* or *Portugals*, which they meant to have killed, and when they have bought them, they let them flee and runne away.

They have a custome in *Cambaia*, in the High-wayes, and Woods, to set Pots with water, and to cast Corne, and other Granie upon the ground to feed Birds and Beasts withall: and throughout *Cambina* they have Hospitals to cure and heale all manner of Beasts and Birds, therein whatsoever they ayle, and receive them thither as if they were Men, and when they are healed, they let them flie or runne away whither they will, which among them is a worke of great Charitie, saying, it is done to their even neighbours. And if they take a Flea or a Louse, they will not kill it, but take or put into some hole or corner in the wall and so let it goe, and you can doe them no greater injurie then to kill it in their presence, for they will never leave intreating and desiring with all curtesie not to kill it, and that man should not seeme to commit so great a sinne, as to take away the life of that, to whom God had given both Soule and Bodie: yea, and they will offer much money to a man to let it liue, and goe away.

They eate no Radishes, Onions, Garlick, nor any kind of Herbe that hath any colour of Red in it, nor Egges, for they thinke there is blood in them. They drinke not any Wine, nor vse any Vineger, but onely water. They are so dangerous of eating and drinking with other men which are not their Countrimen, that they would rather starue to death then once to do it. It happenneth oftentimes that they sayle in the *Portugals* ships from *Goa* to *Cochin*, to sell their Wares, and to traffique with the *Portugals*, and then they make their prouisions for so long time as they thinke to stay vpon the way, which they take aboord with them, and thereupon they feed. And if the time falleth out longer, then they made account of, their water and prouision being all spent, as it happened, when I sailed from Goa to *Cochin*, they had rather die for hunger and thirst then once to touch the *Christians* meat. They wash themselues before they eate, as the *Bramenes* doe. They are of a yellow colour like the *Bramenes*, and somewhat whiter, and there Women among them which are much whiter and clearer of Complection then the *Portugall* women. They are formed and made both in Face, Limbes, and in all other things like men of *Europe*, colour onely excepted. Their Apparell is a thinne white Gowne vpon their naked bodies, from the head to the feet, and made fast on the side vnder their armes, their Shooes of red leather, sharpe at the toes, and turning vp like hookes, their Beards shauen like the *Turkes*, sauing onely their Moustachios, they weare on their Heads a white cloth three or foure times wrapped about like the *Bramenes*, and vnder their haire a Starre vpon their foreheads, which they rub euery morning with a little white Sanders tempered with water, and three or foure graines of Rice among it, which the *Bramenes* also doe as a superstitious Ceremonie of their Law. Their Bodies are commonly anoynted with Sanders and other sweet Woods, which they doe verie much vse, as also all the *Indians*.

Their Women are apparelled like the *Bramenes* wiues; they eate like the *Mahometans*, and all other *Indians* vpon the ground. In their Houses or Assemblies they sit on the ground vpon Mats or Carpets, and always leaue their Shooes without the doore, so that they are alwayes barefoot in their Houses: wherefore commonly the heeles of their shooes are neuer pulled vp, to saue labour of vntying or vndoing them, they haue a thousand other Heathenish superstitions which are not worth the rehearsall.

The *Canaras* and *Decanyns* are of the Country of *Decam*, commonly called *Ballagate*, lying behind *Goa*: many of them dwell in *Goa*. Their apparel is like the *Gusurates* and *Benianes*, except their Shooes, which they weare like Antiques with cut toes, and fastned above upon their naked feet, which they call *Alparcas*. They weare their Beards and haire long, as it groweth without cutting, but onely turne it vp, and dresse it as the *Benianes* and *Bramenes* vse to doe, and are like them for colour, forme, and making. They eate all things except Kine, Hogges, and Buffles, Flesh and Fish. They account the Oxe, Kow or Buffle to bee Holie, which they have commonly in the house with them, and they besmeere, stroke, and handle them with all the friendship in the world, and feed them with the same meat they vse to eate themselues. In the night time they sleepe with them in their Houses, and to conclude, use them as if they were reasonable Creatures, whereby they thinke to doe God great service. In their Eating, sitting in the House, Washing, making Cleane, and other Ceremonies and Superstitions they are altogether like the *Bramenes*, *Gusurates*, and *Banianes*. In their Marriages they contract each with other at seven yeeres, and at eleven or twelve yeeres they are married, and dwell together. When they are to be married, they begin fourteene dayes before to make a great sound with Trumpets, Drummes and Fifes, which continueth day and night for all those fourteen dayes, with so great a noise of songs and Instruments, that men can neither heare, nor see. On the Wedding day, all the freinds and kindered on both sides doe assemble together, and sit upon the ground, round about a Fire, and goe seuen times about it vttering certaine words, whereby the Wedding is done. They giue their Daughters no Household-stuffe, but onely some Iewels, as Bracelets, Eare-rings, and such like of small value, wherewith their Husbands must be content, for the Daughters are no Heyres, but the Sonnes inherite all, but they keepe and maintaine their Daughters and Sisters till they marrie: when they die they are likewise burnt and some of their Wiues with them, but not so many as of the *Bramenes*. Euery one of them followeth his Fathers occupation, and marrieth with the Daughters of such like Trades, which they name Kindreds. They haue their Fasting dayes, and Ceremonies like the *Bramenes* for they are as the Laitie, and the *Bramenes* as the spiritualtie, the Ministers, Priests, and Prophets of their Idols. They hire and farme the Customes and Rents of the *Portugals*, and the Kings revenues in the Land of *Bardes Satsette*, and the Iland of *Goa*, so that oftentimes for any question or strife they must appeare in Law where they alwayes come without Councell or Atturney, and know so well how to place their words, according to the Lawes of Portugall, not only Temporall but Spiritual, that they are able to set downe, and shew where it standeth written as well as any Counsellour could doe, and make their Petitions and Requests without any mans advise, that the *Portugals* doe wonder at their readie wits, as I have oftentimes found in them. When they are to take their Oathes to beare witnesse with any man they are set within a Circle made of Ashes vpon the pavement where they stand still, laying a few Ashes on their bare Heads, holding one hand on their heads, the other on their breasts, and then in their owne speech sweare by their *Pagode*, that they will tell the Truth without dissimulation, whatsoever shall bee asked them, for that they certainly beleeue they should be damned for euer, if as then they should not say the truth, but conceale it.

The *Canarijns* and *Corumbijns* are the Countrimen, and such as deale with Tilling the Land, Fishing and such like labours. These are the most contemptible, and the miserablest people of all *India*, and live very poorly, maintaining themselves with little meat. They eate all kind of things, except Kine, Oxen, Buffles, Hogges, and Hens flesh; their Religion is like the *Decanijns* and *Camaras*, for they are all of one Countrey and Custome, little differing: they goe naked, their middle onely covered with a cloth. The Women goe with a cloth bound about their middle beneath their nauels, and hanging downe to the middle of their thighes, and the other end thereof they cast ouer their shoulders, whereby half their brests are covered. They are in a manner blacke, or of a darke browne colour, many of them are *Christians*, because their chiefe habitation and dwelling places are on the Sea-side, in the Countries bordering upon *Goa*, for that the Palme-trees doe grow vpon the Sea coasts, or upon the banks by Riuer sides. The Rice is sowed vpon low ground, which in Winter time is covered with water, wherewith those *Canarijns* doe maintaine themselves: these bring Hennes, Fruit, Milke, Egges, and other such like wares into the Towne to sell. They dwell in little straw Houses, the doores whereof are so low, that men must creepe in and out, their houshold-stuffe is a Mat upon the ground to sleepe vpon, and a Pit or hole in the ground to beat their Rice in, with a Pot or two to seeth it in, and so they live and gaine so much as it is a wonder. For commonly their Houses are full of small Children, which crall and creepe about all naked, vntill they are seven or eight yeares old, and then they cover their middle. When the women are readie to trauell with Child, they are commonly delivered when they are all alone, and their Husbands in the fields as it fortuned vpon a time, as I and some other of my freinds went to walke in the fields, and into the Villages where the *Canarijns* dwell, and hauing thirst, I went to one of the *Canarijns* houses to aske some water, therewith to refresh vs, and because I was very thirstie, I stooped downe and thrust my head in at the doore, asking for some water, where I espied Woman alone within the house, tying her cloth fast about her middle, and before her hauing a woodden Trough (by the *Portugals* called *Gamello*) full of water, where shee stood and washed a Child, whereof as then she had newly beene deliuered without any helpe: which having washt, she laid it Naked on the ground vpon a great *Indian* Figge leafe, and desired me to stay and she would presently give me water. When I understood by her that she had as then newly beene deliuered of that Child without any helpe, I had no desire to drinke of the water, but went vnto another to aske water, and perceived the same woman not long after going about her house, as if there had beene no such matter, and the Children are brought up in that manner cleane naked, nothing done vnto them, but onely washed, and made cleane in a little cold water, and doe in that sort prosper and come vp as well as man would wish, or as any Child within these Countries can doe with all the tending they haue, and liue many times vntill they be a hundreth yeares old, without any Head-ach, or Tooth-ach, or losing any of their Teeth. They weare onely a tuske of haire on the tops of their Heads, which they suffer to grow long: the rest of their haire is cut short, they are very expert in Swimming and Diuing, they row vp and downe the Riuers in Boates called *Almadias*, whereof some of them are hewen out of a peece of wood, and so narrow that a man can hardly sit in them, and it chanceth oftentimes that they turne ouer and ouer twice or thrice before they passe the Riuer, and then they leape out into the water and turne them vp, and so powering out the water they get into them againe. They are so miserable, that for a Penie they would indure to be Whipped, and they eate so little, that it seemeth they liue by the Aire, they are likewise most of them leane, and weake of limbes, of little strength and very Cowards, whereby the *Portugals* doe them great outrage and villanie, vsing them like Dogs and Beasts.

In their Marriages and Deaths they obserue the manner of the *Decanijns* and *Canaras*, as also in their Religion and Ceremonies. When the Man is dead his body is burnt, and the Woman cuts her haire off, and breaketh all her Iewels, although they bee but few and small, for they are most of Glasse.

There are many *Arabians* and *Abexijns* in *India*. The *Arabians* obserue *Mahomets* Law, and the *Abexijns*, some are *Mahometans*, some *Christians*, after their manner, for they are of *Prester Iohns* land. The *Abexijns* that are Christians, haue on their Faces foure burnt markes in manner of a Crosse, one ouer their Nose in the middle of the forehead, betweene both their eies, on each of their Cheekes one, between their eyes and their eares, and one vnder their nether Lip downe to the chinne. These *Abexijns*, and *Arabians*, such as are free doe serue in all *India* for Saylers and Sea-faring men. The *Portugals* (although they serue for Saylers in the *Portugals* Ships) that come into *India*, and haue neuer beene other in *Portugall* but Saylers, yet are they ashamed to liue in that order, and thinke it a great discredit vnto them, together with a great diminishing of their Authorities and estimations, which they account themselues to hold in *India*, so that they giue themselues out for Maisters of ships, and by their Captaines are also called Pilots and chiefe Boatswaines, but not lower: for if they should descend but one step lower, it would be a great blot and blemish vnto them all their liues after, which they would not indure for any thing in the world. These *Abexijns* and *Arabians*, serue for small money, and being hired are verie lowly and subiect, so that oftentimes they are beaten and smitten, not as Slaues, but like Dogs, which they beare very patiently, not once speaking a word: they commonly haue their Wiues and Children with them in the ship wherein they are hired, which continually stay with them, what Voyage soeuer they make, and dresse their owne meat, which is Rice sodden in water with salt Fish among it. The cause why the Women saile in the ship, is that for in Summer their ships goe to Sea, when they alwaies haue calme water and faire weather, with good windes: they haue commonly but one *Portugall* or two for Captaine, Master and Pilot, and they haue a chiefe Boatswaine, which is an *Arabian*, which they call *Mocadon*, and he is ruler of the *Arabians* and *Abexijns*, that are Sailers, whom he hath vnder his subiection, euen as if they were his Slaues or Subiects.

This *Mocadon* is hee that conditioneth and maketh bargaine with the owners of the Ship, to haue so many Sailers, and hee receiueth the monethlie money for their wages, and accounteth with the Sailers particulary, but for Government of the ship hee hath not to doe, neither troubleth himselfe therewith. The ships when they saile, vse no Caske for water, because there is not any throughout all *India*, nor any made there, saue onely such as come out of *Portugall*, and vsed in the *Portugall* shippes: but insteade of Pipes they vse a great foure cornered wooden Cesterne, that standeth by the maine-Mast, at the very foot thereof, vpon the keele of the ship, which is very well pitched, and made fast, wherein they lade as much water as they thinke will serue them for their Voyage. The Captain, Master or Pilot, Marchants and Passengers, haue euerie man their meat by themselves, and their water in great *Indian* pots called *Martauns*.

The Blacke people or *Caffares* of the Land of *Mosambique*, and all the Coast of *Ethiopia*, and within the land to the *Capede bona Speranza*, goe all naked, although those of *Mosambique* (that is the Women) doe a little couer themselves, which they doe by meanes of the daily conuersation they haue with the *Portugals*. Some haue all their bodies rased and seared with Irons, and all figured like rased Satten and Damaske, wherein they take great pride, thinking there are no fairer people then they in all the world, so that when they see any white people, that weare Apparell on their bodies, they laugh and Mock at them, thinking vs to bee Monsters and ugly people : and when they will make any diuilish forme and Picture, then they inuent one after the forme of a White man in his apparell. There are among them that file there Teeth as sharpe as Needles, which they likewise esteem for a great ornament.

They haue a Custome among them, that when they goe to Warre against their enemies, if they winne the Battle, or ouerthrow each other, he that taketh or killeth most men, is holden and accounted for the best and brauest man among them, and much respected, and to witnesse the same before their Kings, of as many as they haue slaine or taken Prisoners, they cut off their priuie members, that is they bee let goe againe, they may no more beget Children which in processe of time might mischiefe them and with they drie them well, because they should not rot: which being so dryed, they come before their Kings with great reuerence, in the presence of the principall men in the Village, and there take these members so dried one by one in their mouthes, and spit them on the ground at the Kings feet, which the King with great thankes accepteth, and the more to reward and recompence their Valour, causeth them all to be taken vp and giuen to them againe, for a sign and token of Honour, whereby ever after from that time forwards they are accounted as Knights, and they take all those members, wherewith the King hath thus honoured them, and tie them all vpon a string like a

Bracelet or Chaine, and when they Marrie, or goe to any Wedding, or Feasts, the Bride or Wiues of those Knights doe weare that Chaine of mens members about their neckes, which among them is as great an Honour, as it is with us, to weare the Golden Fleece.

There are some of them that are become *Christians* since the *Portugals* came thither, but there is no great paines taken about it in those Countries, because there is no profite to bee had, as also that it is an infectious and vnholsome Countrey: And therefore the *Iesuites* are warie enough not to make any Houses or habitations therein, for they see no great profite to be reaped there for them, as they doe in *India* and the Ilands of *Japan*, and in other places, where they find great quantities of Riches, with the sappe whereof they increase much and fill there Beehiues, therewith to satisfie their thirstie and insatiable desires.

From *Mosambique* great numbers of these *Caffares* are carried into *India*, and many times they sell a Man or Woman that is growne to their full strength, for two or three Duckets. When the *Portugals* ships put in there for fresh Water and other necessaries, then they are dearer. In time of Pouertie or Dearth the Fathers may sell their Children, as it happened in my time, that there was such a dearth, and scarsitie of Victuals in the firme land, and Countries bordering vpon *Goa*, that the men of *India* came to *Goa* (and other places where the *Portugals* are resident) to sell their Children in great numbers, and for small prices, to buy them victuals. I haue seene Boyes of eight or ten yeares, giuen in exchange for fiue or six measures of Rice, and some for three or foure Duckets the peece, and some came with their Wiues and Children to offer themselves to bee Slaves so that they might haue meate and drinke to nourish their bodies.

And because the *Portugals* haue Traffique in all places

(as wee haue beene in many) it is the cause why so many are brought out of all Countries to be sold, for the *Portugals* doe make a liuing by buying and selling of them, as they doe with other wares.

The *Malabares* are those that dwell on the Sea-coast, betweene *Goa*, and the Cape *de Comoriyn* Southward from *Goa*, where the Pepper groweth. They have a speech by themselves, and their Countrey is divided into many Kingdomes, they goe all naked onely their middle covered, the Women likewise haue but a cloth from their Nauell downe to their knees, all the rest is naked, they are strong of limbes, and verie arrogant and proud, of colour altogether blacke, yet verie smooth both of haire and skinne, which commonly they anoynt with Oyle, to make it shine; they weare their haire as long as it will grow, tyed on the top or crowne of their heads with a Lace, both men and women: the lappes of their Eares are open and are so long that they hang downe to their shoulders, and the longer and wider they are, the more they are esteemed among them, and it is thonght to be a beautie in them. Of Face, Bodie, and Limbes, they are altogether like men of *Europe*, without any difference, but onely in colour, the,men are commonly verie hairie, and rough vpon the breast, and on their bodies, and are the most Leacherous and vnchaste Nation in all the Orient, so that there are verie few Children among them, of seven or eight yeeres old, who are virgins: They are verie readie to catch one from another, though it bee but for a small Penie.

In their Houses they are not verie curious, their houses, and houshold stuffe, differeth not much from the *Canariyns* and *Corumbiyns* of *Goa*. Their Idolatrie, Ceremonies, and Superstitions, are like the Heathens. Of these *Malabares* there are two manner of people, the one is Noblemen or Gentlemen, called *Nayros*, which are Souldiers, that doe onely weare and handle Armes, the other is the common people, called *Polyas*, and they may weare no Weapons nor beare any Armes. The Nayros must in all places where they goe or stand, weare such Armes as are appointed for them, and alwayes be readie at the King's commandment to doe him seruice, some of them doe alwayes beare a naked Rapier or Coutelas in their right hands, and a great Target in their left hand: those Targets are very great, and made of light wood, so that when they will they can cover their whole bodies therewith: they are so well used thereunto, that they esteeme it nothing to beare them, and when they trauell on the way, they may be heard a great way off, for that they commonly make a great knocking with the Hilt of their Rapier against the Target, because they would be heard. There are some that carrie a Bow and a venemous Arrow vpon their shoulder, wherein they are verie expert, others carrie long Pikes, some Pieces, with the Match ready lighted, and wound about their armes, and have the best Lockes that possibly may be found in all *Europe*, which they know so well how to use, that the *Portugals* can have no aduantage against them. Wheresoever they goe, they must alwaies have their Armes with them, both night and day. Not any of them are Married, nor may not marrie during their lives, but they may freely lie with the *Polyas* Daughters, or with any other that liketh them, what women soever they be, yea though they be Married women. When the *Nayro* hath desire thereunto, hee entereth into a house where he thinketh good, and setteth his Armes in the street without the doore, and goeth in and dispatcheth his businesse with the good Wife or the Daughter, the doore standing wide open, not fearing that any man should come in to let him; for whosoeuer passeth by, and seeth the *Nayros* armes standing at the doore, although it be the Goodman himselfe, hee goeth by, and letteth him make an end, and hauing done, he taketh his Armes and departeth thence, and then the Husband may come to the house without making any words, or once mouing question about it. In that manner they goe where they will, and no man may denie them. As these *Nayros* goe in the streets, they vse to crie Po, Po, which is to say, *Take heed looke to yourselues or I come, stand out of the way*, for that the other sort of people called *Polyas*, that are no *Nayros*, may not once touch or trouble one of them ; for if any of the *Polyas* should stand still, and not giue them place, whereby he should chance to touch their bodies, he may freely thrust him through, and no man ask him why he did it. And when they are once touched by any *Polyas*, or by any other Nation except *Nayros*, they must (before they eate, or conuerse with other *Nayros*) wash and cleanse their bodies with great Ceremonies and Superstitions. Likewise they must not be touched by any *Christian* or any other man. And when the *Portugals* came first into *India*, at *Cochin* it was concluded (to pacifie the matter and to keepe peace and quietnesse among them) that two men should be chosen, one for the *Nayros*, and the other for the *Portugals*, that should Fight bodie to bodie, and hee that should be ouerthrowne, that Nation should giue place vnto the other, this was done in the presence of both Nations, and the *Portugall* ouercame the *Nayro*, whom he slew ; whereupon it was agreed, that the *Nayros* should giue place vnto the *Portugall*, and stand aside vntill he be past wheresoeuer they meet. The *Nayros* weare the nails of their hands very long, whereby they shew that they are Gentlemen, because the longnesse of the Nailes doth let and hinder men from working or doing any labour. They say likewise that they doe it, the better and faster to gripe a thing in their hands and to hold their Rapiers, which some *Portugals* and *Mesticos* doe likewise vse, and hold the same opinion with the *Nayros*, whereof there are many in *India*, which let their Nails grow for the same cause.

The principallest or chiefest of those *Nayros*, which are Leaders or Captaines of certaine numbers of *Nayros* weare a Gold or Silver bracelet, or Ring, about their armes, above their elbowes: as also their Governours, Ambassadours, and Kings, whereby they are knowne from other men, for otherwise they goe all naked. Also their Kings, Rulers, and other Captaines and Leaders, when they goe abroad, are guarded and accompained by other Nayros. They are verie good and stout Souldiers, and will set vpon a man very fiercely, they are also verie full of revenge, so that whensoeuer they fight against their enemies either by water or by land, and that they chance to be thrust into the bodie with a Pike, they are not presently therewith content to lie downe, but if they cannot speedily plucke the Pike forth, they will not spare to pull it forth with both their hands, and draw it through their bodies, therewith to set vpon them that gaue them the wounds, and to be revenged on them.

The King may not Iudge or execute those *Nayros* openly, for if they haue deserued Death, he causeth them by other *Nayros* to be put to death. The Daughters of the *Nayros* may not haue the companie of any man, but onley of *Nayros*, although secretly they haue the company of many *Portugals* and *Christians*, but if the *Nayros* once perceiued it, or finde them in the deed doing, they might kill them without further question. In euery place where they dwell, they haue a Pit or Well digged, wherein they doe hold water, which standeth openly in the way where euery man passeth by, wherein euery morning when they rise, they wash themselues all ouer, beginning first at the Foot and so rising vp to the Head, as well Men as Women without being ashamed to be seene of such as goe by, or looke vpon them, and the king himselfe likewise: which water is so greene, slimie and stinking, that a man can not chuse but stop his Nose as he goeth by it: and they certainly belieue, that whensoeuer they should forget to wash themselues in that water, that they should then be whollie vncleane and full of sinne: and this washing or making cleane, must not be done in any running water, but it must be in a place where the water standeth in a Pit or Well, and by their *Bramenes* conjured with many Words and Ceremonies, otherwise it were of no vertue but whollie vnprofitable, for their Idolatrous seruices. They are like the other Heathens, and are burned when they are Dead: their Sonnes may not be their Heyres because they haue no Wiues, but vse all women, where and when they will, doubting which is their owne Sonne: for the *Bramenes* also haue the Kings wiues at their pleasures, and doe him great honour when it pleaseth them to lie with their Queen. Their heyres are their Sisters sonnes, for they say, although they doubt of their Fathers, yet they know their Sisters are the Mothers of them. Thus much touching the *Nayros* and Gentlemen or Souldiers.

The other common people of the *Malabares*, called *Polyas*, are such as are the Countrey Husbandmen and Labourers, men of Occupations, Fishers, and such like: those are much contemned and despised, they liue meiserably and may weare no kind of Weapon, neither yet touch or bee conversant with the *Nayros*, for as the *Nayros* goe on the streets, and they heare him call, they step aside, bowing their Armes, and stooping with their Heads down to the ground, not daring so much as once look up before the *Nayros* be past: in other things they observe the Customes of the other *Indians*, for that euery man followeth the Occupation of his Elders, and may not change it for any thing.

There are great numbers of *Moores* and *Iewes* in all places of *India*, as at *Goa*, *Cochin*, and within the Land. In their Houses and Apparell they follow the manner of the Land wherein they are resident: amongst the *Indians* they haue their Churches, Sinagogues, and *Mesquitas*, wherein they vse all Ceremonies according to their Law: but in the places where the *Portugals* inhabite and gouerne, it is not permitted vnto them to vse them openly, neither to any *Indian*, although they haue their Families and dwelling Houses and get their liuings, and deale one with the other: but secretly in their Houses they may doe what they will, so that no man take offence thereat: without the Townes and where the *Portugals* haue no commandment, they may freely vse and exercise their Ceremonies and Superstitions, euery one as liketh him best, without any man to let or denie them: but if they bee found openly doing it in the *Portugals* Townes and Jurisdictions, or that they haue any point of Christian ceremonies mingled among theirs, both men and women die for it, vnlesse they turne vnto the *Christian* Faith: they are most white of colour, like men of *Europe*, and have many faire Women. There are many of them that came out of the Countrey of *Palestina* and *Ierusalem* thither, and speake ouer all the Exchange verie perfect and good *Spanish*.

The *Moores* likewise haue their *Mesquitos*, wherein they pray, and aboue the Church they have many Sellers and Galleries, where they learne their Children their principles of Religion before they goe to Church: they wash their Feet, for the which purpose they haue alwayes a Cisterne with water standing without the Church, and leaue their *Alparcos* (which are their Shooes) standing at the Church doore before they goe in, and being in the Church they fall flat on the ground vpon their faces, and so with their armes and hands lifted vp, make many counterfeit faces. They are also Circumcised like the *Iewes*, and eate no Hogs-flesh, and when they are dead they are buried. In their Churches they haue not any Images, but onely some Stones or round Pillers standing vpright with certaine *Chaldean* letters (out of their *Alcaron*) grauen vpon them. As I and a friend of mine chanced to goe out of the Towne, wee were desirous to see their *Mahometicall* Church, and their manner of Service, which was denied vs by the keeper of the doore, that bad vs put off our Shooes, but because we would not, hee said it was not lawfull for vs to enter in that sort into the Church: but to let vs see it, hee suffered vs to stand within the doore, and opened some of the windowes, that wee might see what was within it: then the *Portugall* asked him for their God and their Saints which they vsed to pray vnto, because he saw the Church emptie, as I said before: then the *Moore* answered him that *They vsed not to pray to Stockes and Stones, but to the liuing God, which is in Heaven, and said that the proud* Portugall *Christians, and the Heathens were all of one Religion, for that they pray to Images made of Wood and Stones and giue them the Glorie which onely appertaineth to the liuing God*: with the which answer the *Portugall* was so angrie, that hee began to chide, so that there had growne a great qarrell had it not beene for me.

In the Kingdome of *Narsinga*, or the Coast called *Choramandel*, there standeth a *Pagode*, that is very great, exceeding rich, and holden in great estimation, hauing many Pilgrimages & Visitations made vnto it from all the Countries bordering about it, where euery yeere they haue many Faires, Feasts, and Processions, and there they haue a Waggon or a Cart, which is so great and heauie, that three or foure Elephants can hardly draw it, and this brought forth at Faires, Feasts, and Processions. At this Cart hang likewise many Cabels or Ropes, whereat also all the Countrey people, both men and women of pure deuotion doe pull and hale. In the vpper part of this Cart standeth a Tabernacle or Seat, wherein sitteth the Idoll, and vnder it sit the Kings Wives, which after their manner play on all Instruments, making a most sweet melodie, and in that sort is the Cart drawne forth, with great Deuotions and Processions: there are some of them, that of great zeale and pure deuotion doe cut peeces of flesh out of their bodies, and throw them downe before the *Pagode* : others lay themselues vnder the wheels of the Cart, and let the Cart runne ouer them, whereby they are all crushed to pieces, and pressed to death, and they that thus die, are accounted for holy and deuout Martyrs, and from that time forwards are kept and preserued for great and holy Reliques, besides a thousand other such like beastly Superstitions, which they vse, as one of my Chamber fellowes that had seene it shewed me, and it is also well knowne throughout all *India*.

Upon a time I and certaine *Portugals*, my freinds, having licence from the Viceroy, were at a Banquet and meeting, about fiue or sixe miles within the firme Land, and with vs wee had certaine *Decanijns*, and naturall borne *Indians*, that were acquainted with the Countrey. The chiefe cause of our going, was to see their manner of burning the dead *Bramene*, and his Wife with him being alive, because we had beene advertised, that such a thing was to bee done. And there, among other strange devises that we saw, we came into some Villages, and places inhabited by the *Indians*, where in the way, and at euerie Hill, stonie Rocke or hole, almost within a *Pater noster* length, we found a Carved *Pagode*, or rather Devils, and monsters in hellish shapes. At the last we came into a Village, where stood a great Church of stone, wherein wee entred, and found nothing in it but a great Table that hung in the middle of the Church, with the Image of a *Pagode* painted therein so mishaped and deformed, that more monstrous was neuer seene, for it had many Hornes, and long Teeth that hung out of his mouth downe to the knees, and beneath his nauell and belly, it had another such like face, with many hornes and tuskes. Upon the head thereof stood a triple Crowned Myter, not much unlike the Popes triple Crowne, so that in effect it seemed to be a Monster, such as are described in the *Apocalips*. It hung before a Wall, which made a partition from another Chamber, in manner of a

Quier, yet was it close made up without windowes, or any place for light, in the middle whereof was a little narrow close doore, and on both sides of the doore, stood a small furnace made within the wall, wherein were certaine holes or Lattices, thereby to let the smoke or sauour of the fire to enter into that place, when any Offering should be made. Whereof we found some there, as Rice, Corne, Fruits, Hennes, and such like things, which the *Indians* daily offered, but there came so filthie a smoke and stinke out of the place, that whosoever went neere it, was almost ready to choke, the said place being all black, smeerie and foule therewith. Before this doore being shut, in the middle of the Church, there stood a Calfe of stone, whereon one of our companie leaped, and laughing, began to crie out, which the *Bramene* that kept the Church perceiuing, began to call and crie for help, so that presently many of the neighbours ranne thither, to see what the cause might be, but before the throng of people came, we dealt so well with the *Bramene* (acknowledging our fault, and saying it was vnaduisedly done) that he was well content, and the people went home againe. Then we desired the *Bramene* to open vs the doore that stood shut, which after much intreatie hee yeelded vnto, offering first to throw certaine Ashes vpon our foreheads, which we refused, so that before he would open vs the doore, we were forced to promise him that we would not enter further in, then to the doore.

The doore of their *Sancta Sanctorum*, or rather *Diabolorum*, being opened, it shewed within like a Lime-kill, being close vaulted round about, ouer the head without either hole or window to cast in light, but onely at the doore, neither was there any light in all the Church, but that which came in at the doore we entred by. Within the said Cell or Vault, there hung at the least one hundred burning Lamps, in the middle wherof stood a little Altar, & couered ouer with cloth made of Cotton-wooll, and ouer that with pure Gold, vnder the which (as the *Bramene* told vs) sate the *Pagode* being of cleane Gold, of the bignesse of a Puppet or a Babie sold in Faires: hard by the Church without the great doore, stood within the earth a great foure cornered or square Cesterne, hewed out of Free stone, with stayres on each side to goe downe into it, full of greene, filthie and stinking water, wherein they wash themselues when they meane to enter into the Church to pray. From thence wee went further, and still as we went, in euery place we found *Pagodes* hewed out of hard Stones, and standing in their holes, of such liuely shapes and figures as we told you before. These stand in the wayes vnder certaine couertures, without the Churches, and haue hard by each of them a small Cesterne of water, cut out of the stone, to wash their feet, with halfe an *Indian* Nut, that hath a handle and hangeth there to take vp water withall. And this is ordayned for Trauellers that passe by, who commonly at euery one of those *Pagodes* doe fall downe and make their Prayers, and wash their feet in those Cesternes. By the said *Pagodes*, commonly doe stand two little Furnaces, with a Calfe or Cow of stone, before the which they set their offerings, which are of such things, as are to bee eaten, euery man as his Deuotion serueth, which they think the *Pagode* eateth in the Night, but it is taken away by the *Bramene*. We found in euery place such Offerings standing, but we had little desire once to taste thereof, it looked so filthily, and as we had sufficiently beholden their mishapen figures and monstrous Images, we returned againe into the Village, wherein we saw the stone Church, because the *Bramene* had aduertised vs, that the same day about Euening, the *Pagode* should be carried in Procession, to sport itselfe in the Fields, and to fetch a circuit, which wee desired to see. And about the time which hee appointed they rung a little Bell, which they had gotten of the *Christians*, wherewith all the people began to assemble, and tooke the *Pagode* out of his diabolicall Cell, which with great reuerence, they set in a *Palamkin* borne by the chiefe men of the Towne, all the rest with great deuotion following after, with their vsuall noyse and sound of Trumpets and other Instruments, wherewith they went a reasonable way round about a Field, and then brought him to the stone Cisterne, where washing him very cleane (although he were very filthie stinking) they carried him againe into his Cell, leauing him shut herein with all his Lampes, to make good cheere, and hauing made a foule smoake and stink about him and euery man left his Offering behind him, they went home to their houses, leauing the *Bramene* alone, who instead of the *Pagode*, made good cheere at their costs with his Wife and Familie.

There is ouer all *India* great store of Cattell, as Oxen, Kine, Sheepe, Hogges, Goates, Kids, and such like, and very good, cheape, and in great abundance, although the flesh is not of so good a taste as that in *Europe*, which proceedeth from the heat of the Countrey, and therefore it is not much esteemed. A man may buy the best Kow in *Goa*, for fiue or sixe *Pardawes*. Oxen are there little killed to eate, but are most kept to till the Land, all other things as Hogs, Sheepe, Goates, are sold after the rate. Mutton is little esteemed of, and not much vsed to be eaten, for it is forbidden to such as are sicke, and the Hogs flesh is much better and sounder, which is rather permitted vnto sicke persons then Mutton. There are Sheepe in that Country of fiue quarters in quantitie, for that the tayle is as great, and hath as much flesh vpon it as any of the quarters. There are many Buffles, but nothing good to bee eaten, vnlesse it be by poore people, but their Milke is very good, and is very well sold and ordinarily eaten, for you shall see the Slaues and *Canariyns* in great numbers, all day going about the streets to sell the Milke of Buffles, and Goates, and excellent sweet Creame, and fresh Butter in small peeces. They make likewise some small white Cheeses, but they are very salt and drie: wilde Bores, some Hares, Conies, Harts, and Hindes are there also to be found, but not many. Cockes, Capons, Pheasants, and Doues are there in great abundance and good cheape. In the Iland of Goa and thereabout are Sparrowes, and some other small Birds, yet not many: but on the Coast of *Cochin* and *Malabar*, there are very few Sparrowes, nor any such like small birds. There are in *India* many Battes, and some of them so great, that it is incredible to tell. They doe great mischiefe to Trees, Fruits and Herbes, whereby the *Canariyns* are constrained to set men to watch in their Trees, and yet they can hardly rid them away. The *Indians* eate them, and say they are as good meat as a Partridge.

There is a most wonderfull number of blacke Crowes, which doe much hurt, and are so bold that often times they come flying in at their windowes, and take the meat out of the dish, as it standeth vpon the Table, before them that are set downe to eate: and as I myselfe sate writting aboue in a Chamber of the house, the windowes being open, one of those Crowes flew in at the window, and picked the Cotton out of mine Inke-horne, and blotted all the paper that lay on my Table, doe what I could to let him. They sit commonly upon the Buffles backes, and pecke of their haire, so that you shall find very few Buffles that have any haires upon there backes, and therefore to anoye the Crowes they get themselues into Marshes, and watrie places, where they stand in the water vp to the neckes, otherwise they could never be rid of them.

There are likewise great numbers of Rats, and some as bigge as young Pigges, so that the Cats dare not touch them. Sometimes they digge downe the Houses, for that they vndermine the walles and foundations through, whereby many times the houses fall downe and are spoyled. There is another sort of Rats, that are little and reddish of haire. They are called sweet smelling Rats, for they haue a smell as if they were full of Muske.

Of Ants there is so great abundance throughout all *India*, and so noisome, that it is incredible to such as haue not seene it: for that men may set nothing, whatsoeuer it be, that is to be eaten, or fatty, nor yet their clothes nor linen, but you shall presently find at the least a thousand upon it: and in the twinkling of an eye they will presently consume a loafe of bread: wherefore it is the manner throughout *India*, to make all the Cup-boords wherein they keepe their victuals, and Chests, where their linen and apparell lieth, with four feet or pillars, and vnder every foot or pillar a stone or wooden Cesterne full of water, and place the Cupboord or Chest in the middle of the roome, not neere the wall, whereby they cannot come at it, otherwise it would be spoiled, and if they doe neuer so little forget to powre water into the Cesterns, if it be but a *Pater noster* while, presently there will be so many ants crawling all ouer it, that it is wonderfull: so that it seemeth to be a curse or plague of God sent vpon that Countrie. There are some likewise that vse such Cesternes of water vnder their beadstead, because they would not be troubled with them as they lie in their beds, and also vnder their Tables. Some men which keepe *Canarie* birds, or such small fowles (what are brought thither from *Portugall*, or out of *Turkie* and *Persia* for their pleasures) are forced to set them on a stike or pearch made for the purpose, with a Cesterne of water vnder it, otherwise it would presently be killed by the ants: and though it hangeth in the top of the house, yet they will come at it if it have a string, to hold it by. The Souldiers and poore people that have not the means to buy Cup-boords, with Cesternes put the bread and other victuals which they leave (which is not ouermuch) in a cloth tied on knots, and hang it on a naile against the wall, and make a circle about it of Charcole, so that the ants cannot get ower nor come at it. There is another sort of ants which are almost a finger long, and reddish of colour: they runne into the fields, and doe great hurt to the herbes, fruits, and plants.

Moths and wormes which creepe and eate through mens cloths, are there in great abundance, whereby men must vse no more clothes nor linnen in those Countries then that he necessarily and daily weareth on his backe, otherwise they are presently moth-eaten and spoiled. They can hardly keepe any Paper or Bookes from wormes, which are like care wormes, but they doe often spoile and consume many Papers and euidences of great importance. There are also many *Wall-lice.* There is a kind of beast that flieth, twice as bigge as a Bee, and is called *Baratta*: These creatures also doe much hurt, and are commonly in Sugar, Honie, Butter, Oile, and all fat wares and sweet meates. Many of them likewise come into their Chests among their clothes and linnen, which they doe also spoile and spot. They are in great numbers and very hurtfull. There can be nothing so close shut or made fast, but they will get in and spoile it, for where they lie or be they spot all things with their egges, which sticke as fast as sirop vpon a Paper, so that they may be esteemed as a plague like to the Pismires.

Within the Land there are also Tigres: other cruell beasts, as Lions, Beares, and such like there are few or none: but venomous beasts and Snakes, Lizards, and such like there are many, for the Lizards will clime and creepe vpon the walls in their houses, and oftentimes fall vpon men, as they lie in their Beds and sleep, and therefore many men that are of abilitie, doe hang Testers and Curtaines ouer and about their Beds. There are likewise many Chamelions, which are said to liue by the aire, but they are not hurtfull.

There are many Monkies or Marmosets, that doe great hurt to the Palme trees, wherein the *Indian* Nut or Cocus doth growe. In those trees you shall commonly see certaine little beasts called *Bichos de Palmeyras*, that is, *Beasts of the Palme trees*: They are much like Ferrets, wherewith men vse to hunt and catch Cunnies, and have a taile like the Penner of an Inke-horne, and grayish speckled haire: they are pretie beasts to keepe and to passe the time withall. Parrots, are there in great numbers, and flie abroad in the Woods. There commeth in *India* out of the Iland of *Molucas* beyond *Malaca*, a kind of birds, called *Noyras*: they are like Parrots, but they haue many red feathers, and speake like Parrots: they are worth in *India* twenty or thirty Pardawes the piece: they are very faire to looke on, and speake sweetly: they claw or tickle men with their tongues vpon their heads and beards, and make them cleane at the roots, as also their eares and their teeth, so that they are very pleasant to keepe in a house, for that both in colour and beauty of feathers they surpasse all birds and Parrots whatsoeuer: but there could neuer yet be any of them brought living into *Portugall*, although they haue sought and vsed all the meanes they could to bring them for a Present to the King which he greatly desireth: but they die vpon the way, for they are very delicate, and will hardly be brought vp.

Elephants are in many places of *India*. In the Iland of *Seylon* there are also great numbers, which are esteemed the best and sensiblest of all the world, for wheresoeuer they meet with any other Elephants (the *Indians* report for a truth, that they haue tried it) those Elephants of other Countries doe reuerence and honour to the Elephants of *Seylon*. The most seruice that they vse them for in *India*, is to draw their Pipes, Buts, Packes, and other goods, and to ship them, all which they doe with Elephants. They are kept at the Kings charges, and he that needeth them, speaketh to their Keepers, and agreeth with them for a price to haue their labour: Then the

Keeper getteth vpon the necke of the Elephant, and thrusteth his feet vnder his eares, hauing a hooke in his hand, which he striketh on his head, that is to say, aboue betweene both his eares, which is the cause, that they are so well able to rule them : and coming to the things which they are to draw, they bind the But or Packe with a rope that he may feele the weight thereof, and then the Keeper speaketh vnto him : whereupon hee taketh the corde with his snout and windeth it about his teeth, and thrusteth the end into his mouth, and so draweth it hanging after him, whither they desire to haue it. If it be to be put into a Boat, then they bring the Boat close to the shoare of the Key, and the Elephant putteth it into the Boat himself, and with his snout gathereth stones together, which he layeth vnder the But, Pipe or Packe, and with his teethe striketh and thrusteth the Packe or Vessell, to see if it lie fast or not. It will draw any great shot or other Irone worke, or metall being made fast vnto it, be it neuer so heavie. They draw Fusts, small Gallies, and other great Boats, as Caruels, and such like, as easily out of the water vpon the land, as if no man were in them : so that they serve their turnes there, euen as our Sleds or Carts with Horses doe heere, to carrie our warres and merchandises. Their meate is Rice and water, they sleepe like Kine, Oxen, Horses, and all foure-footed beasts, and bow their knees and all their members as other beasts doe. In Winter when it beginneth to raine, then they are vnquiet, and altogether mad, so that their Keepers cannot rule them, and then they are led some whither out of the Towne to a great tree, and there tied vnto it by the legs with a great Iron chaine where they carrie him meate, and so he lieth in the open aire, as long as he is mad, which is from April to September, all the Winter time when it raineth, and then he commeth to himself, and beginneth to serue againe as tamely, that a man may lie vnder his bellie, so you doe him to hurt: but he that hurteth him, he must take heed, for they neuer forget when any man doth them iniurie, vntill they be reuenged. They are very fearfull of a Rat or Mouse, and also of the ants, because they feare they would creepe into their snouts. They are likewise afraide of gun-shot and of fire vnlesse by length of time they be vsed vnto them. As they goe alone the way, although you see them not, you may heare them a farre off by the noise of their feet and clapping of their eares, which they continually vse. They are as swift in going almost as a Horse, and are very proude, and desirous of honour. When there is any great Feast or Holiday kept in *Goa*, with solemne Procession commonly the Elephants goe with them, the young before, and the old behind, and are all painted vpon their bodies with the Armes and Crosses of *Portugall*, and haue euery one fiue or sixe Trumpetters or Players vpon the Shalmes, sitting vpon them that sound very pleasantly, wherewith they are as well pleased, and goe with as great grauitie, and in as good order, as if they were men. It happened in *Goa*, that an Elephant should draw a great Fust out of the water vnto the land, which Fust was so great and heauie, that he could not doe it alone, so that they must haue another to help him: whereupon the Keeper chid him, vsing many hard words saying, that *he was idle and weake, and that it would be an euerlasting shame for him, that they must fetch another to help him,* wherewith the Elephant was so desperate, that hee thrust away his fellow (which was brought to help him) and beganne freshly againe to draw, with so great force, more than he was well able to doe, that with extreme labour he burst and felle downe starke dead in the place. At such time as I was to make my Voyage from *Cochin* to *Portugall*, the Rudder of our ship was out of order so that it must of force be brought on land to make it fit againe, and so it was drawne to the Riuers side at the sterne of the Boat, when the Elephant should draw on land vpon two boords that it might slide vp, and because it was heauie, (as the Rudder of a ship *(a)* of fourteene hundred or sixteene hundred tunnes requireth) as also that the Elephant was as yet but young, and not growne to his full strength, so that he could not draw it out alone, yet he did the best he could: but seeing he could not doe it, he fell on his fore-legs, and beganne to crie and weepe, that the teares ranne out of his eyes, and because many of vs stood vpon the shoare to behold this sight, the Keeper began to chide him, and with hard words to curse him, because he shamed him thus in presence of so many men, not to be able to draw vp such a thing: but what strength or labour soeuer the Elephant vsed, he could not doe it alone, but when they brought another Elephant to help him, they both together drew it halfe out of the water, so that it lay partly vpon the boords. The first Elephant perceiuing that, with his head and teeth thrust the other Elephant away, and would haue no more help, but drew it out himselfe.

They are likewise very thankful & mindful of any good done vnto them. When new yerees day commeth, their keepers vse of common custome to ask new yeeres gifts of the Viceroy, the Archbishop, and other Gouernours and Gentlemen, and then the Elephants come to the doore and bow their heads downe, and when any thing is given, they kneele on their knees with great lowlinesse, and thankfulnesse, for the good deeds so done vnto their keepers (which they thinke to be done vnto themselues.) They vse as they passe by such houses, to bow their heads at the dores, as also when they passe by the Church dores, and by Crosses, which their Masters teach them. They haue a

(*a*) The Portuguese East Indiamen must have been of an enormous size in comparison with English vessels of the period, which averaged 250 or 300 tons, and very rarely reached 500 tons.

custome that they goe often into the Market where hearbs are sold, as Reddish, Lettice, Coleworts, and such like stuffe, and those that are liberall to the Elephant, doe vse to throw something before him. Among the rest these was one hearbe wife which alwayes vsed to throw something of her wares before the Elephant. Now when the time came on that the Elephant groweth mad, as I said before, they vse to goe with them three or foure dayes, or a weeke about the streets before they binde them vp (being as then but halfe mad) to aske something of euery bodie for the feeding of the mad Elephant in the winter time. And going thus about the streets, the Master is not able to rule him, for he runneth about with his head downward, and by his roaring giveth the people warning to beware, and when he findeth or seeth no man, hee leapeth and overthroweth whatsoeuer he meeteth withall, whereby hee maketh great sport and pastime, much like to the baiting of Oxen in *Spaine*, which never ceaseth, vntill one, two, or more of them be slaine, the like rule is kept with the mad Elephant in *India*. It chanced in this running about that the Elephant ranne through the streets, and in haste at vnawares came into the market, throwing downe all that was in his way, whereat euery man was abasht, and leaving their ware, ranne to saue themselues from being ouer runne by the Elephant, and by meanes of the noyse and prease of people, they fell one ouer another, as in such cases is commonly seene. Among them was this woman, that alwayes used to give the Elephant something to eate, which had a little child in the market lying by her in a basket, and by the hastie rising vp and throng of the people, tho woman ranne into a House, not hauing time to snatch vp her Child, and take it with her; and when the Elephant was alone in the Market place, where he roared vp and downe, ouerthrowing all things that were before him, hee came by the Child (that is I said) lay still in the Market, and as euerie man looked, specially the

Mother, which cried out, and verily thought that the Elephant had taken it and cast it on his shoulder and spoyled it as he did all other things. He on the contrarie notwithstanding all his madnesse, being mindfull of the good will and liberalitie of the Childes Mother dayly vsed vnto him, took vp the Child handsomely and tenderly with his Snout, and laid it softly vpon a Stall by a Shop side, which done, he began again to vse the same order of stamping, crying, and clapping as he had done at the first, to the great wondering of all that beheld it, specially to the ease and ioy of the Mother, that had recovered her Child sound and well againe.

THE END.